Teaching
the
Native American

Hap Gilliland
Council for Indian Education
with

Jon Reyhner
Eastern Montana College

and others

KENDALL/HUNT PUBLISHING COMPANY
2460 Kerper Boulevard P.O. Box 539 Dubuque, Iowa 52004-0539

Dedicated to the many excellent teachers who have inspired Native American students to achieve, and whose creative ideas have aided in the writing of this book.

Edited by
Hap Gilliland
Jon Reyhner and
Rachel Schaffer

CL
A4   30c

Contents

Chapter 3
Discovering and Emphasizing the Positive Aspects of the Culture
Hap Gilliland

Chapter 4
Learning Through Cooperation and Sharing
Hap Gilliland

Chapter 5
Growth Through Native American Learning Styles
Hap Gilliland

Chapter 10
Selecting and Producing Valid Material for Reading and Social Studies
Hap Gilliland

Chapter 11
A Whole Language Approach to the Communication Skills
Sandra J. Fox

Chapter 12
Developing Reading Skills
Daniel L. Pearce and Hap Gilliland

Chapter 13
Inspiring Creative Writing
Perie Longo

Chapter 14
Teaching English to the Native American Student
Rachel Schaffer

Chapter 19
Teaching the Indian Child Art
Lori Sargent and Jo Reid Smith

Chapter 20
Incorporating Native American Activities Into the Physical Education Program
Robert W. Grueninger

Preface

Teaching the Native American is a book of ideas—not abstract, theoretical concerns, but practical information and suggestions for educators working with Native American students. The book's central focus is on how the cultural differences between white and native American societies affect the educational progress and development of Native American students. While it is intended to be an enlightening, thought-provoking, and above all helpful reference work for teachers and teachers-in-training from Head Start to High School, the issues discussed by the individual chapter authors also provide valuable insights for parents, teacher aides, administrators, and college faculty teaching Native American students or teaching courses in Native American Studies, Bilingual Education, or cross-cultural studies.

The first chapters of *Teaching the Native American* deal with specific areas of Native American culture that affect the education of Native American students: self-image, learning styles, discipline, and others. The rest of the book discusses cultural concerns and cultural relevance in a wide variety of academic areas: the language arts, social studies, mathematics, science, computers, art, and physical education. Each chapter suggests references for further reading and other types of resource materials. The authors of these chapters come from a wide variety of backgrounds, and all have experience with teaching Native American students at different grade levels. The editors have worked extensively with several different North American and South American tribes, and bring special insight to a book which is personal, practical, and immediately relevant to all concerned educators of Native American students.

Introduction

The purpose in writing this book has been to provide a practical guide for teachers either already teaching or planning to teach Native American students. We have endeavored to make it easy for the busy classroom teacher to read and apply.

The writing of the book began several years ago when, with the help of local Indian translators and interviewers, Dr. Hap Gilliland interviewed parents on seven Indian reservations to determine what these parents thought teachers should know before teaching their children. Other interviews followed with all the teachers who the parents thought were effective teachers of their children. As Dr. Gilliland began organizing courses in Native American education at Eastern Montana College, using the results of these surveys and his extensive experience in Indian education, the need for the publication of a good guide for teachers became obvious. There was plenty of material on what was wrong with Indian education, but very little on positive ideas of how to make education more relevant to the needs of these students.

By the time Dr. Jon Reyhner, who also had broad experience in Indian education, joined the faculty at EMC, Dr. Gilliland had two four-drawer files of notes and materials to go into the book, but still had not completed it, so they decided to join forces and also ask specialists in various academic areas who had also worked with Native American education to add their ideas.

Knowledgeable Indian people from various tribes offered to read and evaluate the material as it was written. We appreciate the assistance of the following people in checking the validity of the material and making helpful suggestions throughout.

Rosalie BearCrane—Crow

Lynda LimberHand—Northern Cheyenne

Marie Reyhner—Navajo

Esther Peralez—Aztec

Therese WoodenLegs—Cheyenne

Sandra Fox—Oglala Sioux

Pete Hill—Athapascan

Sharon BowMan—Hidatsa

Sharon BearComesOut—Assiniboin

Ray Mace—Sioux

Diane Bakun—Teacher of Eskimos

Betty Clark—Council for Indian Education

We also thank Erma Gilliland for her proofreading and general assistance, and Rachel Schaffer who assisted with editing throughout.

USE OF THE PRONOUN "SHE" TO DENOTE THE TEACHER

Recently many people have attempted to find a substitute for the word "he" when we do not know the sex of the subject. None of them are satisfactory. He/she or she/he interfere with the flow of the sentence and distract the reader's mind from the meaning. So does the change in number when "they" is used as singular. Alternating between "he" and "she" can also confuse the reader. "He" is still defined as the word used to denote "a person of unspecified sex" (Oxford American Dictionary) and is probably the only really "correct" word for formal English. However, since this is not a formal book, but is written in a "from me to you" style, we hope the readers will bear with us if we sometimes substitute "she" for clarity. When a paragraph is talking about both a teacher and student the meaning is often clearer if different pronouns are used for the two people. Since in actual practice, more elementary teachers are still female and more students with problems are male, we have taken the authors prerogative of sometimes using "she" to denote the teacher (when no specific individual is indicated), and "he" to denote the student. We hope our readers will understand.

Chapter 1

A Culturally Relevant Education

by Hap Gilliland

"Only by being true to the full growth of all the individuals who make it up, can society by any chance be true to itself."

—John Dewey

There are classrooms in which native American youth are happy, highly successful students who are growing into beneficial, contributing members of society. There are many more classrooms in which they are at the bottom of the line academically, socially, and emotionally; where neither teacher nor student expect anything but failure from the Indian students.

Will our Native American students use their full potential in our classrooms? Will they reach their own individual goals and grow into adults who believe in themselves, who consider themselves successful? That depends partly upon how well we learn to understand their backgrounds and values, their ways of learning, and whether or not we can adapt to their needs.

The emphasis in teaching must be on the positive, the good things that can be done to help the student, and that is what we will emphasize in this manual. However, we cannot remedy a problem until we see that the problem exists, and know why. An alcoholic cannot recover from his drinking problem until he recognizes it and admits he had a problem; a school will not change its approach to Indian and Eskimo education until the teachers recognize a need for change.

THE NEED FOR A RELEVANT EDUCATION

There is a great deal of evidence that the majority of schools with Native American students are not adequately adapting to the needs of the students and making their instruction effective. Educational statistics indicate underachievement, absenteeism, over-aged students, and high drop-out rates for Indian students. More subjective evaluations add negative educational goals, low levels of aspiration, and low socio-economic status.

In an educational survey of the Crow Indian Reservation, I found 50 percent of the Crow students two or more years below the national average in reading.

The high school students in a Denáina Indian village in Alaska, with which I worked in 1984, averaged 5th grade reading level.

A study by the Northwest Regional Educational Laboratory reported the dropout rate from 8th to 12th grade of American Indian students from six western states at 48 percent.

1

Sandra Fox, a Sioux Indian educator says, "We cannot deny that Indian students, as a group, do not score as well on tests of educational achievement as most other students do, according to national norms. In 1985, 75 percent of the students in Bureau of Indian Affairs schools were scoring below grade level, as compared to the national average. The records of the Bureau's Higher Education Program report many students failing or dropping out of school because they do not have adequate basic skills."

As S. W. Johnson (1984) says, in describing Eskimo and Alaskan Indian education, "The native student who aspires to success is faced with the difficult and often dissonant task of marching to more than one drum. The dilemma of not rejecting one's own rich cultural heritage, while preparing to be successful in a context which at best ignores or at worst contradicts such a heritage along with its inherent values and ethics is not a simple one. It is little wonder that the native and non-native student (or teacher) find it difficult to recognize, least of all appreciate, each other's orientation, efforts, purpose and values."

The lot of Canadian Native students is no better. The Canadian Education Association found in 1984 that less than 20 percent of Native Indian students finished grade 12. This high dropout rate was attributed to lack of mastery of reading and other basic skills needed to continue in school.

I could go on and cite volumes of research and evidence that proves the need for change, but to those of you who are in the classrooms teaching Indian children, the need is obvious. You see it in the eyes of the student who doesn't understand your explanation because his experiences are different. You see it in the lack of effort of the student who is convinced that he cannot achieve and that even the teachers are against him. You see it in the silence of the student who does not believe you will accept his kind of reasoning or who won't speak up because he would be putting down his friend who already gave the wrong answer.

Too much of the literature on Indian education is devoted to enumerating the problems. We have recognized the problems; let us look for solutions.

RECOMMENDATIONS FOR ACTION

There are no easy answers, no simple changes that would give all native Americans an equal opportunity for the success that others achieve, but there are teachers who have been innovative and understanding enough to succeed. Throughout the rest of this chapter and the chapters that follow are suggestions—ideas that have proven effective for individual teachers. It is up to you to select and adapt from them, to meet the needs of the individual students in your classroom.

1. Become Familiar with, and Accept, Native American Ways

Most of us assume that the Indian child will find that some of the ways of the non-Indian have value for him, and that he will want to adopt them for himself. Then we must also assume that the non-Indian child will see and want to adopt some of the values and ways of his Indian neighbors. Until we really believe that this is good, so that we make it plain in our daily attitudes in the classrooms, we will not give every student an equal opportunity; we are not ready to teach Indian students.

To be effective teachers of culturally diverse students, we must be prepared to understand and accept as equally valid values and ways of life very different from our own. If we become aware of the differences, then learn to know and understand the child's culture well enough to accept it as equally good and equally valid, then neither teacher nor child will be pressured to adopt the other's culture, and mutual respect and understanding can develop.

Educators sometimes speak of Native American students as being "disadvantaged." In reality these Native people have the double advantage of knowing and living in two cultures. The teacher, on the other hand, may know only one culture, and may have accepted that culture as being superior without any real thought or study. *It is the teacher, then, who is disadvantaged.* However, if the teacher does not know, understand, and respect the culture of the students, then the students are at a disadvantage *in this teacher's class.*

We have all heard unknowing people speak of Native students as being "culturally deprived". The very use of the term indicates the speaker's lack of understanding of their very rich cultures. A Blackfeet Indian told me, "A man stood on the top of the pass in Glacier National Park and said, 'I've heard there is some really fantastic scenery around here. Where is it?' The person who lives on an Indian reservation and calls his neighbors culturally deprived is like that man."

Don't let your actions or attitudes imply that one culture is superior to another. The purpose of education is not to turn all students into middle class citizens, or carbon copies of the teacher, but to prepare each student to live in a multicultural society. For this the student needs to gain enough knowledge of various people and cultures to be independent, to choose from each culture that which is best for him, so that he can be successful in his own way.

One Navajo told his daughter's teacher, "Don't try to make every child over like you. One like you is enough!"

If you, as the teacher, are to be respected by your students, then you must first demonstrate your respect for the children and their culture. However rich and worthwhile the culture of a people, if you, the teacher, do not know and understand both your own cultural background and that of your students, those students will be at a disadvantage in your classroom. You not only will fail to adapt to their experiential background, their motivations, and their values, but whether or not you are aware of it you will be exerting pressure for change, and giving the students the feeling that you do not respect either them or their culture.

The need for mutual respect seems obvious, yet in actual practice it is rare. Throughout the world, wherever the Native people have become the minority, they have found themselves under great pressure to adopt the culture, values, and ways of life of the dominant society. In most cases there has been very little respect for mores and values of the Native culture. Nowhere is this more evident than in the schools. In the classroom, the Native culture is seldom used, valued, or even understood.

Fortunately, in spite of all the pressures to change, many Native people have been able to retain their essential values, and some of the more important aspects of their old cultures. American Indians, Chicanos, Eskimos, Aleuts, Hawaiians, New Zealand Maoris, Aboriginal Australians, Camorros of Guam, Lapps of Norway, the Tribal people of the Philippines, the Natives of American Samoa, and the Gaelic speaking people of Ireland all have very rich and beautiful cultures. It would be a great loss to them, and to the world, if these cultures were to disappear. Yet the children of all of these cultures are often disrespected by people from the dominant culture and are pressured to change.

As Raymond Muessig says, "The observation that all people are different and capable of countless patterns of living is obvious and timeworn. What one does about variations in human beings is another matter. One can choose to ignore individual and cultural diversities in the hope that they disappear. Or he can acknowledge their presence and do everything possible to obscure, reduce, overrule, or eliminate multiformities in values, feelings, capabilities, wants, and actions. Sill a third alternative—the one that seems most compatible with an open society—is to enjoy, prize, foster, and protect distinctness in man. Would that all teachers opt for the third possibility."

How well do you really know the culture in which your students were raised? Until you know the culture, you will have prejudices, even if you are not aware of them, for *"prejudice is being down on what you are not up on."*

As an Aboriginal once told me, "You can't expect a person to see eye to eye with you if you are looking down on him."

2. Value the Student's Background and Provide Additional Experience

"Do not do unto others as you would want that they should do unto you. Their tastes may not be the same."

—Bernard Shaw

Clarence Wesley, Chairman of the San Carlos Apache Tribe in Arizona says: "The School curriculum is geared to a whole set of concepts and literary background too often totally unfamiliar to an Indian child. Few teachers have the time . . . or know how to go back and supply that deficiency or to teach the reading skills necessary to catch up. So the Indian child becomes confused and lost, and sits unchallenged while the non-Indian part of the class moves eagerly ahead."

Because the things the Native students know, as a result of their experiences outside school, are very different from the things which you might expect them to know, much of the material you present may be meaningless to them.

As you study, observe, and become well acquainted with the people of the community, learn how your students' background of experiences differs from your own so you will be able to adapt your instruction to their needs. Where students need additional background to understand specific subject matter, you have to help them build that background. Develop instructional materials which are related to student experiences, and present to the students problem assignments which relate to their backgrounds. Choose culturally related reading material for part of the instruction in reading and comprehension skills.

3. Identify and Emphasize Positive Indian Values

"Indian culture has not been wiped out. This culture has been greatly modified since 1492 but those cultural essences which have filtered down to the 1980s are still integral, shaping forces in Indian society, and these essences must be included in Indian education programs if they are to be relevant."

—Dick Little Bear, Northern Cheyenne (1986)

You cannot assume that any student believes in or follows all the values of what we might consider the "typical Indian culture" (if there ever was such a thing), or that he follows the patterns of the non-Indian society. Each student is somewhere in between, though he is usually nearer one end of the scale than the other. Even the Native American student who appears to have lost contact with the old culture of his people will usually vary from the student from the dominant society in his background of experience, the vocabulary he uses and understands, his ways of communicating, his willingness to talk and express ideas, his concept of time, his willingness to compete with his classmates, and his attitudes toward property, future and success.

If you are observant you will find many valuable and useful ideas and values that are integral parts of the traditional culture. Then be creative and you will find many ways of incorporating these into your classroom activities. This does not mean down-grading the dominant society. It means honoring the good in both societies, recognizing that two opposite approaches can both be right, that either can be best, depending upon the individual and the circumstances. It means teaching students to think for themselves, to know the alternatives, and to make their own choices.

4. Develop the Student's Self-concept

"How glorious it is—and also how painful—to be an exception."

—Alfred DeMusse

The importance of developing a good self concept cannot be overemphasized. To do well in school or in life, each person must know who he is and be proud of his background. He must have a positive self-image. Much of the curriculum and reading material of the typical school are designed to build this positive self-image on the part of the middle-class white student. The Native American may not get any of this positive reinforcement.

The high incidence of teen age suicide in tribal groups in which suicide was, in the past completely unknown, indicates that school is not leading to satisfaction and happy lives. Whereas the suicide rate for most teenagers is highest in mid-winter, for Native American students it is highest at the beginning and end of the school term. Suicide and poor achievement are both indicators of poor self-concept.

Since the self-image of the students is such an important factor in the success of education, the entire second chapter of this manual will be devoted to its development.

5. Promote Relaxed Communication

"Oh, the comfort, the inexpressible comfort of feeling safe with a person; having neither to weigh thoughts nor measure words. . . ."

—George Elliot

Communication, real communication, between teacher and student is essential to effective teaching. Misunderstandings, discipline problems, dislike for school, and lack of effort can all be caused by lack of understanding. If children feel that they can communicate with the teacher, that they can ask questions without hesitation, that they and the teacher can discuss their problems freely without emotional upset, that they can be relaxed with the teacher, then many of these problems will not arise.

With some Native students this will be our most difficult job. Many of them have been taught that they should not express an opinion, that they should not make a statement unless they are positive they are correct, or that silence in the company of an adult denotes respect. Others have already been in several classrooms in which their ideas were not respected or used, but were criticized by the teacher or ridiculed by other students.

How good a listener are you? To develop communication with your students you have to listen—really listen, both to their ideas and their questions. In group discussions and individually, in and out of class, let them see that you are really listening, that you are really interested in their ideas. You will never do this with one hand on the door knob and your eyes on the clock.

Show students that much of learning is trial and error. Show them that errors are a good way of learning. Instead of criticizing the mistakes and failures of your students, congratulate them on a good learning experience. Let them see that you, too, learn by experience. Don't try to conceal your own errors, weaknesses, and faults. Admit that you, too, can be wrong, that you make mistakes. Students need to hear a teacher say, "I'm sorry that I . . ." or "I was wrong about that," or "It was unkind of me to say that." Teachers gain, not lose, standing when they admit being human.

Listen to students' questions too. As Muessig says: "A student's request for help—almost any kind of assistance, however unimportant it may appear on the surface—is a genuine compliment and an unusual opportunity. It says, 'I am reaching out to you, and I trust you.' The pupil's appeal for aid can open future possibilities for a deeper relationship and more significant, enduring service. A teacher should, therefore, think twice before ignoring any plea that comes his way."

Part of listening is giving help when it is needed. "Few people ever get dizzy from doing too many good turns." This doesn't mean jumping in and giving final answers. Sometimes, as Erica Jong says, "Advice is what we ask for when we already know the answer but wish we didn't." More often, talking is a way of clarifying a question and the alternatives, and/or making a decision. Whenever a student can come to a conclusion for himself, he should have the opportunity to do so.

Eventually, if you listen well enough, students will share their feelings with you. Then you will know that you have developed real communication. Remember the Swedish proverb: "Shared joy is double joy and shared sorrow is half sorrow."

6. Develop a Culturally Relevant Curriculum

"If we cannot now end our differences, at least we can help make the world safe for diversity."

—John F. Kennedy

The Indian culture should become an integral part of basic instruction. Bring the Indian heritage, Indian values, Indian contributions to thought and knowledge into the discussions in every subject whenever possible. Show the students that you value their heritage. Impress upon the students that they have a great heritage and that their values are important. Help them to put their values into words that they can use to defend these values. Give them assurance that they can learn to live in the dominant society without rejecting the culture and heritage of their families and their community. Make the Native American culture a visable part of your instructional program. Give it a place of honor.

6

Too often teachers think they have given their Native American students a relevant curriculum by emphasizing Indian history in their social studies class, or by using some cultural material in the reading program. To really make your instruction relevant to the children's lives you need to use local examples in every subject, to use Native American values and examples in all of your instruction, and show how they apply to whatever subject you are studying.

7. Adapt Instruction to Students Learning Styles

"The Indian educational enterprise is peculiarly in need of the kind of approach that . . . is less concerned with a conventional school system and more with the understanding of human beings."

—William Byler (Then Executive director, Association on American Indian Affairs)

Every child has his own learning style, the way in which he learns most easily. Some are auditory learners, others visual. Some find kinesthetic experience most effective. Some of these differences are differences in innate ability. Others are caused by a learning disability in one area. For most children, however, the differences are cultural. That is, they are caused by a difference in early learning experience.

The majority of non-Indian urban students start school as auditory learners who are accustomed to much verbal communication and have acquired most of their knowledge through listening. They picture life in a linear fashion and learn well by starting with small parts and building from a larger concept. This is the kind of learning for which most of the school curriculum is designed. The majority of Native American students, however, are visual learners who have developed their knowledge by observation and their skills through demonstration and imitation. They learn best by starting with the larger concept, the whole picture, then learning to see the parts. Much more information will be found in the chapter on Growth through Native American Learning Styles.

Consider carefully the learning styles of each student. Present new learnings through as many different learning modes as possible and give your Native American students a fair chance.

8. Work with Parents and the Community

Know the homes from which your students come. Understand that there may be no place where a student can sit down and do homework, isolated from the extended family and from the TV.

Meet the parents. Let them know what you are doing in the classroom. Show them how it relates to daily life in the community. Many Indian parents make little effort to motivate their children's school work because the schools have not found ways of involving them in the school curriculum or of keeping them informed.

Attend community functions, expecially pow-wows or other cultural activities so children and their parents know that you are interested. Then in the classroom, help the students see how the material you are teaching relates to life in their community—that it has meaning in life outside of school. Make your instruction relevant to their immediate needs.

SUMMARY

J. Francis Rummel summarizes a great deal in one sentence: "Now that we have achieved education for all, let us now seek education for each."

There is much evidence of a need for improvement in the educational experience of Native children. Low levels of achievement, teenage suicide, and adult unemployment all indicate a need for better education.

There are many causes for this lack of achievement. Poor self concept and lack of motivation on the part of the students may be largely responsible. However these are brought about by many other factors inside and outside the school. Alcoholism and lack of community support are problems in many communities. But an education that is not relevant to the needs of the community is equally to blame.

There is no quick cure for the problems. You have to learn to understand your students and their culture before you can adapt to their needs. This takes hard work and a willingness to be flexible in both your thinking and your instructional procedures.

Start by learning about the culture, the backgrounds, and the learning styles of your students; learn them well enough so you can treasure them and use them in developing relevant instruction and in building effective communication and the self-esteem that will motivate your students to learn. Knowledge and understanding will help you to accept language differences and new ways of thinking. By meeting parents and taking part in community activities you can continue to learn and grow in the understandings needed to teach in your community.

Each of the chapters that follow will discuss some of the problems and will recommend ways in which positive changes can make instruction more relevant to the needs of Native students. Implementation of these suggestions will depend upon your ability to adapt these ideas to the needs of individual students.

The fact that many Native American students are not reaching their potential should not be a cause for discouragement, but a challenge: a challenge to every teacher to find ways of adapting to the needs of each student, to give every student an equal opportunity to succeed.

REFERENCES FOR FURTHER READING

Cheyney, Arnold B. *Teaching Children of Different Cultures in the Classroom.* Charles E. Merrill, 1986.

Finley, D. "Why Eskimo Education Isn't Working." *Phil Delta Kappan,* 64–8, 1983, pp 580–81.

Gilliland, Hap. "A Fable for Americans." *Chant of the Red Man.* Council for Indian Eduction, 1976, pp 24–36 & 74–83.

Jaimes, M.A. "The Myth of Indian Education in the American Education System." *Action Teacher Education,* Fall 1983, pp 15–19.

Johnson, W.S. and R.N. Suetopka-Duerre. "Contributary Factors in Alaska Native Educational Success: A Research Strategy," *Educational Reserch Quarterly,* 8–4, 1984, pp 47–51.

Little Bear, Dick. "Teachers and Parents Working Together." in Jon Reyhner, *Teaching the Indian Child: A Bilingual/Multicultural Approach.* Eastern Montana College Bilingual Education. 1986.

Mahan, J. M. "Major Concerns of Anglo Teachers Serving in Native American Communities," *Journal of American Indian Education.* Vol. 23, May 1984, pp 19–24.

Musig, Raymond. *Aphorisms on Education.* Phi Delta Kappa.

Reyhner, Jon Allan. "The Self-determined Curriculum: Indian Teachers as Cultural Translators," *Journal of American Indian Education,* Vol 21, Nov. 1981, pp 19–23.

Chapter 2

Promoting a Positive Self-Image

by Hap Gilliland

"A man can stand a lot as long as he can stand himself."

—Axel Munthe, *The Story of San Michelle.* Dutton.

Are your students happy with themselves? Do they have high self-esteem? This is the real measure of the success of any teacher. Achievement in school is more highly related to self-concept than to mental ability or any other factor. Give the student self-esteem, show him that he has the ability to succeed, let him believe that he is a worthwhile person who has and deserves your respect and the respect of his fellow students, and he will work, he will cooperate, he will succeed. Take away this self-esteem, leave him without hope, and he has no reason to try. To every student in any culture, self-respect is essential to success and a good life.

THE NEED FOR IMPROVED SELF-CONCEPT

"The greatest need among Native Americans today is having positive attitudes toward themselves."

—Carol Black Eagle (Crow Indian)

A child's concept of his own worth is the most significant factor in the development of his personality and his ability to work and play with others. Academic performance is also directly related to self-esteem.

As Father John Bryde said, "Practically all educators will agree that, basically, the overall purpose of education is to turn out happy and socially contributing human beings. This means that as a result of his education, the student feels that he is on top of his environment, is contributing to its development, and has a joyful sense of achievement according to his ability."

A child with self-esteem likes himself. He has a good feeling about his own personal-worth. Self-esteem is not only the key to motivation; it is necessary to clear thinking and to concentrated effort; yet as Floy Pepper (1985) says, "Many discouraged Indian children believe that they have little possibility of solving their problems, or even of moving toward a solution. They lack confidence and approach each challenge with the anticipation that they will perform poorly or fail."

11

Indian students are ahead of other students on self-concept before they begin first grade, but they fall far behind later (Bruneau 1985).

Suicide is now the second most common cause of teenage death in the United States, and suicide is several times as prevalent among reservation Indian students as in the general population. In the past year alone, one of every 200 Indian students attempted suicide. This is sure evidence of the great need for the schools to build the self-concept of the Native students. Yet as Edward Wynne, professor of education, University of Illinois, Chicago, stated in U.S. News and World Report, "When Scholastic Aptitude Test scores drop 5%, people hit the roof. But when the suicide rate of youth goes up almost 250%, you barely get a nod."

It is of critical importance that we, as teachers, recognize that if we are to be successful in teaching Native American students, we must, first and foremost, find ways to raise the self-esteem of the students.

NINE WAYS OF BUILDING A POSITIVE SELF-IMAGE

Although many Native students are lacking in self esteem, there are many others who are excellent students who attack their work with confidence. What are the reasons for the differences? Can some of the following suggestions help you to build the self-confidence and self-esteem of your students?

1. Start with a Happy, Accepting Classroom Climate

"I saw a child today who didn't have a smile—so I gave him one of mine!"

—Unknown

The climate you set in the morning may be the most important thing you do all day. Let your students learn from experience that when they walk into the classroom in the morning they will be greeted by a smile, a touch, the body language that says, "I'm glad you are here." This means you must go to the classroom as a happy, loving, caring adult. It means controlling your own life so that it includes recreation and self-fulfillment, so that you can be the caring, cheerful, confident, and compassionate person your students deserve for a teacher. And it means starting the day with some social thing to set the climate. It means letting your students know, through actions as well as words, that they are important to you.

Meet your students in the morning with a cheerful, positive greeting that says this day will be good. Remember that a smile produces a smile in return. Your attitude is more contagious than chicken-pox or measles.

2. Expect Every Student to Succeed

"Give me the benefit of your convictions, if you have any; but keep your doubts to yourself, for I have enough of my own."

—Goethe

A student gains an opinion of himself through "reflected appraisals"; his idea of what others think of him; his concept of the opinions of friends, parents, peers, teachers, and other individuals who are significant to him. What concept of himself will the Native student have when he reflects your opinions? Our attitudes and feelings are expressed in every action when our pupils are present. Native American students are exceptionally skilled in reading these actions, especially if there is any indication that they are being rejected.

A student will believe that he can succeed if he can see that *you* believe that he will. Let your approach to every student reflect your confidence that he will succeed. When teachers like their students and expect the best from them those students just naturally expect more of themselves.

3. Recognize Students' Strengths

"The dream begins most of the time with a teacher who believes in you, who tugs and pushes and leads you on to the next plateau, sometimes even poking you with a sharp stick called truth."

—Dan Rather, *The Camera Never Blinks* (Ballantine)

One of the ways in which we can lead a student to believe in himself is to identify and recognize his strengths. Every child has strengths. It is up to us to find them, to let him know about them, then to use his strengths to help him learn.

We must make sure that every student has success every single day. Call the student's attention to his successes. Make sure he is aware of them. Every person *must* have the memory of a series of successes to build the self-confidence to sustain his efforts when he has difficulty.

If you want to be respected by your students, remember that the pupil's opinion of you depends not on what he sees in you, but what you help him see in himself.

You can produce more gains in a week by proving to your students how much *they* know, than you can in a year by showing them how much *you* know.

A mother asked, "You say you think Miss Timber is a better teacher than Miss Jones. Why?" Her son answered, "When I'm in Miss Jones's class I think she is the smartest person I know, but when I'm in Miss Timber's class I think *I* am."

One teacher, in order to help her second graders see their own strengths, had each student write a statement beginning with, "I like myself because . . . "The statements she got were simple but revealing, and they helped her to find good things to emphasize. A typical statement was, "I like myself because I'm an Indian boy. I can ride a bicycle, and I take good care of my teeth."

There was one very gifted student in the class, who completely outshown the other students in a hundred ways. The teacher was anxious to see what kind of a list she would make. Her answer was very short and very instructive for the teacher who was just learning the Indian culture: "I like myself because I know how to make friends."

As Bennett Cerf says, "A pat on the back, though only a few vertebrae removed from a kick in the pants, is miles ahead in results."

4. Compliment Instead of Criticizing

"If a child lives with criticism, He learns to condemn. . . .
If a child lives with encouragement, He learns confidence.
If a child lives with praise, He learns to appreciate. . . .
If a child lives with approval, He learns to like himself.
If a child lives with acceptance and friendship, He learns to find love in the world."

—author unknown

Your attitude toward your students is mirrored in the students' thinking. They can build the self respect that is necessary to a happy life and to success in school only if they live in a school atmosphere that is warm and supportive, where each child is recognized by himself and others as a worthy individual who is wanted, respected, and liked.

Children look to others to confirm or deny that they are important or significant. Let your actions tell each child that he, as an individual, has your respect, that you respect those qualities that make him special and different. Let him know that what he does or says is special to you.

"Praise is like seven-up; it should be served while it is still bubbling." Praise given to a Native student for a job well done should be given immediately but unobtrusively. Don't wait until afternoon to praise a student for what he did in the morning. Speak to the student individually, unobtrusively, and let him know your approval, but don't hold him up before the class in a way that will separate him from his classmates. This not only can be humiliating to him but may cause other students to react negatively and thereby force him to quit trying. Remember that too the Native student the approval of his friends is more important than the approval of the teacher. Don't force him to choose between you and his friends. If you do, you are the one who will lose.

Can you find new and different ways of complimenting your students, and of reminding yourself of their need for praise, not criticism?

One teacher had an "I'm glad you're here" rubber stamp made. She used it on each paper that showed student effort.

One year when I felt I was not complimenting students enough I put a stick-on pad on the corner of my desk. Whenever I complimented one of my unsure-of-himself students I put a tally mark on the pad. My goal for myself was to have five tally marks for complements (and not more than one criticism) before noon.

Pointing out the students' good points and achievements will not completely counterbalance the ridicule of other children if it goes on in your class. You may have to teach your children to look for the good in each other. For those who have the problem of ridicule in their classes there are some suggestions in the chapter on discipline.

Gary Herman, editor of *The Love Letter*, says that there is a "language of encouragement" that we should all learn to speak. He lists the following basic phrases of "the second language that with careful practice we can learn to use like a real expert:"

"I like the way you handled that."
"I have confidence in your judgement."
"If anyone can figure it out I'm sure you can."
"What do you think would be the best way to . . .?"

"I like the way you tackle a problem."
"I can tell that you really worked hard on this project."
"Thanks, that was very thoughtful of you."
"I need your help on . . ."

Herman also points out that "effective phrases of encouragement seldom focus on judging or evaluating performance, but instead they are aimed at recognizing effort put forth, designed to build confidence, used to demonstrate acceptance, focus on contributions or assets, and show appreciation."

A calm atmosphere, in which students are respected will also do much to help the Native student get over his natural shyness. The kind of shyness that the Maoris call "whakama," the hesitant feeling where we don't quite belong, is natural for the Native student in the environment of the classroom. To pressure the child only increases it. "Feelings are everywhere—be gentle."

If your Native students are unsure of themselves and of your attitude toward them, they will "retreat into whispers and hide their lack of confidence behind impassive faces."

Students seldom express their feelings to teachers who are not caring, but one Aboriginal student blurted out to his teacher, "You don't care for me. No one cares for anybody! The whole world is crazy!"

Along with giving your students understanding, don't be afraid to show affection for them. Will Rogers said, "What constitutes a life well spent? Love and admiration from our fellow men is all that anyone could ask." Be sure, of course, that they *all* feel it, not just the good students. As one teacher said, "To love the world is no big chore. It's that miserable students in the corner of my room who is the problem."

In a study of Indian dropouts, a third of them mentioned that their teachers didn't care about them, or give them sufficient help (Coladarci 1983). Might your students feel that the only time they get any feedback from you is when they do the wrong thing? Why not ignore the mistakes and have fun trying to catch them doing something right!

5. Give Your Students Respect. Show Them That You Need Their Help

Too many teachers and other well-intentioned individuals look at the physical surroundings in which a child lives, the prejudice he faces, his problems in school, and they sympathize. They feel sorry for him. He does not need sympathy; he needs something to be proud of. Pity and pride do not go together. Building sympathy for a group of people may be a good way to raise money for a mission or a school, but it has no place in the work within the school or mission.

Chief Dan George (1970) expressed the idea much more clearly than I can:

"Do you know what it is like to be without pride in your race, pride in your family, pride and confidence in yourself? You don't know, for you never tasted its bitterness. .

". . . You hold out your hand and you beckon me to come over. Come and integrate you say. But how can I come? . . . How can I come in dignity? I have no presents. I have no gifts. What is there in my culture you value? My poor treasure you can only scorn.

"Am I to come as beggar and receive all from your omnipotent hand? Somehow, I must wait. I must delay. I must wait until you want something of me

. . . until you need something that is me. Then I can raise my head and say to my wife and family: Listen . . They are calling. They need me. I must go. Then I can walk across the street and I will hold my head high for I will meet you as an equal . . . . you will not receive me in pity. Pity I can do without. My manhood I cannot do without!"

How do we show our students that they have our respect—that we need them? We must develop our powers of observation and learn to see and assess each student correctly and fully. Every student has good points of which he can be proud. *We* have to learn to see them before we can help *him* to see them. Bring out his strengths and talk about what he does well.

The language experience method of teaching reading is one way of showing the child that you respect his ideas and of giving him something to be proud of. He sees that you consider his ideas worth listening to, recording, and using as reading material.

It hardly seems necessary to mention that helping students to become good readers, to solve math problems well, to achieve academically is one of the important means of building self-esteem. This can be enhanced even further if the student can also share his knowledge, and help another student to achieve.

One teacher I know can always identify the student who doesn't believe in his own ability, and she can identify the things that student can do well. She asks the student for help. She takes him to another student who is having difficulty and asks him to help that student. Both students are benefitted. Helping each other is an important part of Indian culture, why not use it more?

Ideas on helping students help each other will be discussed more throughly in the chapter on Learning Through Cooperation and Sharing.

6. Give Students a Voice in Decision Making

"Where the people posses no authority, their rights obtain no respect."

—George Bancroft [To Workingmen of Northhampton, Boston Courier, Oct. 22, 1834.]

One important way in which the self-esteem of any group of students can be improved is by showing them how to assume responsibility for their actions and trusting them to do so. Many Native students have not learned to take this responsibility because they have not been given the opportunity.

Students need to make decisions and choices. This really is another effective way of showing respect for each of them. Students must learn to see the consequences of their actions, not only to themselves, but also to others. They need to see themselves as responsible people. They can only learn this if we, their teachers, give them an opportunity to learn early how to solve their problems and give them experience in making their own decisions. They need to be asked their opinions, to have their questions answered, and to see their ideas put to use so they can learn to see the consequences, good or bad. Only in this way can they learn to make decisions based upon reasoning and thinking and develop the self-confidence necessary to be willing to make their own decisions.

Students will be afraid to make decisions until they trust their teacher, and our Native American students will hesitate to trust us unless we trust them.

The teaching of decision making skills will be discussed in the chapter on discipline.

7. Help the Students Develop Their Own Realistic Goals

If Indian students have no personal goals, they have little reason for effort. The tribe or community may enforce cumpulsory education laws and keep the child in the classroom, but they cannot force anyone to learn. The student needs a goal, an immediate goal, not vague talk about the future.

When you have recognized the students' strengths and shown them that they can succeed, then they will be ready to sit down with you individually and discuss where they have been, how far they have advanced, and where *they* want to go from here. Encourage the students to set goals that fit their talents and way of life, not those that fit your dreams. The goals must be *short range,* specific, measurable, attainable, and they must be *the students'* goals. *They* must see a reason for them and want to attain them. Otherwise the goals are yours, not theirs.

8. Understand Community and Individual Problems and Seek Solutions

No matter how positive your approach, or how great your desire to help your students, there will be problems within your school and your community that will interfere with student progress and will drag down the self-concept of some students.

One of these problems will be alcoholism. There is probably not any Native American student who is not adversely effected by alcoholism. No matter how good the curriculum, if the child, the members of his extended family, or his close friends are being physically or emotionally abused as a result of alcoholism, his self-esteem will be damaged.

High dropout rates, poor achievement, and behavior problems are all correlated with alcoholism in the home. The greater the amount of unemployment, poverty, and helplessness in the community, the greater the amount of alcoholism.

You need to really understand the disease of alcoholism to understand what is going on in the lives of your students. And you need to teach the children about it, to help them understand it as a disease, along with the destructive behavior that goes with it. But you must teach for understanding, without condemnation of the victims. If the students understand it as a disease, they can learn to cope better, and alcoholism in their families will have less effect on their self-esteem. If both you and your students understand the problem; the students can discuss it openly, along with their individual problems that go with it.

Some teachers have looked at this and the other problems and said, "what's the use?" and given up. Don't let this happen to you. Anywhere you teach, some of your students will have serious problems, and some will be the victims of drugs, alcohol, or abuse.

It is essential that you try to understand the problems effecting your students, whatever they are; that you be willing to discuss them openly in a non-condemning way, and that you help your students to adapt. Part of the students' self-esteem is in realising that they must not hold themselves responsible for their relatives but that they can take charge of their own lives.

9. Give Your Students Pride in Their People and Their Heritage

"Too many teachers, unfortunately, seem to see their role as rescuer. My child does not need to be rescued; he does not consider being Indian a misfortune. He has a culture, probably older than yours; he has meaningful values and a rich and varied experiential background. However strange or incomprehensible it may seem to you, you have no right to do or say anything that implies to him that it is less than satisfactory."

—an Indian mother*

To develop self-esteem the student must have pride in his people, and know that they are worthy of respect. For the student to develop this pride, you must show in your actions, and develop within your class as a whole, a respect for Indian culture and for Indian people as a group.

Give your students pride in their heritage by using the values of the culture in your classroom. Emphasize the positive aspects of the culture in your discussions. This is so important that Chapters 3, 4, and 5 will be devoted to learning the culture and using its positive forces in the classroom.

Show your respect for the language by learning and using at least some important words or phrases.

Teach about native history and culture. Use ideas from the culture in teaching other subjects. Use cultural objects as prominent parts of the classroom environment. Make the crafts, games, and music an integral part of your instruction.

Provide acceptable reading materials. Your students will quickly identify prejudice and stereotypical expressions. If you give them biased material to read, they will assume you agree with what is said, unless you precede the reading with adequate discussion of the author's bias.

SUMMARY

Self-esteem is the most important factor in achievement. Since may Native students have become convinced that they will not succeed, this must be a major concern of every teacher of Native students. How do we bring self-esteem to Native American students? How do we make them believe in themselves and want to achieve?

We must expect success and ignore weaknesses. In place of criticism we must recognize and emphasize the individual's strengths. Help the students develop their own goals—goals in which they *can* succeed, then *expect* success. Teach with encouragement, humor, and enthusiasm.

We must have respect for the students and show it in our actions. We have to treat them with the same kind of respect that we would like from them. Give them understanding and help preserve their identity, their self-fulfillment as worthwhile individuals.

*An excerpt from a letter written by an Indian mother to teachers of Indian children, published in the *Powell River News* of British Columbia. Reprinted in the *Navajo Times,* April, 1974.

We must teach students to face and understand the problems in their own lives and in their communities. Teach them decision making skills, then give them a voice in decision making, and responsibility for their own actions.

We must develop good communication. *Listen* to the students. Show them respect and let them know they are worthwhile as individuals, regardless of their academic achievement.

We must respect the students' people and their way of life, see the good things in the culture, learn its values, then show our respect for these values in the way we teach.

REFERENCES FOR FURTHER READING

Baird, Clifford G. *The Power of a Positive Self-Image.* Victor Books, 1985.

Bruneau, Odette J. "Self Concept." *Psychology in the Schools,* Oct. 1985. pp. 378–379.

Coladarci, Theodore. "High School Dropout among Native Americans." *Journal of American Indian Education,* Oct. 1983, pp 15–21.

Erlandson, Ray et al. *Character Education Curriculum.* American Institute for Character Education, 1985.

Herman, Gary. *The Love Letter.* Published monthly by Schoolmaster Educational Services, 412 South Second Street, Olivia, MN 56277.

George, Chief Dan. "What Will You Teach My Children?: Excerpts from a speech at the conference of the Canadian Association of Indian and Eskimo Education, Banf, May 1970." in Hap Gilliland, *Chant of the Red Man.* Council for Indian Education, 1976.

Gilliland, Hap. "Building Self Confidence." *A Practical Guide to Remedial Reading.* Charles E Merrill, 1978, pp 164–168.

Gilliland, Hap and Harriet Mauritsen. "Humor in the Classroom." *The Reading Teacher,* 24–8, May 1971, pp 753–756+.

Martin, James C. "Locus of Control and Self Esteem in Indian and White Students." *Journal of American Indian Education,* Oct. 1978, pp. 23–29.

McGinnis, Alan Loy. *Bringing out the Best in People.* Augsburg Publishing House, 1985.

Muller, D. G. and Leonetti R. Muller. "Self-Concept of Primary Level Chicano and Anglo Students." *California Journal of Education,* 1947, pp 56–60.

Pepper, Floy C. *Effective Practices in Indian Education: A Teacher's Monograph.* Northwest Regional Educational Laboratory, 1985.

Quandt, Ivan *Self-Concept and Reading.* International Reading Association, undated, 39 pages.

Phyllis Tempest. "The Navajo Student and the Tennesee Self Concept," *Journal of American Indian Education.* 24, July 1985.

Chapter 3

Discovering and Emphasizing the Positive Aspects of the Culture

by Hap Gilliland

"We must learn to appreciate diversity, not suppress it. How devastating to think of a world in which everyone is the same!"

—Janice LaFountain, Crow

Cultural diversity is like an orchestra. Each cultural group, like each instrument, retains its identity, making its own kind of music. But it becomes part of the whole, which would not be as good without it. As Garcia (1982) says, "There exist in the teaching-learning universe many progressive cultures, each rich complex, and worthy of knowing."

We must lead our students to understand that though cultures are different, no one culture is superior or inferior to another; that each not only is best for the people within that society, but that each culture benefits our society as a whole; that we all benefit from the ethnic and cultural diversity of American society. We must work toward the continuing development of a society which has a wholesome respect for the intrinsic worth of every individual. We must make allowances for difference. Let people be glad to be different.

LEARNING STUDENTS' BACKGROUNDS IN CULTURE AND EXPERIENCE

"If the dream of equal educational opportunity for Native Americans is to be realized, then education must be studied as a cultural process and this process must be made compatible with the Indian way of life. The Indian student dances to a different drummer. He/she hears Indian drums, not white man's drums."

—Dale Little Soldier (1981)

Teachers are often not aware of the seriousness of the problems children have in being Indian in the non-Indian world of the school, problems rooted in the difference in cultures. When main-stream children enter school, the ways, ideals, and values they are taught reinforce and build on the teaching they have received since birth. The same ideas and behaviors are rewarded. However, entering school for the native American can be a shocking experience. Many of the behaviors and expressed values are in direct opposition to what the child has been taught at home.

Before we can be really effective as teachers, we have to first be learners. We have to know the cultural values and experiential background of our students.

1. Recognize the Need to Know

Each cultural group has developed instructional techniques through which the children are taught from infancy until school age and in out of school situations throughout their growing years. By the time children enter school, many of their values, skills, and ways of learning are firmly established. These have served the cultural group over a long period of time. There is no reason to feel that they will not serve well in the future.

Before a person teaches children within any social group, that person should think seriously about how the mores, the values, the learning methods of that group can be applied in the classroom. Imposing on children ways of thinking and acting that are foreign to their group may make these children less well adapted to living within their own culture. If the school uses methods appropriate to the children's background there is no reason that children of any minority group should make less progress educationally than those of the dominant society.

Even though you may be an expert teacher, failure to learn the local culture can doom you to failure in the Indian community. Orvando (1986) reported that only 10 percent of Eskimo children in his study felt that any large portion of their school instruction was of use in their native village life, and 72 percent felt that the curriculum should include more Eskimo cultural activities. This is typical of studies of American Indians also.

Don't make the mistake of thinking that the old tribal ways and values no longer have meaning for your students, or conversely, of expecting that most of your students are well grounded in their own tribal heritage. Every Native child is somewhere between the two cultures. He may be doing everything the way of the dominant culture and appear to have lost all the Native culture; still he may deep down feel the way he is doing things is wrong. His inner feelings may still be Indian.

We can easily get some idea of the background of our students in general, and some idea of the experience of each student, but what is more essential is that we learn the cultural values around which our students build their lives. These influence their learning, attitudes, and behaviors even more than their experiences, but they are much harder to discover. They lie deep within the child's subconscious mind. They influence his behavior without his being aware of them, and he cannot express them clearly. The outward experiences of the Native child may not be much different from those of children from the dominant society, but the majority of Native children still retain many of the old values of their people. What are those values? Some are common to most Native groups. Others will vary with each cultural group and each community.

A culture is a way of life of a group of people, developed around a set of customs, beliefs, values, assumptions, attitudes, expectations, and behaviors. (A culture does not consist of physical surroundings.) All of us accept changes in culture and technology, yet our old values persist. These are taught consciously and unconsciously from infancy. Following them brings harmony and acceptance within the group.

In talking about differences in cultures, there is always danger of developing a stereotyped picture of a group of people and assuming that all those within that group fit the pattern. We recognize that danger, and the lack of understanding that can come from it, but we also recognize that we cannot develop understanding without talking about some generalities. An individual Chippewa is probably no more like his neighbor than you are like yours, but they have each been exposed to some of the same values, beliefs, and ideals. The more you can learn about the culture the more you will understand each individual.

2. Actively Promote Positive Values

Like people, cultures have good and bad points. As you learn the culture of your community, you are sure to find some things that are so good that you will want to accept them for yourself. As Gelett Burgess said, "If in the last few years you haven't discarded a major opinion or acquired a new one, check your pulse. You man be dead."

You are just as sure to find other things of which you disapprove. However, most values and ways of the traditional culture have the potential to be either helpful or detrimental in our classrooms, depending upon our attitudes and our adaptation of our instructional methods. For example, the children's willingness to share and to help each other may cause real problems for some teachers, but it can be a great benefit in most classrooms, particularly if the teacher plans her instruction to make use of it.

It is vital that you emphasize the *positive* and de-emphasize (not deny) the negative aspects of the culture at all times; not only in class but in your conversations with students, with people in the community, and with other teachers. If there are things about the culture of which you disapprove, talking about them will help neither you nor your students, especially in the lower grades. Cultural values develop because they are useful. Perhaps you disagree because you do not yet have enough knowledge to understand them.

As an example, two customs of the old life were frequently criticized in the books I read as a child. They criticized the men for letting the women carry the loads and for walking in front, "making the woman follow." I learned the reasons for these customs dramatically when I was living with the Yanowamo Indians of South America shortly after their first contact with the "outside world." A group of us had been gathering food and wood in the rain-forest. When we were ready to return to the village, one of the women had a huge basket of wood on her back, her baby on her hip, and still had to carry bananas and another bundle of food. I thought I could be helpful so I picked up her stalk of bananas to carry it for her. She became extremely angry. I soon learned that I had in effect told her, "You are not of any value. You are not worth protecting." I should have been concerned enough to have my bow and arrows in my hands ready to protect the women when we started down the trail. I was also expected to lead the way. Believe me, I was glad when, on other occasions, a young warrior went ahead and was the first to face the jaguar, the bushmaster snake, or the raider from another village, and let me take the "woman's position," several yards behind. . . . Now I understand these customs, and the importance of understanding the reasons for a custom before we judge it.

As teachers we should endeavor to know Native American cultural traits, as well as our local culture, well enough so we will know which ones apply locally. Then we can not only keep from being in conflict with the culture, but be able to discuss it and frequently point out to the students some of the values, the good things about the culture. We should put the values into words frequently, in a way that students can understand, and discuss them, so that our students learn to express them in their own words and can make their own comparisons and choices.

To help children eliminate prejudice, we can talk over with our students the stereotypes of Native Americans and other minorities portrayed on TV and in books. We can help them look at these from the viewpoint of the person being described. In many groups there are still traditional clothing, braids, and so forth which some students wear to identify themselves with their cherished heritage. These help them in keeping their identity. They do no harm to the school.

23

As we explore the different cultures throughout the world and their value systems we help rid our students of prejudice against any group of people who are different. Whether we intend to or not, we will teach what we value. Our students learn from our actions.

3. Become Part of Your Community

As Dick Little Bear says, "Teachers should try to grow while they are on Indian reservations. Many teachers who have had long tenure on Indian reservations negate that length by repeating the same experiences over and over again each succeeding year. The children deserve teachers who are willing to keep learning."

We have talked about the need for knowing the culture and background of our students. But how do we go about getting that knowledge? The next step should be to study information available about Native American cultures in general, including that contained in this and the following chapters, but giving special attention to any information you can locate which focuses on the local culture and the local community.

Of course some of the teachers who have been in the community for some time will have valuable information to share. The ones who are responsive to the community can provide you with valuable ideas about the culture, the things that work with the children, and even the political forces in the community. But remember that there are also many teachers, even with reservation experience, who still hold biases and prejudices.

Visit with the people in the community at every opportunity. Stop and talk when you see people in their yard. Let them see that you respect them and their culture, that you will be honest with them, that you are an open person easy to talk to, interested in other things in the community besides the school. Ask questions. Not intrusive personal questions, but questions about any upcoming community activity, anything of interest in the area, about their opinions, or questions like "How did you do this in the old days?"

Naturally, the most important people to visit with are the parents and grandparents. Don't wait to talk to them until there is a problem to talk about. First impressions are long lasting. Don't make them negative. Don't wait for parents to come and visit you. It doesn't happen that way. Involve the parents and other community members in the school whenever, and in whatever ways you can. Let them help you by working with projects and field trips, teaching crafts, and telling the children about their work. And make every contact an opportunity for you to learn as much as the children do.

Most important of all is visiting the children's homes. No other thing you can do will provide as much information about both the culture and the child as a visit to a home. No matter what you do to encourage them, some parents will never get to the school. The only way you will learn about their child is to visit their home. Even with parents and guardians who willingly come to the school, you will learn much more by a home visit.

In every school in which I have taught, I have visited the homes of most of the students. I have been told when I arrived in the community, "Not here—you can't visit homes here—a lot of the parents are ashamed to have the teacher see their homes." But I have always been welcomed; even more in the poor homes than in the well-to-do ones. But then, I happen to believe there is as much love in a poor home as a rich one—not as much love of money perhaps, but sometimes more love of children!

Many parents have told me, "You are the first teacher that was interested enough to come to see us." Of course a positive attitude is essential. I have known critical teachers who even I would not have welcomed to my home!

24

EMPHASIZING THE POSITIVE ASPECTS OF THE CULTURE

Certain psychological traits occur frequently among many different Native groups and are highly valued by them. These are cultural characteristics of which Native American people can be proud. They are the positive characteristics which we can bring out, and which will be helpful in our classrooms.

It is very important that we emphasize these *positive* aspects at all times, not only in the class, but in our discussions with students, with people in the community, and with other teachers.

Some of these values, customs and characteristics which are common to many Native American groups are listed below. These are the values of the traditional Indian. Each Native child will be living somewhere between the traditional Native American way and the traditional middle class Anglo way. Often a Native student acts more like the white child, but feels more akin to the Indian way.

In addition to the great difference between the culture and values of the urban middle-class and the reservation Indian, there are big differences between the many Native American cultural groups. Not all of these values will apply to any one group.

Dick Little Bear (1986) gives a good example related to his own tribe the Northern Cheyenne: "What is acceptable in one tribe may be taboo in another. For instance, in all Plains Indian cultures, eagle feathers are sacred. Yet among the Cheyennes, eagle feathers must not be touched by Cheyenne females. So for something that seems logical for a teacher to do, like awarding an eagle feather, or a likeness of one, to a Cheyenne female for an athletic or academic accomplishment is violating Cheyenne beliefs. Yet, doing so in a classroom with students from another Indian tribe might be perfectly acceptable."

Remember also that all of these concepts are continually changing, both in the Indian and non-Indian societies. Each child has a positive gift to be developed in his growth process as an Indian.

The list includes many characteristics common to many native people, but this is only a beginning. It is intended to give you some background, some ideas of what to look for as you learn about your own community. No matter how much you have learned from outside sources about the Native culture in general, or even about the tribe with whom you work, you must realize that your community and your students are different. This listing is intended only as a guide to help you study and observe your own community. You must determine which items apply to the Native American children with whom you work.

1. Eye Contact

A good example of misunderstandings and conflict that come from not knowing some detail of the culture is the attitude toward eye contact.

Many teachers insist that when they talk to a student, he must look them in the eye. They consider this a sign of trust and respect, and looking around a sign of disinterest or dishonesty. A child who continues to look down is considered stubborn.

To most Indians looking down is a sign of respect. In some groups, a person can only look you in the eye if you are on an equal footing. A parent with whom you become good friends and who has taught you some Indian skills may reach the point where he can look you in the eye, but a child—never. What happens when you insist that a student look you in the eye? You make it even more impossible for him to do so. In some Indian groups a person only looks another in the eye to show defiance. To do so is considered aggression. A Navajo stares at another person only when he is angry. The downcast eye is courteous. Persistently looking at a person is intrusive so being stared at is very disturbing. Unless they are quite acculturated, Indians in conversation are more likely to look off in the same direction than at each other.

A teacher told me about one student who would never say a word, nor even answer when she greeted him. Then one day when he came in she looked in the other direction and said, "Hello Jimmy." He answered enthusiastically, "Why hello Miss Jacobs." She found that he would always talk if she looked at a book or at the wall, but when she looked at him, he appeared frightened.

Kent Cook, principal of the Lame Deer School on the Northern Cheyenne Reservation, has students who come in to see him sit near his desk facing the opposite wall, and they will talk to him. If he has them turn and look at him, many of them will never speak.

2. Lack of Pressure from Time

"Do not be anxious about tomorrow. Tomorrow will be anxious for itself. Let today's own trouble be sufficient for today."

—Matthew 6–34

The Native American characteristic which is probably most misunderstood is their concept of time. To European-Americans time is very important. It must be used to the fullest. Hurry is the by-word. Get things done. Prepare for the future. They feel guilty if they are idle. They say, "Time flies." To the Mexican, "time walks." However, the Indian tells me, "time is with us." Life should be easy going, with little pressure. There is no need to watch clocks. In fact, many Indian languages have no word for time. Things should be done when they need to be done. Exactness of time is of little importance. When an activity should be done is better determined by when the thing that precedes it is completed or when circumstances are right than by what the clock says.

The fact that Indians habitually give less thought to time lapse than non-Indians was evidenced by an experiment which indicated that Indian adolescents' estimates of the time required to do a job were less than half as accurate as the estimates of their non-Indian counterparts (Anderson 1980).

Non-Indians often mistakenly interpret an Indian's relaxed attitude toward time as being a sign of indifference or irresponsibility, while some Indians think non-Indians are so dissatisfied with the present, and concerned about the future, that they never really live in the present or enjoy it to the fullest.

Time to the traditional Indian and non-Indian may be a very different concept. European-Americans accept time as a straight line from past to present to future. Our language emphasizes this concept and helps us think in this way. We use the past tense most of the time in our descriptions and also put a great emphasis on the future. Many Indian people describe time as a circle, and many Indian languages are based almost entirely on the present. In some there are no future tense verbs. The future has to be indicated by the rest of the content, and the past tense is seldom used.

I arrived at a meeting and asked a traditional Indian what time he thought it would start. He appeared puzzled about why I asked. After a moment he said, "What difference could it possibly make? You're not going to miss it. You are already here!" Ask an Eskimo what time an event is to take place, and his typical answer is "It will happen when we get there." He does not look at the clock; he looks at the weather. That is what decides his actions.

Patience and the ability to wait quietly are valued characteristics among Indian people. They may not understand the non-Indian's compulsion for continuous action and getting things done. Look carefully at the beadwork, quillwork, weaving, and other art works of the Indian people. Watch them at work. Understand the patience that is necessary to do these things.

When the typical non-Indian has a criticism to make he is often quite blunt. He gets to the point and expresses his feelings quickly. He may offend the Indian who is accustomed to much talk about the good things first. A teacher seldom has the patience to listen long enough to hear the concerns.

Pepper (1985, p. 182) suggests that Indian students have a unit of study on time, which would include use of time in the old cultures as well as in modern life. We have to teach the students that if they are to work successfully in the economic system of the dominant society, they must recognize the importance that others put on time and learn to work according to schedules; and they have to think ahead, to the affect of their present actions on the future. But we do not have to teach them that time is more important than people and human relationships.

Keep your scheduling flexible, so that there is not a feeling of pressure to finish at a certain time—or to stop in the middle of an unfinished task.

3. Time for Thought

"A man without patience is a lamp without oil."

—Andrés Segovia

During a discussion, Indian etiquette often requires a lapse of time before a response. A person should take time to think about a question. Grover Wolf Voice, a Northern Cheyenne elder told me, "Even if I had a quick answer to your question, I would never answer immediately. That would be saying that your question was not worth thinking about." Throughout a conversation, taking time and deliberating, imply that what the other person says is worthy of consideration.

Appreciate the patience of your students. Don't expect immediate answers that come without thought. Appreciate, rather than becoming impatient with their slow, deliberate, unhurried discussions.

Nationwide, approximately 25 percent of Indian students start school with little or no English, so also keep in mind that the Indian child may need a longer time to formulate an answer because, especially with a difficult question, he may have to translate into his own language, think it over, and then translate back into English.

In the classroom which contains both Indian and non-Indian students, the Indian student may never have a chance to speak. This may cause the non-Indian students and teachers to think the Indian is shy, withdrawn, disinterested, obstinate, unsociable, or that he is sulking or trying to ignore the teacher. When asking questions, few teachers allow enough time even for highly verbal urban children. What about the Indian children who are taught to wait, to think before answering? Many teachers never discover that some of their brightest students have answers because the verbal children with quick answers are the only ones who ever have an opportunity to answer. To motivate Indian children to take part in class discussions we must give them time to think out their answers—time to be right.

4. Respect for the Elderly

Modern Americans often value youth and wish they were younger. Books and magazines are filled with advice on how to look young, feel young, and act young. Both Eskimos and Indians respect the elderly for their knowledge, which comes from many years of experience. In the old life, when a person could no longer do hard physical work, he was given a place of social prominance and was searched out for guidance and advice. Even today, young educated Indians are often ignored and given few opportunities in their own communities because they have not yet the age for respect. However, some of the traditional Indians who twenty years age looked forward to the time when they would be sought out as they reached the wisdom of age now find that todays youth have accepted the White culture's emphasis upon youth.

Elders, both male and female, although they may be somewhat shy about coming to the schools are a good source of cultural information and wisdom, and they have many interesting experiences to tell students.

5. Valuing Leisure

In the old life, and in the present life of the rural Navajo and others, there is no distinct line between work and play. They will both bring happiness if they are in harmony with nature.

Traditionally Indian people depended on nature to satisfy their needs. They used what was available. They grew what crops were necessary. They hunted only as much game as was needed. To take more was wasteful of both Nature, time, and energy. They were not concerned with producing beyond their needs, acquiring materials, or saving what they would not soon use. People did not work just to be working or to look busy. They worked when there was work to be done and enjoyed relaxation when there was not. The puritan work ethic had no place in their culture.

Indian students and their parents may well be frustrated when children are assigned work for the sake of work. Homework assigned just because you think they should have homework goes against their principles and will probably discourage them from being serious about assignments that are really important.

6. Sense of Humor

Many early explorers reported that "No other people laugh as much as the Eskimos." Since I knew the Yanowamo Indians of Venezuela before they had any contact with the outside world, I am more inclined to think that no one laughs as frequently as a Yanowamo. Native Americans have always had a deep sense of humor related to life, to inner feelings. It is one of the things that makes difficult situations bearable. But humor is different in each society. Some teachers actually think that their Indian friends have no sense of humor. But that is not surprising since it is often claimed that the humor of a culture is usually the last part of the culture to be really understood. Modern Indians have accepted our light jokes, our open obvious humor, but much of their real humor is hard for the person new to the culture to detect. Jokes do not translate well, especially those that include idioms or puns.

Many Indians are especially good at condensing a statement into a few words, saying much with a verbal picture and a bit of humor. Often an Indian will listen to a long discourse of a white man, and repeat it to his friends in two or three sentences which convey the over all idea, plus his own sense of humor.

Listen to the humor of your students and their parents. Learn to enjoy it. If you can put humor into your classroom, if you can let the students see you laugh at your own mistakes and problems, and if you can encourage them to laugh at theirs, you will have moved a long way toward understanding Indian humor, building mutual understanding with your students, and having a smooth running, enjoyable classroom.

7. The Extended Family

The extended family has an important place in the lives of nearly all Native American children. Crow and Navajo mothers consider their sisters children as close as their own. In Cheyenne and many other Native languages there are no words for aunt or uncle because they, in addition to the actual parents, are called mother and father. Cousins are called brother and sister. Most Indian children are welcome to move in with an aunt or uncle because these are their "other parents." In the Indian community, kinship is identified with even the remotest family tie. All clan members are considered relatives. Therefore in traditional families, since all share responsibility, deaths and family breakups seldom result in homeless children.

In many Native families, the grandparents play a greater part than the parents in training the child. The larger group of close relatives gives the children a sense of security and protection which they do not find in the world outside their homes. Among their relatives they can feel accepted and safe. Because of this extended family there is less chance of jealousy, sibling rivalry, or of emotional upset when a baby is expected.

The child whose parents have moved to a new location to obtain better opportunities for employment may have lost the benefits of the extended family. This may be a great loss especially if the child is a member of a broken home. If, however, the family remains in the community with the extended family, a broken home may not be nearly as serious for the Indian child as for the more mobile middle class.

A Crow mother told me that Old Man Coyote noticed how driftwood clings together in the river and how strong that bundle of driftwood becomes, so he realized that people too should band together. So he put the people in groups and called them clans. To the Crow and the Navajo, the clan is very important. They consider themselves responsible for the actions of their clansmen.

Teachers should not be surprised if aunts or grandparents show up for conferences in place of the parents, or if they show as much concern about the child as the parents. Nor should they consider the child's living with another relative an indication of problems at home. These are normal relationships. Appreciate the fact that the child has numerous people to whom he can go for help or emotional support.

Indian children may have trouble relating to the basic reader stories in which each family stays within a separate house except upon very special occasions, where a family consists only of two parents and two or three children, and where life is child centered and adults frequently participate in children's activities. To them, the family consists of many relatives. Life is adult centered, and although children and adults do many things together, the children are participating in adult activities.

Most Indian parents are affectionate people. Touching and closeness are part of the relationship between parents and children. Some of them watch non-Indian parents and teachers and think they are "cold."

8. Courtesy, Privacy, and Autonomy

Indian children are taught not to interfere in other people's affairs or their rights as individuals. They should have respect for the individual's privacy, autonomy, and personal dignity. A person seldom gives advice unless it is asked for. You may find that Indian people will resent freely given advice, especially if it does not pertain directly to the instruction given in class. They may resist advice on personal matters of future planning. No one should presume to make a decision for another person or for the group, but cooperation with the group and concensus on group decisions is important. To the Navajo, good behavior means fulfilling their duties to the extended family, being generous, keeping their self-control, and minding their own business.

Indian children may not willingly share information about their families, expecially their problems. In counseling sessions, Indian students are less likely than others to reveal either family or school problems. Counseling will require much patience because it usually takes a long time for the student to get down to the real problem. Non-Indians often think Indians seem aloof and reserved, while to Indians, European-Americans may appear to be superficial and hence untrustworthy. However, Sharon BearComesOut, an Indian councelor, tells me that her students are "becoming much more open and trusting when it comes to sharing family concerns and exploring ways to help themselves."

9. Harmony with Nature, Spirituality, and Health

In the old culture great effort was made to live in balance with nature. People were part of nature, so health and well being were possible only if they lived in harmony with nature. Early Indians did not understand people who wanted to own the land, to control it, to change it, to use it, and to be masters of it. Air, water, and land could not be owned. They were part of nature and people were to live with them, not control or change them.

Marie Reyhner says that the Navajo regard nature as the best teacher. Nature is the basic source of knowledge of the natural order of things. It teaches us through the stars, seasons, wind, and animals to observe, and respect, and learn from nature without disturbing the natural order.

European-American society since the industrial revolution, has been more concerned with controlling nature. But we are moving rapidly toward the old Indian point of view. We should give the Indian people credit for their emphasis on the ecology, If we talk about this emphasis in the old life, perhaps we can combat some of the present live for now attitudes toward the ecology, especially in Alaska. The advent of cross country vehicles is promoting great irreparable damage to the tuntra and to all of bush Alaska. Discussions and school projects could bring community wide recognition and action on these issues.

In science classes we should give the Native people credit for their knowledge of nature, of animal ways, and the uses of plants. Nature, and the observation of nature, should be an integral part of our study. What better way could we begin the study of science than by honoring and using the Native people's knowledge of nature?

However, we have to be cautious about requiring Native children to pick, capture, handle, or disect either plants or animals if they are hesitant. Check first to make sure you are not forcing them to go against the taboos of their people. Even the "thoroughly assimilated" child may have strong feelings in this area.

Since all of the Indian's old way of life was surrounded by nature, and nature was spiritual, spiritual considerations were important in everything that was done. For the traditional Indian, religion, spirituality, still has a place in every act, and every decision, every day. Don't underestimate the importance of the spiritual in the lives of even the most modern of Indians. For most of them, it is much more important than for the majority of the general population. Lack of spiritual concerns and failure to cooperate with nature are considered better explanations for poor health, misfortune, or poor hunting, than are scientific explanations. We should not try to avoid the spiritual aspect of life in the students' discussions, or downgrade it in any way. Accept the spiritual explanations for things along with the scientific. They can provide two acceptable viewpoints that often go hand in hand.

Harmony with nature, and spirituality, are also necessary to good health. The main purpose of many Navajo healing ceremonials is to restore harmony between man and nature. Poor health results from disharmony with Nature. It affects a person, physically, spiritually, psychologically. Indian "medicine men" treated not just the affected part of the body, but the whole person. They believed that the mind and body were so closely linked that it would be foolish to treat one without the other. They were the early psychosomatic physicians.

Modern medicine is just beginning to recognize the importance of this. In 1984, St Mary's Hospital and Health Center in Tuscon hired Indian medicine man Edgar Monetathchi to teach their staff traditional Indian techniques of treating the sick with holistic medicine, relying on improvement of mental state along with treatment of physical ills. Since then medical personnel have come from as far away as Mexico and Europe to study their methods, and other medicine men are training people in California and other places. Paul Ortega, Mescalero Apache medicine man, says that ancient healing methods, healing the mind as well as the body, speed the recovery of patients after their treatment with modern medical techniques.

If teachers as well as medical personnel recognize the validity of Indian medicine, it will be possible for individuals to have the advantages of both the old and the new, rather than having to make either/or choices.

10. Respect for Ceremonies

Most Indian groups still carry on many traditional ceremonies and other activities. These are a very important part of the life of the community and the teaching of the children.

Marie Reyhner, a Navajo mother, told me:

"Traditionally, the teachings of the Navajo were handed down orally. Knowledge was regarded as sacred, and the teaching was not left to just anyone, who may not respect the teachings. Navajo children are taught by the mother, father,

31

uncles, aunts, and grandparents. The grandparents usually teach about the ceremonials, getting help from other elders if needed. Some of the ceremonials the Navajo grandparents would emphasize are a ritual for all at three months of age, a special ceremony for the baby's first laugh, the puberty ceremony for girls, healing ceremonies, welcome home ceremonies, thanksgiving ceremonies, and ceremonies of birth, marriage, death, protection, and others. They also teach about every area of family life: manners, personal relations, kinships, behavior, dress, not to be rude or immodest, to be gracious of relatives, considerate, and never stingy. Religion is very important—daily prayers of thanksgiving for food, clothing, family, relatives, for healing or wholeness, and for celebration.

"Many of these knowledges are important to the Navajo that may not be important to others. If one has determination to be good or to be accepted as one with knowledge, he learns what is essential for a Navajo to know, always stressing the good, suppressing the bad; encouraging sharing, giving, and compassion for your fellow men."

In most plains Indian groups, the sun dance and the vision quest are the most spiritual of the ceremonials. There are many other ceremonies, pow-wows, and other traditional activities which range from the highly spiritual to largely recreational and social. These are all important parts of the lives of our students.

It hardly seems necessary to say that teachers should always show respect for the ceremonies or that comments or actions that can be interpreted as disrespectful could permanently damage a teacher's standing and effectiveness in the community. Rather, why not ask an elder to come and teach your class about the ceremonies. He could help the students to see that it is much more important to understand the values than the actions or costumes.

11. Honesty

In most Native cultures of the past, honesty—telling the truth and keeping one's word—was one of the most important of all human characteristics. This was especially true of most North American Indian tribes. In other societies, such as the Yanowamo Indian tribe of South America, a person is supposed to tell the truth only to the people of his village and his personal friends. Lying to others is a respected practice, so it is important to know if the person speaking considers you a personal friend, someone worthy of hearing the truth.

To the Indian child, trust must go both ways. The person who does not trust others is considered untrustworthy. To be trusted, a person must trust the respect others. Watching closely to see that a person does the right thing is disrespectful and destroys his self-esteem.

12. Emotional Control

In most Native American groups, it is considered inappropriate for a person to express strong feeling openly in public. Actions that would evoke loud expressions of anger in most non-Natives are more likely to bring a shaking of the head and an expression of sorrow. Adults do not normally cry in the presence of others except in mourning.

SUMMARY

Teachers should endeavor to learn as much as possible about the cultures of the communities in which they live. The chart below summarizes some of the common values and preferences of many Native American people, contrasted with those of the dominant society. Just as it is obvious that all the items in the first column do not apply to any one non-Indian, the items in the second column should not be construed as all applying to any one Indian, and only to an extent to any group of Indians. These are generalities—and there are no "general" Indians. The cultural patterns of each tribe are different, and each Native American is an individual with his own ways and his own personality. Instead of assuming that any particular statements apply to your students, use the list as a guide to aid you in knowing what to look for as you study your own community.

EUROPEAN AMERICAN VALUES	NATIVE AMERICAN VALUES
Acquire, save. Possessions bring status. Wealth & security sought after.	Share. Honor in giving. Suspicious of those with too much.
Compete. Excel. Be the best.	Cooperate. Help each other. Work together.
Assertive, do-er. Dominate.	Passive. Let others dominate.
Vocal. Must Talk. Embarrassed by silence. Be noticed.	Quiet. Say what is necessary. Enjoy silent companionship. Stay in background.
Time is extremely important. Get things done. Watch the clock, schedules, priorities.	Time is here. Be patient. Enjoy life.
Prepare. Live for the future.	Enjoy today; it is all we have. Live now.
Keep busy. Idleness is undesirable. Produce to acquire and build reserves.	Enjoy leisure. Depend on nature and use what is available.
Give instant answers.	Allow time for thought.
Emphasis on youth.	Respect for wisdom of the elderly.
Work is a virtue.	Work for survival.
Light humor. Jokes.	Deep sense of humor. See humor in life.
Few strong ties beyond the single family unit.	Close ties to entire extended family including many relatives.
Analyze and control nature.	Live in harmony with nature.
Science. Reason.	Spirituality.
Act according to logic.	Act according to what feels right.
Health: concern for germs, cleanliness.	Health results from harmony with nature.
Traditions of varying importance.	Great respect for ceremonials and traditions.
Always look a person in the eye. Looking away means disinterest or dishonesty.	Looking in eye means aggression or anger. Looking down is a sign of respect.

Criticism is immediate, blunt, to the point.	Talk about good things before criticism.
Honor for the sports figure and individual achievement.	Respect for bravery, especially if for group benefit.
Personal space required.	Touching, closeness, affection.
Accept public show of emotions: anger, sorrow, affection.	Little evidence of emotion in public.
Visitors, associates, teachers must be welcomed inside the home.	Yard is appropriate place to visit teacher until well acquainted and accepted.
Monolingual. English is the best and only important language.	Bilingual. Values of culture are best expressed in the language of that culture.

REFERENCES FOR FURTHER READING

American Association of colleges for Teacher Education, "No One Model American." *Journal of Teacher Education.* Winter 1973. pp 264–265.

Beers, David. *It Happens When We Get There: Conversations with Teachers in Alaskan Villages.* Alaska Department of Education. 1978.

Brooks Anderson, Larry Burd, John Dodd, & Katharin Kelker. "A Comparative Study in Estimating Time." *Journal of American Indian Education.* Vol. 19, Number 3, May 1980.

Fiordo, R. "The soft Spoken way v.s. the Outspoken Way: A Bicultural Approach to Teaching Speech Communication to Native People in Alberta." *Journal of American Indian Education.* Vol. 24. July 1985. pp 35–48.

Fuchs, Estelle and Robert J. Havighurst. "Indian Education as Seen by community Leaders." Chapter 8 of *To Live on This Earth: American Indian Education.* University of New Mexico Press. 1983. p 182–190.

Galloway, Charles. Silent Language in the Classroom. Phi Delta Kappa Educational Foundation. 1976. 33 p.

Gilliland, Hap and Harriett Muaritsen. "Humor in the Classroom." *The Reading Teacher.* Vol 24, No. i, May 1971, pp 753–756+.

Grudin, Robert. *Time and the Art of Living.* Harper and Row. 1982. 225 p.

Little Bear, Dick. "Teachers and Parents: Working Together." in Jon Reyhner, ed. *Teaching the Indian Child: A Bilingual/Multicultural Approach.* Eastern Montana College. 1986. pp 222–231.

Little Soldier, Dale and Leona M. Forester. "Applying Anthropology to Educational Problems." *Journal of American Indian Education,* Vol. 20, No. 3, May 1981. pp 1–6.

Maloney, Ray. "Ten ways to Turn Out Terrific Kids." *Vibrant Life.* Jan/Feb. 1985.

Pell, Sarah J. "A Communication Skill Project for Disadvantaged Aleut, Eskimo, and Indian Ninth and Tenth Graders." *Journal of Reading.* Vol. 22, No. 5, Feb 1979. pp 404–407.

Pepper, Floy C. *Effective Practices in Indian Education: A Teacher's Monograph.* Northwest Regional Educational Laboratory. 1985.

Schaffer, Rachel. "English as a Second Language for the Indian Student." in Jon Reyhner, ed, *Teaching the Indian Child: A Bilingual/Multicultural Approach.* Eastern Montana College, 1986. pp 114–134.

Tiedt, Pamela L. and Iris M. Tiedt. *Multicultural Teaching: A Handbook of Activities, Information, and Resources.* Allyn and Bacon, Inc. 1979. 353 p.

Chapter 4

Learning Through Cooperation and Sharing
by Hap Gilliland

"What's wrong with this world? There ain't but one word will tell you what's wrong, and that's selfishness."

—Will Rogers

In that one sentence, Will Rogers, a Cherokee, expressed the Indian viewpoint that you must be aware of if you are to understand the Indian way of life.

If you are a teacher who has never lived among Native American people, and who is not familiar with the Native way of thought you may not realize, at first, the importance of cooperation and sharing. You may expect to motivate children through competition, and you probably assume that any person would work to become better off than his neighbors. In the Native American community you may become acquainted with a whole new orientation to life.

Let's look for a minute at the familiar middle-class urban child. He lives in a world of things. He is always much aware of the things around him and a desire for possessions. He knows that a person is supposed to work hard to acquire things. There is honor in getting, and even in keeping. His people unconsciously measure a person's value in terms of having fine possessions, which are status symbols and are considered highly desirable. A person should save for the future. "A penny saved is a penny earned." A person must "Put something away for a rainy day." In this middle class student's home, discussions center on things, on time, and on the past and the future.

Now picture a Native American child who lives in a world of people. To him, people are all-important. He may have few possessions, and they are of value mainly because they can be shared. Family members may be suspicious of the person who collects many personal possessions. "You can't get rich if you look after your relatives right." He has learned that having more than your neighbors may be undesirable. A person is not likely to be fond of the person he envies. This Indian child's interests are in the present and his goals center around people. Conversations in his home are about people and activities, and more often about people's qualities than about their accomplishments. His actions are based on people and their relationships. Many Native people cannot understand a person who puts possessions above relationships with friends and relatives. It has been said, "It is more important to be human than to be important."

I am not implying that owning the necessities is not important to the American Indian or that the dominant society is disregarding of people. It is the emphasis in life that is different. This difference in priorities is noticeable and important. Since these attitudes

37

affect the whole community as well as the children's relationships with the teacher and with their peers, as well as their motivation for school achievement, it is very important for us, as teachers, to understand the way of thinking that the Native child has learned in his home. To which of these ways of thinking should we gear our instruction?

THE SHARING WAY

"It is well to give when asked, but it is better to give unasked, through under-standing.

—Kahlil Gibran, *The Prophet,* (Knopf)

A look at the past will help us understand the Indian way of sharing. When the Plains Indian killed a buffalo, he shared the meat, not only with his relatives, but with all who needed it. He could do this with confidence, knowing that they would also share with him. One Indian, in describing his ancestors said, "They were all fat or they were all thin." How better could you describe a society in which anyone who had food made sure that no one went hungry?

Sharing in the old days was not only for friends. It was for anyone in need. In 1882, Sitting Bull and the last of his followers were returned to the reservation in South Dakota, where they lived in abject poverty. Four years later, Sitting Bull and about a hundred Sioux got permission to travel 500 miles West to visit the Crows who were relatively well off. The Sioux had always been among the worst enemies of the Crows, so government personnel expected the Crows to turn a cold shoulder and send them away. Instead, the Crows, knowing the condition of the Sioux people, loaded their wagons with blankets, food, and other needs, and sent them home with several hundred horses. Even today, the custom is alive. In 1987 the Crow tribe sent the Sioux several truck loads of coal to heat their homes. An Indian who butchers a cow or shoots an elk will nearly always give at least half of the meat to his friends and relatives.

Of course we are talking about the traditional Indian. In the last few years we have seen many of the children losing this feeling of wanting to share, but they still feel it is "right," and the parents and other adults still want their children to feel this way. Some say the sharing way no longer works because there are now too many "red apples" who will take, without sharing in return. A group of us were talking about this on the Northern Cheyenne reservation recently when Don Little, a Sioux, told us that although it may be true that sharing will not always result in others sharing with you at a later date, it does result in happiness, in health, in spiritual well being. It improves your mental health while it teaches your children your values and gives them good feelings and strength of character.

Today, at any Plains Indian pow-wow or special event, time is set aside as give-away time. Special give-away songs are sung and any person who has gifts to give brings them out and the herald calls out the names of the people who are to receive them. These gifts are often Pendleton blankets, hand made quilts, food, dishes, pots and pans, or bead-work and other crafts painstakingly created in the home. They may even be horses.

Among traditional Indian people, status is acquired through generosity, not thrift; cooperation, not competition. "It is more blessed to give than to receive."

As Marie Reyhner, a Navajo, explained to me, "A person who saves is stingy and should not be respected because he doesn't share his goods. Things that are saved are only spoiled or stolen or lost. A person who shares is happy. He is considered kind and is looked up to and appreciated, while the 'richer' person is feared and distrusted. If a Navajo is stingy, people will say he must have missed his first laugh ceremony while a baby, or they may suspect that he is an orphan."

LIVING COOPERATIVELY

Along with sharing goes living cooperatively. Among the Papago, Sioux, Zuni, and most other Native American groups, cooperation, equalitarianism, and informality are more important than individual achievement, self expression, or competition. The student does not feel any urge to out-do his neighbors, so competition does not produce motivation. In some groups, the individual who shows himself to be superior, rather than an equal and cooperating member of the group, could be ostracized. Students who excel are often belittled by others.

Students from a cooperative society will try to make every member of the group feel worthwhile. This may even include the teacher. A teacher on the Northern Cheyenne reservation told me, "I never felt like an Olympic star till I played basketball with my Cheyenne students. They were all so well coordinated and such good players I hesitated to play, but they immediately could see my skill level and what I could do and adjusted their playing to make me feel that I was doing my part and was an important part of the team."

A teacher in a Hopi school put a chart on the wall with the names of all the students on it. He told them, "Every time someone gets a perfect score in math I will put a star after his name." The first day about a third of the students received stars. The next day a few others earned theirs. No one produced another perfect paper until the teacher finally took the chart down. You see, any student who had already gotten a star could not turn in a perfect paper and get a second star, as there were some in the class who had not yet received their first. Fortunately, this was an all-Indian class. If there had been non-Indians in the class they would have built up a series of stars and the Indians would probably have had to follow their example. The teacher could have destroyed something very valuable without ever becoming aware of it.

SHOULD STUDENTS BE TAUGHT TO COMPETE?

"Man's unique agony as a species consists in his perpetual conflict between the desire to stand out and the need to blend in."

—Sidney J. Harris. *Field Newspaper Synbdicate*

Whenever we talk about eliminating competition and encouraging students to help each other, someone asks, "Shouldn't the students learn to compete so they can compete in the adult world?" Vince Lombardi, the football coach stated the attitudes of many schools when he said, "Getting a high grade isn't everything—it's the only thing." And others agree. Jules Henry says, in this book, *Culture Against Man:* "I deplore the fact that the elementary school pitches motivation at an intensely competitive level, but I see no sense in altering that approach, because children have to live in a competitive world."

Do they really? I have heard teachers use this same excuse for making unfair comparisons between the achievement of the brightest students and that of the average or low ability students. The teacher says the students will all have to compete as adults. But will they have to compete against people of all abilities and interests as the teacher forces them to do? Does the rancher compete against the medical student? Or does each compete only against another of his own ability and his own occupational choice? How much does either have to compete? In some occupations, like selling insurance, a person may compete daily, but he is only competing with himself, or against that segment of the population that has *chosen* to compete in the same occupation. Perhaps, in a way, you compete with other teachers to get your job, but you compete only against other teachers—and not face to face. Your success as a teacher depends greatly upon your ability to get along with and work with other teachers cooperatively, your willingness to share with them rather than compete with them.

A student can learn about urban society. He can be taught consumer wisdom. He can know what to expect from urban society and how to protect himself from unscrupulous business without adopting all the ways of the urban society. He does not have to compete with his friends or quit sharing with them. He simply has to learn what to expect and how to make intelligent choices. If you do get a child to compete and then reward him so that he is envied, he will probably have to pay the price by being ridiculed and picked upon.

Which kind of adults do you want your students to become?—those who will push anyone down to get to the top, or those who are always anxious to help their friends and co-workers? Go ahead—teach your own children to develop ulcers and be nervous wrecks when someone else gets the promotion, to lose the fun of the game because they have to have the highest bowling score, the prize in bridge, and the biggest house on the block. Teach it to your own children if you must—but don't teach it to mine!

EIGHT WAYS OF APPLYING NATIVE VALUES IN THE CLASSROOM

"Light is the task where many share the toil"

—Homer

In a day when every child is bombarded with TV ads aimed at making him want many things, and dramas that reflect the "get for yourself" thinking, it is important that we do all we can to encourage the Native American ethic of giving, sharing, and cooperation.

We can stress the Native strengths: the enjoyment of self created activities, the lack of keep up with the Joneses pressures, the freedom from the tensions of the competitive society. If we discuss with the students the Native society's emphasis on cooperation and helping others, they can develop pride in their culture.

There are many ways of using cooperative effort in the classroom. Here are eight that you might want to try.

1. Use Group Problem Solving

"By first doing a job together, each helper learns to do the job alone."

—Unknown

As a teacher, you will eliminate much frustration for both yourself and for the Native child if you do not expect him to be quick to respond individually. He will perform best as a member of a group.

In a group oriented, cooperative society the most effective assignments are problem solving assignments in which the students work on group solutions. Let two to six students work together on an assignment. Even in subjects like mathematics many of the assignments can be given as group assignments that the pupils are to solve together. In science and social studies, assignments can be set up as group problems with small groups working together to find solutions.

Instead of individual oral reports, a group can have a panel discussion in front of the class. When one person does give a report for a group, shouldn't the entire group stand together with him while he gives his report? He will find it much easier to talk in front of the class and each student will feel a part of the achievement.

When it is necessary that each student work on a different topic, after each student has chosen his own topic, the topics and who is working on them can be discussed with the whole class, and they can all be asked to watch for information on the other topics and to help each other find information. It is then the responsibility of the whole group to see that everyone is successful. The group is responsible for helping anyone who is having trouble. I tell my students that if anyone does poorly, they are all responsible—they didn't give him enough help! Individual praise, given quietly, should express appreciation for the help given to another, more often than emphasizing individual achievement.

We must be very sure that before the students begin to work, their plans are very specific and are understood by each student, but that they are group oriented rather than task oriented. The plans are more likely to be understood and carried out if they are developed cooperatively by the teacher and the students.

2. Try Peer Tutoring

"If you would thoroughly know anything, teach it to others."

—Tryon Edwards

The use of peer tutoring makes the students responsible for each other's learning. Both the tutor and the one being tutored feel responsible for doing as well as they can. Neither wants to disappoint the other. Helping each other becomes motivation for achievement, rather than a reason for holding back to keep from being resented by their friends.

Students boost their self-concepts by teaching each other. Nothing gives a student more confidence in his ability to do a task than to know he has taught someone else to do it too, or that his teacher had enough confidence in him to ask him to help.

The best students are often not the best people to use as tutors, especially if the class consists of a racially and culturally mixed group. Often the gifted student cannot relate to the problems of the student who has real difficulty and may also be impatient with him or make remarks about his ignorance. The child who has had difficulty with a certain concept

41

but finally has come to understand it, is often better able to understand and to help clarify the problems that another child is having with the concept than anyone else. In addition, he needs to clarify the concept in his own mind by putting it into words and explaining it.

One high school remedial reading teacher lets some of her remedial high school students practice reading books they have chosen for younger children. They then are excused from her English class to go to the lower elementary classrooms to read to the students. Everyone benefits.

Some parents, and a few teachers, think that peer tutors should not be used because they fear that this will be wasting the time of the students who are doing the tutoring and that the ones being taught are being deprived of the expert help of the teacher. This is the opposite from the truth. Every teacher who thinks about it realizes that when she teaches a skill for the first time, she learns even more than the pupils do. McWhorter (1971) found that when students tutored other students in reading, the tutors raised their own reading levels by an average of 2.4 years in four months, while those being tutored gained 1.1 years in the same period.

Older children tutoring younger or less skilled children can have double benefits if the older child, himself, needs practice. A sixth grader reading at first grade level may be indignant if asked to use primer type material for practice in reading. However, if he is asked to help a first or second grade child who is having trouble, reading this same material takes on status and responsibility. He builds his self concept and self confidence as he builds his reading skills.

Students should also be encouraged to get together to help each other outside of class.

3. Apply Cooperative Effort to Learn Writing Skills

Another good opportunity for students to help each other is through the use of peer evaluation during the teaching of writing skills. When students are doing any type of creative writing, give each student an opportunity to write something, then let the students divide into groups and read and evaluate the writing of each student in their group, helping them with suggestions of how they can improve their work. Thus the students are the final authority. The teacher does not criticize the writing. Each student has a real audience and a reason to write well. What he writes becomes important.

Thorough planning is essential and must include an explanation of the importance of *helping* each other by pointing out the *good* things in the writing, rather than down-grading it; of helping a person to correct his errors, rather than criticizing them. The group must accept responsibility for seeing that each person ends up with a paper he can be proud of.

4. Develop Group Pride in Achievement

There are some teachers who are able to develop in their students a group feeling of pride in belonging to a group of hard working students. They build in their students a loyalty to one another. In effect, this loyalty to the group includes the teacher. When someone does good work, the whole group takes pride in it instead of envying or criticizing as they do in other classrooms. This group feeling seldom comes about through the influence of a good leader among the students. It more often develops through the attitudes shown by the teacher, the comments she makes to the students in and out of class.

5. Lessen Competition for Grades

In any group in which peer approval and peer relationships are important, some good students will intentionally make poor grades on tests or will refuse to turn in homework to prevent getting a better grade than their friends. Grades based on final tests of knowledge are unfair measures in any case. The tests are largely a measure of previous knowledge rather than of how much was learned in this class or how much effort was put into the learning. The child who has no knowledge of a subject to begin with has no chance of competing with the one who already knew more than other students will when they finish. The slow learner knows that no matter how hard he works he can not compete with the gifted student who can make a good grade almost without ever opening a book.

Emphasis upon learning, on the fun of learning, on helping each other, and on making use of the knowledge in some immediate way, is much more effective. I taught for seven years in a school that gave no grades, so I understand the increased motivation when children are taught by the attitude of the whole school that the object is to learn as much as possible, not to get grades. Most of us are forced to give grades, even if we teach in a cooperative, non-competitive society, but we can put the emphasis on the student's improvement in his own work, on interesting ideas, and on the fun of learning.

One teacher eliminates individual competition for grades in this way. She tests the students when they begin the study of an area of learning. She then teaches and gives study material to the entire group. Each student receives a study worksheet which covers the information they are expected to know. The students are assigned to groups, each of which contains students of all ability levels. The students help each other complete their worksheets and learn the material. It is the responsibility of the entire group to see that each one has learned as much of the material as possible. They are then tested over the material. The scores of the group are totaled for a group grade based, not on comparison with other groups or expected knowledge, but on improvement over that group's original score.

6. Replace Competition with Others with Self-Competition

"There is nothing noble in being superior to some other man. True nobility is being superior to your former self."

—Hindu proverb

While students should never be required to compete with their friends, each one should be competing with himself, trying to surpass his own record. If tests are used for evaluation, they should be tests of individual *improvement*, and the results should be discussed in that light.

In my elementary classes, at the beginning of any new study in Social Studies or Science, I give a test over the entire unit of work. This is not only a basis for evaluating improvement, but a guide for study. When the students come to anything that was in the pre-test, they remember having seen it and know this is important. It is something to remember. Sometimes when I am talking to the class someone will draw in their breath. "Oh! You gave that away!"

At the end of the unit I give the same test again. I do not put a grade on the test. I mark the *correct* answers on both the pre- and post-test and return them to the student

43

together. The only comparisons made are those each student makes between his final test and his beginning test. A common reaction from children of all ability levels, as they compare the two tests, is "You mean I *didn't even know that!?*" Both the lowest and the highest ability students can see that they have learned, and this encourages them to work hard on the next unit.

It is only through this kind of comparison with their previous work that children realize how much they really do learn. Without this evidence they are unconscious of their increase in knowledge because no one can remember not knowing a thing. (Try naming some of the things about Indian education that you do not yet know!)

7. Encourage Students to Help Each Other

"To teach is to learn twice."

—Joseph Joubert

Whenever I talk about cooperative learning, some teacher will ask, "But how do you keep them from cheating? How do you know they are doing their own work?". . Instead of being forced to go it on their own, shouldn't students be learning how to help each other? Cheating is impossible if every student is *supposed* to help his neighbors!

In his own family and neighborhood, when a child sees a brother, a sister, or a friend who is having trouble, whether it is with another person or with a task he is attempting to do, the child knows that he should try to help him. Yet when he is in class and his friend is squirming because he does not know an answer, this child is told that helping is not allowed. Why? Couldn't we, the teachers, show the students that we appreciate their willingness to help? Couldn't the children learn form each other?

A group of third grade Indian students who I taught had been so drilled in not helping each other, and the evil of "cheating" by getting information from someone else, that they refused to ever let anyone see the work they were doing. They would even cover up the page they were reading when someone tried to look at it for fear that person would get some information. It took three months to get them to the point where they were willing to help each other, to work together on projects, and to take pride in group achievement.

The successful teacher of Native American students, and perhaps all students, is the one who encourages students to help each other, who teaches them how to help and emphasizes cooperation and mutual help, who can demonstrate self improvement to each student, without making comparisons with other students.

People are at their best when they are helping each other and working together. Regardless of race or cultural group, two heads are better than one. Working together is fun; it stimulates thinking; it helps us develop children's thinking skills; it motivates the students because each feels a responsibility to the group; and it makes the individual feel that others care. Since cooperative learning requires communication, it also improves language and self expression. This practice in communication skills is needed by many Native students.

8. Honor the Sharing Way

"The more you give, the more good things come to you."

—Crow Indian saying

If you look for them, there are ways that you can let the community see that the Native American way of sharing and cooperation is important in your school.

On graduation day 1987, at the Lame Deer school on the Northern Cheyenne reservation, graduation was combined with a pow-wow and give away. The school picnic was held in the morning with most of the fun being non-competitive (no winner or loser) Indian games. In the afternoon was the assembly at which students were honored for scholarship, athletic achievement, and so forth. This was followed by the graduation ceremony. Next came a traditional Cheyenne feast. Following this was a traditional pow-wow with the entire community taking part. After two or three traditional Indian dances with everyone taking part, the singer/drummers would begin an honoring song and one of the graduates and his family would lead the dance around the floor with all those who wanted to honor that student joining in behind. At the end of the dance that family would bring out all kinds of gifts—star quilts, home-made beadwork, and others—that they had been gathering or making for the last year, and these were given to all those who the family wanted to honor for having been in some way helpful to the student, and to other people as well. This is the Cheyenne way—the person being honored honoring others and giving the gifts instead of receiving them.

Each community had its own activities which honor the sharing, cooperative way of life. Could these be incorporated in some way into the school program?

There is a "new" game that has recently become very popular with American youth. Actually, it is a very old traditional Pacific Island game. An American visiting a Micronesian island chanced upon a group of people in a big circle playing a game. One person kicked a rattan ball high into the air with a fancy backward kick. While it was in the air everyone clapped their hands three times in rhythm. Before the ball hit the ground on the other side of the circle someone kicked it high in the air again, and so it continued.

The American asked a bystander, "Is this a popular game?"
"Oh yes, It is our most popular sport."
"But how do you know who wins?"
"Wins! That would ruin the game! Nobody wins. The fun is to keep the rhythm going."

The Plains Indians describe life as being (like this game) a circle, with rhythm that keeps it going. That rhythm is dependent upon people cooperating with each other and with nature. Let's help to keep the rhythm going!

SUMMARY

The Native American way of life is based upon sharing and cooperation, not upon acquiring and competing. Teachers who practice cooperative learning have found that in addition to raising achievement, it builds better attitudes toward school, it raises the self esteem of the students, and it increases their concern for others.

Some of the ways in which cooperative methods can be applied in the classroom are: encouraging students to help each other, the use of group problem solving, the observation and application of local family instructional techniques, peer tutoring, group effort in improving creative writing, lessening competition for grades, having students compete only with their own past records, and the development of school wide activities which emphasize generosity, sharing, or cooperation.

REFERENCES FOR FURTHER READING

Cathie Jordan. "Cultural Compatibility and the Education of Hawaiian Children: Implications for Mainland Educators." *Education Research Quarterly,* 8–4, 1984. pp. 59–71.

Kathleen McWhorter and Jean Leve. "The Influence of a Tutorial Program on the Tutors. *Journal of Reading,* 14, January 1971, pp. 221–24.

Chapter 5

Growth Through Native American Learning Styles

by Hap Gilliland

"There is nothing so unequal as the equal treatment of unequals."

—unknown

The way in which a person most easily learns and remembers new or difficult information is his learning style. It is our responsibility to learn as much as possible about the learning styles of each student in our classrooms and to adapt our instruction to those learning styles. Smith and Rensulli (1984) found that students taught through their preferred learning style achieved better academically, were more interested in the subject matter, liked the way the subject was taught, and wanted to learn other school subjects in the same way.

Each person in every culture has a unique learning style which results from his own reaction to his innate temperament, his inherent abilities and disabilities, combined with the conditioning he has received from his culture, his family, and his school.

There is in every cultural group a great variety of learning styles, but there is also a difference between cultural groups as to which mode of learning is easiest for the majority of the students. Teachers have found that some learning styles are more prevalent among Native Americans than among the general population. Being aware of these can help us to help these children more effectively.

Tests* can give us clues to the learning styles of children, but mostly we have to rely on observation of the children at work and discussion with them. Many children, when asked questions about specific ways of learning, can tell us which is easiest for them. The important thing is to learn the learning styles of the students and teach them *through their strengths.*

Whereas the larger proportion of European-Americans learn easily through listening and speaking, math, science, and sequence, the majority of Native Americans learn more easily when observation, artistic and spatial skills, and physical activity are emphasized. Many of them begin with a holistic view of a subject and are more concerned with feelings than with cold evidence.

---

*Red Fox Test & Learning Potential Examination (Council for Indian Education.) The variation between the various tests within the Wechsler Intelligence Scale for Children (Psychological Corporation) also provides clues.

Below are eight suggestions for ways in which we can find out about the learning styles of our students and adapt our classroom instruction.

1. Learn About the Children's Early Training

"An area of potential conflict in teaching Native children is the clash between the learning styles they have been exposed to at home and those used in the classroom."

—Rachel Schaffer (1986)

Since lifetime learning patterns are learned early, it will pay us to learn as much as possible about the instructional methods used in the homes of the community in which we teach.

Wax and Thomas (1961) say that "Sioux and other Indians begin to train their children to be highly sensitive social beings long before they can talk . . . Indian training in social sensitivity and in respect for others begins at birth, and apparenty, is reinforced with every interpersonal experience." They also suggest "that in both cultures parents and elders subject infants and children to an intensive and careful training, but that they use very different methods and emphasize very different skills."

Education in most Native American homes is much more casual, informal, and unstructured than in homes of the dominant society, therefore the majority of Native American children work more effectively in an informal atmosphere. Rigid formal arrangements of the classroom may be inappropriate. This does not mean that your lessons should not be structured or well planned, but after assignments are understood, letting the students sit on the floor to read or write, if they prefer, may promote better thinking. Try grouping around a table or putting desks in groups and allowing freedom of movement when students are studying.

Talk to the mothers of your community. Learn about their children's early training. See what can apply to your classroom. It is possible to expect concentrated effort and high quality work, and still be warm, accepting, informal, and democratic.

2. Use Family Instructional Techniques: Demonstration and Imitation

"There are only three ways to teach a child. The first is by example. The second is by example. The third is by example."

—Albert Schweitzer

In many Native American homes, the mother guides the learning by modeling household duties expected of the children. A child learns through observing over a long period of time, then begins to practice the skill as he feels secure in doing so. Verbal interchange and explanation are not a major part of this process. The process takes longer than the method of most classrooms, which is to listen and then learn through trial and error, but the child retains his feeling of confidence and security throughout.

Indian children taught in this way are usually reluctant to exhibit before others clumsiness or inability to do a task. Only when they have observed until they feel competent do they feel that it is appropriate to take over and do the task. Nash (1958) relates how a Mayan girl learns to operate a weaving machine in a factory. "She will not try her hand until she feels competent, for to fumble and make mistakes is a cause for . . . public shame. She does not ask questions because that would annoy the person teaching her, and they might also think she is stupid."

It can be expected, then, that children accustomed to learning through imitation may appear hesitant when expected to do a task after only being told how to do it. And it is not surprising that teachers unfamiliar with the instructional techniques of the Native American family mistakenly interpret the children's reaction as shyness or sullenness.

Is there any reason why these family instructional techniques cannot be used in the classroom? Many tasks can be taught through demonstration, letting the children learn through their superior skills in observation. This can be followed by practice in small group, letting those students who have learned the skill and feel more secure perform the task first and help the others.

Philips (1972) says that on the Warm Springs reservation, when teachers used small group, students directed, watch and learn instruction, the Indian students were more cooperative than non-Indian students.

3. Let Children Learn from Children

Nearly all Native American children are a part of an extended family. Therefore, children are accustomed to spending much time with a small group of children who play and work together, and who learn with and from each other. They are thoroughly accustomed to a type of "peer tutoring."

In some more traditional groups the small child spends the major portion of his time under the charge of an older child, and by the time he is four or five he is a full-fledged member of the group. The group provides a great deal of the child care and is charged with much of the daily work of the household. Parents relate to the group of siblings and their companions as a group, rather than dealing with each child individually. When an adult is pleased or displeased by what a child has done, the whole group may be rewarded or blamed. Children develop confidence in their own competence and their ability to act independently. This independence is an essential ingredient of their self-concept.

New information and skills are usually learned from siblings and companions. The child learns through both observation and participation. He develops competence gradually, as a part of a group, and his effort is accepted as a part of the group's achievement. By the time he starts to school, he is thoroughly familiar with a type of peer tutoring.

In many Native American communities that once relied on this kind of home training, the situation is changing rapidly, partly because of modern work schedules, but mostly because of television viewing occupying a major portion of the children's time. In some homes, however, the old peer group teaching is still in effect.

Since the Native Hawaiian system of child care is very similar to this American Indian system, the Kamehameha school puts this kind of learning into the classroom. The classroom is divided into a number of learning centers. During the Reading-Language time, the class is divided into several groups and the teacher works with each group for 15 to 20 minutes teaching a skill. She concentrates her efforts on this group, with little interruption from the other students, all of whom are sitting in groups, working. A child does not stay with the group with which he received instruction, but with a group which includes some children who are more skilled and some who are less skilled in the group activity. Each child is practicing a skill in which he has received some instruction, but which he has not mastered. As he needs help, he can usually get it from the other children in the learning center. The children understand that their behavior must not disrupt other groups and that they are to give each other help or feedback as it is needed. No child is forced to work alone. This primary school program has proved very successful, not only in their school, but in a number of other schools with ethnically Native Hawaiian children. They have raised the average reading scores of the children from below the 30th percentile to above the 50th, and achievement in other subjects comparably. Similar methods have been found applicable to other Polynesian and to some American Indian children.

If the extended family system of learning in the home and the community, upon which this instructional system was based, is common to your American Indian community, you may be able to apply much of what has been described. However, this depends upon the home training in your community. The system just described has not been found successful with Navajo students because many of them live apart and learn to work and play alone. What is important is that you look around, see how children are learning skills and responsibilities in your own community, then determine how you could apply some of the home instructional techniques of your own community to make your own classroom more effective for your students.

4. Teach Through Stories and Legends

"Stories are one kind of truth and reality. They are maps of knowledge in memory."

—Sandra Rietz (1986)

The oral literature of the Native American people is much more than something to entertain the children and occupy the grandparents. It is an organized way of passing on the knowledge and behaviors necessary to the society.

Stories also slant the way a person sees the world, and in that way, change the world in which the child lives. The view of the world embodied in the stories of the culture becomes for the child the "natural" view. This is what is real. We experience the world, not with impartial senses, but through our habitual ways of thinking, our memory, imagination, emotions, and will. The truths and the structure of the universe, as each person knows it, are partly the result of his own oral tradition. It has been said that "Myths supply security in an uncertain world."

Traditionally, the teaching of proper behavior and moral values was indirect and informal. Much of this was through the telling of stories and legends. Most of the stories emphasized, but not obviously, one particular value such as generosity, courage, or cooperation.

Just as the child in the traditional Native home learned the values early through stories and legends, the modern Indian child can begin from his first day of school learning proper behavior and values at the same time he is being interested and entertained through stories. There are many good Indian stories and legends in the books available that teach particular values. *Tonweya and the Eagles,* for example, teaches the importance of helping each other rather than competing; *Coyote's Pow-wow,* the need for sharing; *Red Horse and the Buffalo Robe Man,* being kind to animals, and *Northern Cheyenne Fire Fighters* builds the self concept of the Indian while teaching the importance of bravery and being dependable in the modern world. The evil of outdoing friends, or carrying competition too far is taught by the Crow legend *Blue Thunder* in which two boys forget their friendship in competing with each other and end in the distruction of not only the boys but their families as well. In most of the Indian legends now in print, the moral behind them is not obvious to the learner, so discussion of what *the students* think is the value emphasized may be important. Some of the old fables from other cultures are also good to use with Indian children.

The oral literature of the community and story telling within your class can be the basis for your beginning instruction in reading and writing, as well as inspiration for much creative writing of older children. Written versions of stories the children have heard—in their homes and in class—can build the bridge between oral and written communication and make beginning students feel "at home" with the idea of reading, even if they have had no exposure to a reading environment before starting school. Stories from the local culture can also provide the basis for the development of other skills—speaking, writing, creative dramatics, listening, even mathematics.

In addition to the myths and folk stories of our community, another important source of stories we should tap is the real lives of Indian heroes, past and present. These should include the lives of tribal leaders and local elders. Telling the stories of the lives of real people and discussing what made them great can help shape the character of our students.

Traditional stories when told in the native language convey much more meaning and feeling than any translation can convey. The telling of stories can then be a very important part of the responsibility of the bilingual teacher or teacher aide. It can also be an important reason for bringing parents and grandparents into the classroom. Even if most of the students do not speak the Indian language, they will get a surprising amount from listening to stories told by elders in their own language. One school which I visited had children from several different cultures. Parents from each of these cultures came to the school and told stories and taught songs in their own language. While building in each child pride in his own heritage, it unified the class with a pride in their group as a whole and in their ability to cooperate and help everyone in the group.

Stories help people know their place in society. They give them a sense of perspective, a feeling of what is right and good. They help them understand relationships between people, and therefore, between themselves and others. Because these are so important, many of the traditional Native American stories are sacred to the tribe that tells them. Therefore, however useful storytelling can be in our curriculum, we must preserve the traditions connected with it. If there are stories which are to be told only at certain times or places, these constraints must not be ignored.

5. Utilize Visual Learning Skills

"Sometimes you have to be quiet to be heard."

—Swiss Proverb

The majority of middle class Caucasian children begin school as auditory learners. They have been bombarded with verbal information since early childhood. Their parents talk to them a great deal. They are encouraged to talk, to learn new words, to express their ideas. Their parents have taught them many things through verbal explanations.

As shown in the examples given earlier, many Native American students have learned to do things by observing, by imitating. The majority have become visual learners.

This does not mean the teacher can make assumptions as to the learning style of any individual. It does mean that the great emphasis on oral learning in most classrooms will not be appropriate for most Native American students.

Most Indian children are taught very early in life not to interrupt when adults are talking and not to interfere when adults are busy. Even toddlers do not become noisy and attempt to keep the attention of their parents.

Most Indian people value the ability to sit still quietly. They are comfortable with silence. Talking for the sake of talking is discouraged. When they talk the tone should be soft, never harsh or loud. And they should not appear to know more than the others in the group. The soft voices sometimes upset teachers who equate soft speech with secrecy.

When I conducted a survey in which I had local Indian people interview 100 Indian parents on each of six reservations, one of the questions asked was, what are the things your child dislikes about his teacher? The answer given more than four times as often as any other was "She talks too much"! Maybe we should remember the saying, "Nothing is often a good thing to do, and always a clever thing to say."

At an informal party, among strangers, a majority of non-Indians try to make talk with whoever will listen. They feel compelled to act, to make contact, to cover their uneasiness with talk, with action. Traditional Indians, on the other hand, will stand or sit quietly, saying nothing, watching, learning, trying to discover what is expected of them, and speaking only when they are sure of themselves. White people find their place by active experimentation, Indians by quiet alertness. One Indian said about a white acquaintance, "He'd rather be wrong than silent." Little Wolf described the need clearly: "Less mouth thunder; more hand lightning."

All children need to learn all the different reading skills but when the emphasis is on phonetic instruction, linguistic materials, rhyming words, word families, and building words from word parts; when you use formal organized instruction with few choices, much direction, frequent checking of work with specific time limits, and motivation by adults; remember that these are the learning modes of the auditory learners who make up the majority of the non-Indian population.

Most Native Americans are expert observers. They learn easily from demonstration and note every detail. They also are good at reading non-verbal messages from actions, gestures, and facial expressions. They learn much about a subject or a person through observation. They usually do better than their non-Native peers on observation and visual learning tasks, visual discrimination, and spacial configuration. Why not teach through the skills in which they excel? If they do better after seeing a thing done than hearing a description, couldn't we use modeling to encourage learning? Instead of describing what we want done, we could do the task and have the children watch. Show them the right way. Ask the children to imitate what we have done. All children pay more attention to what we do than what we say.

In turn, when the children are reluctant to answer questions, they may respond better if we let them respond with action or demonstration rather than with verbal description.

Reading instruction can emphasize modeling, through oral impress instruction and tape recorded story books. We can use films and filmstrips, concrete objects, pictures, graphs, roll playing, socio-drama, and creative dramatics. Have the children handle objects while talking about them. Teach vocabulary using word games.

Although most Native American students are good visual learners, the more verbal teacher rarely fully utilizes or encourages the observational skills of the students.

6. Employ Active Learning Strategies

"Statistics show that we remember 10 percent of what we read, 20 percent of what we see, 50 percent of what we see and hear, and 90 percent of what we do."

—John Barth

Most Native American children learn much more readily when instruction is multisensory, relevant, and active, so they have several opportunities and alternate means to absorb the information, and they have the memory of concrete experience to which they can tie the principle.

For persons with tactile and kinesthetic learning abilities, we can use tracing of words written in crayon, writing in sand, demonstrating comprehension through action, and group activities. Give them freedom of choice, freedom in organization, and few time limits.

Use a wide variety of three dimensional objects and change these frequently. Provide freedom to move while learning, and use input from the children in planning so that the children have a sense of control. More emphasis should be on teaching students how to think, than what to think, and they can learn it best through materials which they can feel, touch, and manipulate. Remember the Chinese proverb: "I hear and I forget. I see and I remember. I do and I understand."

7. Advance Holistic Intuitive Learning

The majority of urban Caucasion students learn most easily when learning is done step by step, beginning with the parts and building toward the whole. They process information in a logical, sequential, linear, judgmental fashion.

The majority of Indian students, on the other hand, are whole concept learners. They prefer to start with the whole, then move to the details. Explanations are clearer to them when they move from the whole to the part. These children are good at seeing the unity and harmony in the larger situation. Breaking up learning into a series of minute hurdles can be very discouraging to the Indian student who can't see where it is all leading.

Begin with the larger concept, and from that develop the parts, rather than the other way round. For example, in studying the community, it is better to start with the characteristics of the community as a whole, then later, if helpful, discuss separately the social, political, and economic aspects.

In reading, whole word approaches, choral reading, and oral impress should precede breaking words into phonetic parts and comprehension into specific skills.

In social studies, forget about building concepts step by step from small details; look first at whole emerging patterns then let the children learn through stories, parables, pictures, imitation, music, and poetry.

SUMMARY

Each student has his own learning style through which he can learn most easily. Although all learning styles are found in all groups of people, the majority of children learn most easily through the learning styles traditionally practiced by their own cultural group. Below are listed learning styles more common among Native American students, contrasted with those of non-Natives.

SUBURBAN-CAUCASION LEARNING STYLES	NATIVE AMERICAN LEARNING STYLES
Well defined, organized.	Informal atmosphere.
Auditory learner. Prefers verbal instructions, explanations.	Visual learner, prefers demonstrations, illustrations.
Listens to explanation then learns by trial and error. Wants teacher as consultant.	Observes carefully then tries when he feels secure in doing so. Wants teacher as model.
Prefers direct instruction. Likes to try new things.	Prefers to be shown. Likes learning through stories, pictures, activities.
Starts with parts, specific facts, and builds toward the whole.	Starts with general principles, holistic, overall view.
Insists on reason, logic, facts, causes.	Accepts intuition, coincidence, feelings, emotion, hunches.
Competes for recognition.	Cooperates and assists.
Task oriented.	Socially oriented.
Impersonal, formal, structured.	Personal, informal, spontaneous.
Likes discovery approach.	Likes guided approach.
Relies on language for thinking and remembering.	Relies on images for thinking and remembering.
Likes talking and writing.	Likes drawing, manipulation.

REFERENCES FOR FURTHER READING

Bernstein, Norma T. "The Effect of Training in the Congitive Uses of Language Deficit of Disadvantaged Kindergarten Children," in J. Allen Figurel, *Better Reading in Urban Schools.* International Reading Association, 1972.

Cattey, M. "Cultural differences in Processing Information." *Journal of American Indian Education,* 20, Oct. 1980. pp 23–29.

Garcia, Ricardo L. *Teaching in a Pluralistic Society: Concepts, Models, Strategies.* Harper and Row, 1982, 209 p.

Greer, Mary and Bonnie Rubenskin. "Once there was a Student," *Will the Real Teacher Please Stand Up?* Goodyear Publishing Co. 1972, pp. 1–31.

Kersey, Harry A. Jr., Anne Keithley, and F. Ward Brunson. "Improving Reading Skills of Seminole Children." *Journal of American Indian Education,"* 10–3, May 1971.

Lombardi, Gerald and Frances Lombardi. "The Family, the Tribe, and the Human Race." *Circle Without End.* Naturegraph, 1982, pp. 40–67.

Nash, Manning. *Machine Age Maya.* Memoirs of the American Anthropological Association, No. 87. 1958, pp. 26–27.

McGinnis, Alan Loy. *Bringing Out the Best in People.* Augsgurg Publishing House, 1985.

Pepper, Floy C. "What do Teachers do about Learning Styles?" *Effective Practices in Indian Education.* Northwest Regional Laboratory, 1985, pp. 122–129.

Pepper, Floy C. and Steven L. Henry. "Social and Cultural Effects on Indian Learning Style: Classroom Implications." *Canadian Journal of Native Education,* 13–1, June 1987.

Philips, S. U. "Participant Structures and Communicative Competence: Warm Springs Children in Community and Classroom." in S. B. Cazden, V. John, and D. Hymes (Eds.) *Functions of Language in the Classroom.* New York, Teachers College Press, 1972, pp. 370–394.

Rietz, Sandra A. "Preserving Indian Culture Through Oral Literature." in Jon Reyhner, ed. *Teaching the Indian Child: Bilingual/ Multicultural Approach.* Eastern Montana College, 1986, pp 255–280.

Shaffer, Rachel. "English as a Second Language for the Indian Student," in Jon Reyhner, ed, *Teaching the Indian Child: a Bilingual/Multicultural Approach.* Eastern Montana College, 1986, pp. 114–133.

Tharp, Roland G. "The effective Instruction of Comprehension: Results and description of the Kamehameha Early Education Program." *Reading Research Quarterly,* 17–4, 1982, pp. 503–527.

Wax, Rosalie H. and Robert K. Thomas. "American Indians and White People." *Phylon,* 22–4, Winter 1961, pp. 305–317.

Chapter 6

Discipline Through Motivation, Decision Making, and Self-Control

by Hap Gilliland

Classroom Management, the control of the students, is the greatest concern of the majority of teachers throughout the United States and Canada. Every year from 1969 to 1985 lack of discipline was number one on the list of problems of public schools, according to the annual Gallup Pole of Public Attitudes Toward Education (Carter 1987).

Although schools everywhere are having discipline problems, those with a majority of Native American students are less likely to have problems of serious violence, but fighting, picking on each other, ridicule, and poor attitude are common.

Some teachers fear teaching Native American children because they consider them undisciplined. Others prefer them because they find them so cooperative. Which behavior the students exhibit depends largely upon the teacher's understanding of the ability to use culturally acceptable means of control and motivation. Eight means are recommended for maintaining a smooth running classroom.

1. Build Interest, a Love of Learning, and a Desire to Achieve

"Nothing great was ever achieved without enthusiasm."

—Ralph Waldo Emerson

A study of 500 well diciplined U.S. and Canadian Schools found that these schools focused on positive attitudes and prevention, not punishment; problems, not symptoms; faith in their students and their teachers; and they emphasized that their schools were places to do valuable, successful, productive work. (Wayson 1985).

In the traditional Indian home, expectations were often quite definite, perhaps exact, but love combined with gentle discipline was the system of control rather than force. In fact, the Cheyenne, among others, said that the child must always be convinced, not forced. Developing interest, motivating a child to want to learn, is always much more effective than telling him that he has to do a job. There is a saying: "Education makes people easy to lead but difficult to drive, easy to govern but impossible to enslave." Some teachers lead; others attempt to enslave.

Classroom control is about ninety-five percent motivation and interest and only five percent "discipline." Motivation depends upon our learning the students' needs, and their interests. If we meet their needs, students will work willingly. If we provide for their interests they will be enthusiastic. When there are discipline problems, it is well to look at our means of motivation. Have we given the children a reason to want to achieve?

Motivation is the key to a well-behaved classroom in any culture. With Native students, group motivation is at least as important as individual motivation.

If we can develope in our students a real curiosity about the things we teach so that the majority of the students are really interested and motivated, they will take care of discipline. They will work with us and will censure anyone who interferes with what they want to do most, which is learn.

We cannot expect the students to already have the understanding that school is important and that we as teachers are to be respected and obeyed. Many Indian families see little relation between school and the important things in life, and they may have little respect for teachers in general. Any respect we receive, we will have to earn.

The very word *discipline*, as defined in most schools, is a negative concept. It assumes a need for correction. The best prevention of problems is a positive attitude and a tension free classroom. We have to work to make the classroom a friendly place, a home away from home. Look at the classroom and say, "Is this a place I would choose to be if I were a child?" Native children respond quickly to the pleasant classroom. I have seen a lot of students who the teacher had to push out the door at the end of the day to get them to go home. The majority of them were Native children.

Most Native children will work very hard for a few words of approval from parents or an elder, or from their teacher. They may be very insensitive to punishment, but they react very favorably to praise. However, the praise must not be the loud obvious praise which separates them from the group.

The Sioux way is to not be concerned with eliminating bad behavior, but developing positive good behavior. This comes through shared responsibility. You and your students must work as a team to develop a pleasant atmosphere through mutual understanding. The cause of a great many discipline problems is depersonalization. Let the child know that "You belong here. We want you. You are important as an individual." Show him through your actions that you mean this. He will not believe what you say unless he sees it in your actions.

Both positive approval of good behavior and punishment of bad behavior give the child attention. Both reward the behavior. If the only time a child gets any individual attention is when he misbehaves, then it is this attention which gives him the sense of importance that he needs. Naturally, he continues the behavior. The effective means of discipline then, is to recognize and compliment only good behavior. Except in extreme cases, ignore the bad. This also follows the system of control most often used in the homes of Indian children.

The secret is to support and reinforce the kind of behavior of which we approve. There are many ways of doing this: a touch, a smile, a wink, a pat, a helpful comment, giving the child more opportunity to go ahead his own way, laughing with him, or helping him to make his own choices. These are the kinds of rewards that are meaningful in the long run.

Show all the students that you believe in them. Challenge them. Let them know that you consider their misbehavior, like their other mistakes, as opportunity for them to learn and to grow. Show them by your actions that you see them as good worthwhile persons. If you expect them to misbehave, why shouldn't they?—It won't make you think any worse of them than you already do. But if you *know* they will do their best, they will.

The problem free classroom is the one with a teacher who enjoys teaching, and lets the children feel this enjoyment. Are you compassionate? Do you like children? Have an equal liking for children of all cultures? Is this evident from your *actions,* not just from what you say? Let them see that you still like them—even after they have "screwed up." Don't be afraid to like your students and don't be afraid to let them feel it. Be sure they *all* feel it, not just the good students. As one teacher said, "To love the world is no big chore. It's that miserable student in the corner who is the problem." The feeling that nobody loves them is the most common reason teen agers give for attempted suicide, drug abuse, and serious discipline problems in school.

Indian adults treat their children with the same respect that they expect the children to give them. That is what every teacher who wants the cooperation of her students must learn to do.

One of the most serious problems in many Native classes is the way some children ridicule others. Our setting the example, and always complimenting the good instead of pointing out the bad is one way of improving this situation. However it often requires more direct action. Diane Bakun, when teaching a class of Eskimo students, kept a jar of marbles on her desk. Whenever the entire class could get through one period—opening until recess, or recess until noon—without anyone ridiculing anything anyone else did, she put a marble in the jar. When the jar was full, the class had earned a party. She also had a rule that whenever students said anything that down—graded another, they could not do anything else until they had given that person two compliments.

Another teacher I observed, whenever someone made fun of someone else's answer, would say, "I wouldn't do that Jim, or we will have to do it to you."

Occasionally behavior is such that an effective means of control other than the positive *must* be found. Isolation is usually the most effective form of control. Since it removes the child from the group approval which he seeks, it is effective if it is approached as a means of changing behavior, not of punishment for what was done.

2. Follow Cultural Patterns of Control

In areas such as the Northern Plains, the old cultures were largely built around a hunting and warring society. That way of life is largely gone. Children can no longer see that to deviate from the prescribed behavior may endanger the lives or food supply of themselves and the tribe as a whole. However, the practice of giving the child a good understanding of the reasons for and possible results of their actions, then leaving it to them to make the right decision in all but life and death situations, is still the common practice in most Indian homes.

Discipline is unstructured. Children are unfamiliar with the type of discipline in which they simply do as they are told without question. In the home, children are allowed to work together with very little supervision, giving them a feeling of autonomy, trustworthiness, and competence. They are given reasons, a knowledge of needs, then freedom of personal choice. They are responsible for their actions and the consequences. At the time when survival depended on the right choices, this was all that was needed. It is no longer as easy for them to see the importance of doing what adults recommend.

If Native American children have not become accustomed to dictatorial rules or irrelevant punishments, they must know not only what is required, but why it is necessary. If they are punished in any way, they must know for exactly what, and why it resulted in this (hopefully logically related) punishment. And they must understand throughout that the teacher still regards them, not as bad or worthless persons, but as worthy, respected individuals who are being helped to learn.

Wax and Thomas (1961) say, "It is misleading to call Indian child-rearing practices 'Permissive' or 'indulgent.' It might be more accurate to say that is usually does not occur to Indian parents to permit or forbid their children to do anything, much less permit or forbid them to move their bowels. White parents, on the other hand, see themselves as 'permitters' and 'forbidders.' Nevertheless, from the Indian point of view, they [white parents] leave vast and very important areas of their children's behavior completely unstructured."

Discipline problems which are based in resentment toward the teacher, or the system, are hard to cure because it is very difficult to identify the cause. Allowing students to voice their resentments can clear the air.

Before criticizing or punishing children, try to understand the reasons for the problems. For example, with the Indian emphasis on sharing and cooperation, attempting to motivate students through helping individuals obtain something that is not to be shared, or to gain an advantage over another, may produce an inner resentment that will lead to discipline problems. Teachers sometimes instigate classroom problems or playground fights by asking students to compete for a prize. There can be great resentment toward the child who competes and wins, then does not share.

One Indian school checked its records of all punishments meted out during the year and 60 percent were for tardiness or absence from classes! Yet tardiness is usually the fault of the parents rather than the child. If there is no alarm and the home does not run by the urban time schedule, it may be almost impossible for the child to always be on time. If a girl is the only baby sitter and her mother is going to the doctor, responsibilities at home will come before school. The school needs to work with the parents to try to solve these problems, but if the child is continually scolded, punished, or harassed for something he can do nothing about, he cannot be blamed if he makes little or no effort to improve in those or other ways. Let the child know you believe he is doing his best and you will usually see improvement. A system of group and individual rewards for promptness may help.

A few rules are necessary but most discipline can be unstructured. Unstructured discipline is more flexible, and is better understood by the Indian child. Indian children are often "thoughtless" but seldom intentionally disruptive. The reason they seem thoughtless is because school type restrictions are so foreign to their way of life at home. It takes time and patience to develop an understanding of the importance of having a controlled atmosphere at school.

Problems that arise can best be handled through individual non-directive counseling. Once you and your student really know each other, individual discussion can eliminate most of your problems and make life happier for both you and the student.

Be honest with the children about what you are trying to do, and your reasons. Then when it goes wrong, admit that it didn't work, and try something else.

Physical punishment usually had no place in the traditional society. The use of force to obtain discipline was almost unknown, and is rare in most Indian groups today. Most parents believe that both demeaning criticism, and harsh or physical punishment, especially in public, are rude, disrespectful, and harmful to the child's self concept. Frowning, ignoring, or shaming are more common means of showing disapproval. However, shaming in front of others can be devastating to the Indian child.

One way that you can judge any disciplinary action that you plan to use is by asking yourself, how would you, as an adult, react to this same treatment from a superior? Would it maintain your self-respect? Would it make you want to cooperate, or would it make you want to rebel? One Indian said to a teacher, "You have a right to do to a child in class anything you are willing for the principal to do to you during your teacher's meeting." Public criticism destroys the self-respect upon which all your discipline and achievement depend.

Public punishment of a child, even if the rest of the class feel that the child has done wrong, forces the class to take sides. Who has done the greatest wrong, the child or the teacher? It may force the other children to become affiliated with each other against the teacher. Control can never be effective if it is teacher against the children. It must be the class united with the teacher against the wrong do-er.

Most Native American parents never raise their voices to the shrill level. They use a voice that is soft, even in tone, non-judgmental and unemotional but firm. The children are not criticized as people. It is the act, not the child, that is disapproved. When a teacher hears an Indian parent disciplining a child in his Native language, she may not even be aware of what is happening unless she knows the language, because the voice is low and calm, often lower than when just talking with the child. When parents hear the teacher discipline in a loud, harsh tone, they think she has lost self control. The teacher has lost the respect of both the parent and the child.

Open conflict with a student affects the entire group's respect for the teacher. A teacher who displays frequent irritation suffers loss of respect. If criticism must be given, it must be done privately. Criticism and shaming, if used, must not be overwhelming or personal, and must always be accompanied with instruction that will help the student to do better. Humor and good natured teasing are Indian substitutes for direct criticism. Teasing is criticism that is indirect, so the person has the right to accept it or reject it, but he understands its meaning. This is a commonly used means of discipline in many tribes. In some, such as the Crow, the mother's brothers and their children are the "teasing cousins." It is their responsibility to tease the one who gets out of line, to help him to see the error of his ways. In this way, the child does not have to be criticized directly, and the discipline does not have to come from the parents.

Model the behavior you want. If you want children to respect each other, you must show that you respect each of them. Native American children are experts at learning from demonstration and example. This is as true of teaching discipline and attitudes toward each other as it is of teaching subject matter. Having the children roleplay a situation, then discussing how they felt, or would feel in that situation, is one of the best ways of teaching discipline. It is especially effective with problems of ridicule or of interracial conflicts.

A sense of humor is one of your most valuable tools. Don't hesitate to laugh with the children, at yourself as well as at the problems that arise. Indian children have a tremendous sense of humor, and they appreciate it in others. Your sense of humor can relieve a great many tensions that could lead to problems. It can help build your personal relationship with the children.

3. Use Peer Group Control

The power of peer pressure cannot be ignored or overestimated. Students often do things which are against their better judgement because they want the approval of their peer group, or because they want to avoid the criticism or ridicule of their peers. This peer pressure is blamed for a great deal of the present delinquency in our cities. It is an even greater force in the lives of American Indian students who live in a group-oriented society based on cooperation and dependence on each other.

Peer groups are therefore an effective means of social control. Group approval is much more important than teacher approval. If an individual has to make a choice between cooperating with the group or the teacher, the group will win. To the autocratic teacher this means sure trouble. But for the teacher who can motivate the group, get them interested, and work with them, the peer group can greatly decrease the number of disciplinary problems.

Order, or disorder, can be created by the students as a group, depending upon their relationship to the teacher, and their understanding of the value of the classroom activities. Let the students have a part in decisions, and in solving classroom problems. Talk with them, and *listen to their ideas.* If you don't listen to their ideas, you are saying that their ideas are not important; therefore the students are unimportant. When you listen, and expect them to have good ideas for solving the problems, you are giving them respect, and building their self-concept.

Class decisions are better and receive better cooperation if concensus is reached, rather than being decided by a straight vote. Nearly all Indian tribes originally made decisions by concensus and some tribal councils still operate under that system. Instead of taking a vote, and deciding a matter according to which side has a 51 percent vote, each person has an opportunity to voice his opinion. After each opinion is expressed, everyone tries to see how the plan can be changed somewhat to incorporate that person's ideas. In the end everyone should feel that the plan is the nearest they can come to having complete agreement; all opinions have been considered, and everyone has yielded to reach concensus. "Tribal council" consensus type meetings apply Native American values and they are good training in democratic action because they require the involvement of all, with unselfish cooperation and mutual respect. The object of the individuals in the group is not victory. The object is a wise, workable plan, amicably decided upon. Roberts rules of order are more efficient in that they take much less time, but they are not nearly as democratic.

When rules and decisions on action are made by the group, rather than by totalitarian rule, the group will back the decision and control will be fostered rather than opposed by peer group pressure.

4. Let Students Know Your Expectations

"To err is human, to forgive divine—but to forget it altogether is humane."

—Gloria Pitzer's Secret Recipe Report

Whether on the athletic field or in the classroom, the students want to know the rules, but they have to know the reasons for them, and they have to be applied consistently. But the fewer the rules, the better the game, and if the players can help set the rules, they will understand them and remember them better, and be more willing to follow them.

Whenever possible the parents should have a part in developing school-wide rules. This way they will understand the reasons for them and feel that they are important. Otherwise most Native parents consider discipline strictly the problem of the teacher. It has nothing to do with them.

Time spent establishing routines and giving students a sense of responsibility and mutual respect the first two or three days of school is worth more than many hours of correcting students and trying to enforce rules later.

Don't squelch discussion of the rules, and don't hesitate to revise them until all understand and agree with them. Don't assume that the students already know what is unacceptable behavior. You cannot have a rule that covers every specific situation. If the students internalize the principles they should be effective even when they don't apply exactly. Indian children learn best by example. Find, discuss, and role play some examples of situations to which they apply. If students agree that these rules are essential for cooperative living, they soon become effective and automatically obeyed. Whenever it is discovered that a rule is no longer needed, that it is ineffective, or that it causes more problems than it prevents, then eliminate it happily.

Rules must not only be understandable, they must be enforceable. Rules like "Be good," "Behave," and "Act like gentlemen" are neither. They are, therefore, useless. Be sure each rule is reasonable, and that the child is *able* to follow it. Once the rules are agreed upon and understood, insist upon their being carried out. "You cannot love someone you let walk all over you." Nor can the child love the person he walks over. A rule unenforced says: "Rules do not have to be followed."

High standards are essential, both in quality of work and behavior. When you do not have high expectations in class-work, students interpret your attitudes as saying that what you are teaching them is not really important. When behavior standards are low, you are saying to the students, cooperation is not important, and I really don't care about my students.

A teacher should always expect respect from the students, and not accept disrespectful behavior; but it has to go both ways. Indian students are very aware of the kind of respect you are giving them and cannot be expected to give respect if they are not also treated with respect.

Don't condone unacceptable behavior, but let your students know that rules are not to produce punishment, but to set clearly defined limits by which the group can live together more comfortably and effectively. The object is to have the rule followed, not to punish the one who doesn't follow it. Ignore irrelevant behavior. Pay no attention to the tantrum if the rule is followed. The goal has been achieved for this time, regardless of the attitude in achieving it.

If it is necessary to penalize a person for not following a rule, the penalty should be immediate. A penalty to take place later has little meaning to a student oriented to the present, and it makes for a long range disgruntled attitude. In the old days, on the rare occasion when a person had to be punished for not following the rules, as soon as the punishment was over, so were all resentments. The person took his place as if nothing had happened. This is the way it should be in the classroom. If the Indian child understands the reasons for restrictions he will seldom hold any resentments. He will also assume that the incident is gone and forgotten on the teacher's part as well. Both of you can start the relationship fresh.

Once in a while you are bound to make a mistake in the punishment you mete out. Whether the cause is anger, or not having all the facts, or just not considering the child's viewpoint, if you see that it was a mistake, or decide the punishment was unjust, don't ever hesitate to say you were wrong, and apologize to the student. It will raise your standing as a person, identify you as a caring person, and make up for the act which the class has already recognized as unjust. No one should ever try to pose as a person who never makes mistakes.

Unfortunately there are some school rules that must be followed which some students interpret as going against their way of life; there are also skills that students must learn to prepare them to be able to fit into both cultures. The children's attitude and cooperation in these cases depends largely upon the teacher's approach to them. Gloria Moore, a Navajo, described to me one such situation which occurred while she was teaching in a Navajo boarding school. One group of boys were intentionally not following any of the school's regulations for the lunchroom: putting napkins in their laps, eating with forks, etc. When Mrs. Moore reminded them of the rules, they retorted, "We heard you were Navajo. Now we know you're not. No matter what you look like, you're just another white teacher! We're proud of being Navajo."

Gloria's answer was, "I'm as proud of being Navajo as you are, but we all have to learn to live in different cultures if we're going to get along. When I'm in my mother's hogan, we sit on the ground cloth around the kettle. We all eat out of the same pot. That's the right way to do it. I wouldn't want to do it any different. But when I'm here I eat the way they do here, so that when I visit other people I know what to do. This way isn't any better, but it's the right way when you are here, just like the other is the right way when you are home. You need to learn more than one way."

They all cooperated. if she had said, "This is the right way. The way you are doing it is wrong," she would have gotten nowhere.

A teacher who was not Indian might have said, "I am not saying this way is better, but it is something you will need to know when you go other places. I am trying to learn to do things your way, so I can do them correctly when I visit Indian homes. I will help you learn my way, and I hope you will all help me learn the Indian way."

5. Encourage Self-Discipline

"Democracy is the art of disciplining oneself so that one need not be disciplined by others."

—Georges Clemenceau

The person who has real self-esteem and who understands what is expected of him as well as the reasons for the expectations will seldom cause a discipline problem. By doing the wrong thing, he would lose his self-respect. . The important factor in building self discipline, then, is attitude. If the teacher respects the student, he builds that student's self respect.

Children usually live up to the teacher's expectations. Threats indicate to them that instead of having confidence in them, you think they are not going to do the thing requested. If they can see that you expect them to cause trouble, why shouldn't they? It is not going to change your opinion of them. However, if all your actions indicate that you have confidence in their doing the right thing, they won't betray that confidence. They live up to your expectations.

Someone said that Cherokees treated their children as adults. A Cherokee answered, "No, we treat them as human beings. That is a status you only accord to adults, and usually only to adults of your own social status."

6. Help Students Develop Their Own Goals

"I have regretted all my life that I did not take a chance on the fifth grade. It would certainly come in handy right now, and I never go through a day that I am not sorry for the idea I had of how to go to school and not learn anything."

−Will Rogers

Children develop confidence in their own abilities in two ways. One of these is through their perceptions of how well they are fulfilling the personal standards that they have developed for themselves. They look at their abilities, their status, their roles, and they compare these with what they would like to become. They also compare their achievement of their objectives with how well others appear to have achieved those same objectives. As teachers, we must recognize that these standards may be very different for Native American children. Their understanding of success may have little relation to our own. We must help students achieve *their* goals.

When people want something they will work for it. The *want* precedes the achievement. Many Native American students define success in ways unrelated to school. Their only objective in school is to get through it−to endure it. If they are aware of goals in our classrooms, it is because we have set goals and told the students about them. They are not the students' goals.

During my first year of teaching, I told a seventh grader who refused to try to learn math, "In a few years you will be looking for a job, and you will have trouble getting one if you can't do any arithmetic." His reply was, "I can count my sheep. I want to be a sheep herder, and I can be a good one without any more math." His statement made me realize that here was boy with a worthy goal and a belief in his ability to reach it, but it had nothing to do with anything I was trying to teach him.

7. Let Students Make Many Decisions for Themselves

"If the process of education is made gentle and easy and if the students are taught to think for themselves, we may call the man a good teacher."

−Confucius

Students need to make decisions and choices. They need to see themselves as responsible people. They cannot leave their decisions to others. They must learn to make them and live with them. Many Native American students have not learned to take this responsibility because they have not been given the opportunity. They need to be asked their opinions, to have their questions answered, and to see their ideas put to use so they can learn to see the consequences, good or bad. Only in this way can they become willing to make decisions, and to base them upon reasoning and thinking.

SCHOOL OF EDUCATION
CURRICULUM LABORATORY
UM-DEARBORN

It is only if you trust your students to make decisions for themselves that they will grow to be decision makers. Those who have had this opportunity will be in control of their adult lives. They will be the leaders of the community. As Peter Copen (1980) says, "We believe that this is the key to successful adulthood: being self-directed, causing your experience and not merely feeling its effects, realizing that you have the power to choose and that there are clear options available to you."

Most teachers ask questions. Some ask questions about the students' preferences. Only a few *listen*. Make sure your students know that you are listening—that their decisions are being carried out. The secret is constant reinforcement of the students' recognition of their capabilities, their ability to make the right decisions, and letting them know that they have the right and the responsibility. Many Indian students don't believe they can make a difference, that they can decide for themselves and for their group. Help them to eliminate the words "I can't" from their vocabularies.

If Indian students can learn to step forward and voice their opinions they will not allow their people to be oppressed or controlled by the dominant society. They learn this by practice in the classroom.

Of course they need to not only be willing to make decisions for themselves, but to make the right decisions. Not necessarily the decisions we and the dominant society think are right, but reasoned decisions, based on thought and good judgement. This, too, requires practice.

We must continually look for occasions when decisions can be made by the students instead of being handed down by the teacher; times when they can make a contribution, when their ideas can make a difference. I always start every social studies unit with an introduction to the subject to be studied, so the students have some background, then a pupil-teacher planning session, in which the students talk about what *they* want to learn about it. Then we *follow* their suggestions. We do this again throughout the unit, at every opportunity. Do we have discipline problems—students not wanting to cooperate? Not when the children are doing what they planned, when they are carrying out their own decisions.

8. Teach Decision-Making Skills and Character Education

> *"Rare is the teacher who can submit an idea for classroom discussion and then give up possession of it, who can lay a thought on the table for study and see it rejected and revised. . . . But if you can do this, you will be teaching your students how to become responsible citizens. . . . Your students will develop self-discipline and learn to consider the consequences of their actions."*
>
> —Raymond Mussig.

Before our Native students, or any other students, can build self-esteem by knowing they are trusted to make decisions for themselves, we have to do three things: 1. Teach them decision-making skills. 2. Give them a relaxed classroom atmosphere in which no student is afraid to express his ideas, so that there is free and open communication between us and out students. 3. Give them opportunities to make decisions, both individually and as a group, and have those decisions carried out.

Decision-making skills are taught through open discussion in which students not only make decisions for themselves, but discuss many hypothetical situations similar to ones they face daily, then discuss openly and freely all the different possible consequences of the different decisions they might make.

It is much easier to start teaching decision-making skills if you have a planned program in "decision making" or "character development" with which to begin. Two examples of useful materials in this area are the decision-making kits, or "tubs," available to all Alaskan schools from the Alaskan State Department of Education, and the *Character Education Curriculum* kits from the nonprofit American Institute for Character Education—AICE (1987).

The *Character Education Curriculum* contains some excellent material for discussions on making decisions. Among the many concepts covered are 1. the difficulties created by trying to be one of the "in" group; 2. the influences which form a person's reputation; 3. the positive characteristics of a strong leader; 4. the effects of prejudice; 5. the benefits of generous, kind, and helpful behavior to ourselves and others; and 6. the need for trust in a working relationship.

The curriculum emphasizes the value of working cooperatively with others, an important part of the heritage of Native American students. It gives students experience in decision making while endeavoring to shape positive attitudes toward life and school.

It is important that classroom discussions provide opportunities for students to interact with others, explore possible solutions to potential problems, and identify probable consequences of each solution. The seventh, eighth, and ninth grade *Character Education Curriculum* includes causes and effects of substance abuse. The emphasis is on the effects of alcohol, drugs, and other substances on students' minds and bodies; and the effects on the users' families, friends, and society in general. This makes it expecially valuable in Native American communities. It includes guides to discussions of ways in which students may cope with their problems in more positive ways.

These materials were not developed specifically for Native American students, but they are very appropriate, especially if we use local problems in our discussions, and apply the same methods throughout our instruction, rather than just being satisfied with using a decision-making curriculum for twenty minutes three times a week. We must select problems from other subjects, and challenge the students to think and make decisions about them. We should *listen* to the students and observe actual situations they face around the school, in their homes, and the community, then pose questions based on these. "What will you do when someone calls you 'chicken' because you don't accept a drag of marijuana?" "What would you do if you saw one of the tough sixth grade boys forcing tobacco into the mouth of a fourth grade boy at recess?" Let them discuss openly all the possible actions, including doing nothing, and their possible consequences. Ask questions that lead the discussions, but without giving answers, and without sounding judgmental.

The purpose of this process is not to indoctrinate our students in an arbitrary set of values. It should provide an opportunity for them to examine their own choices, to help them develop their own moral conscience.

A good way to start these discussions is through a "story" that presents a difficult situation similar to one the students have faced, then let them discuss and decide what they might do, and what the results would be. The discussion will be most successful in a relaxed, informal, open atmosphere in which every student is encouraged to speak, where every individual's beliefs and inner feelings are respected, and where no preference is shown for the response of one child over another. It may be necessary to teach the students to distinguish between constructive criticism and ridicule before they, too, can encourage everyone's participation. Our role is that of leader and observer. We can aid the discussion most with an occasional question. "How would this affect your family?" "Can you see why other people might feel differently?" "Are you saying this because you think that is what I want to hear?"

You should not hesitate to express your own values and feelings, but you *must* wait until the children have all had their say, then do it without being critical of their ideas. Explain why these values are important to you, being careful not to imply that all of them are right for everyone, or that the values of others are not as valid. Each student should be encouraged to consider values from each of the cultures represented in his community, from his friends and family, and from his teachers. By choosing from all of these, he develops his own life style.

Discussions of values and decision making will become more meaningful if they are supplemented with role-playing of situations in which students must make decisions. To do this, set up a situation, get volunteers, give them time to plan the action, and prepare the class to listen and respond. You can follow with questions: "Was this true to life?" "Would you react the way Bill did?" "How was Wassie affected by this action?" "Are there other ways you could solve this problem?"

Pupil-teacher planning sessions in which the class as a whole makes decisions which will be carried out in the classroom provide practice in real decision making and show students the importance of their own decisions. Students in a democratic classroom in which they have a voice in decision making not only have greater self-esteem, they also have more respect for the opinions of others and are more willing to cooperate. As Booker T. Wachington said: "Few things help an individual more than to place responsibility upon him and to let him know that you trust him."

SUMMARY

If students are interested in their studies there will be few discipline problems. Effective classroom control develops when teachers know and apply the cultural patterns of control from the community, place responsibility on the students as a group, make their expectations clear, and encourage self-discipline. Students should have training in character development and decision making, then have a share in making their own decisions and setting their own goals.

If you continually watch for the good things, complement them, reward the good behavior, most of the problems will disappear. Build each child's self respect, plan with the group and let them help you with control. Then a positive attitude will be easy to maintain, and you can be free to enjoy working with your Native American students.

REFERENCES FOR FURTHER READING

Bahr, Robert. "Instilling Positive Values in Youth." *Kiwanis,* 72–5, May 1987, pp. 26–29.

Beers, David. *It Happens When We Get There: Conversations with Teachers in Alaskan Villages.* Alaska Department of Education. 1977.

Bronfenbrenner, U. "Alienation and the Four Worlds of Childhood." *Phi Delta Kappan,* Feb. 1986. pp 430–436.

Carter, Mildred. *A Model for Effective School Discipline.* The Phi Delta Kappa Educational Foundation, 1987.

Character Education Curriculum. American Institute for Character Education (ACEI) 1987.

Copen, Peter. "Walkabout Lives!" *Phi Delta Kappan,* June 1980, pp 703–705.

Garcia, Ricardo L. "Classroom Management and Human Rights Strategies." Ch. 9, *Teaching in a pluralistic Society.* Harper and Row, 1982, pp 145–152.

Hyman, I.A. and J. D'Alessandro. "Good Old-Fashioned Discipline: The Politics of Punitiveness." *Phy Delta Kappan,* Sept. 1984, pp 39–45.

Little Soldier, Dale, and Leona M. Forester. "Applying Anthropology to Educational Problems," *Journal of American Indian Education,* Vol. 20, No. 3, May 1981, pp 1–6.

Macgregor, Gordon, et. al. *Warriors Without Weapons: A Study of the Society and Personality Development of the Pine Ridge Sioux.* University of Chicago Press. 1975.

Malony, Ray. "Ten Ways to Turn Out Terrific Kids." *Vibrant Life,* Jan/Feb. 1985.

McGinnis, Alan Loy. *Bringing Out the Best in People.* Augsberg Publishing House, 1985.

Mussig, Raymond. *Aphorisms in Education.* Phi Delta Kappa Educational Foundation.

Pepper, Floy C. "Effective Classroom Management Practices," *Effective Practices in Indian Education: A Teacher's Monograph.* Northwest Regional Educational Laboratory, 1985, pp 41–110.

Wax, Rosalie H. and Robert K Thomas. "American Indians and White People." *Phylon.* Vol. 22. No. 4, winter 1961, pp 305–317.

Wayson, W. "The Politics of Violence in School: Doublespeak and Disruptions in Public Confidence." *Phi Delta Kappan,* Oct. 1985, pp 127–132.

Chapter 7

Working with the Parents

by Sandra Kay Streeter

The involvement of parents and grandparents in the education of the children is especially important with Native American people since there has often been a feeling among Native families that school has little relation to "real life" and parents may therefore have little interest in the school. Children learn more when their parents are involved in education (U.S. Dept. Ed. 1986; Lyons 1983). A study of 250 California elementary schools found parent involvement related to student achievement (Herman & Yen, 1980). Umansky (1983) makes the point that when parents and teachers work together the child will identify both the school and the home as places to learn. Native American parents, historically, were systematically excluded from participation during the mission, boarding, and day school era (Little Bear 1986).

In situations where the school and the child come from different cultures the child looks to the people at home to find out if it is "OK" to participate in this new environment. Little Bear points out that the past exclusion of the Indian parent from the education of their children has only served to make Indian parents suspicious of modern American education. This suspicion many times is demonstrated by a hesitancy to participate in the child's classroom. Consequently, the parents may send a message to the child that it is *not* "OK" to participate fully. The classroom teacher is then faced with the problem of encouraging family cooperation. Following are some techniques teachers can use to encourage parental involvement in the child's learning environment.

PREPARING TO INTERACT WITH THE PARENTS

The success of the parent-teacher relationship is based upon mutual self-respect. When teachers move into a new school it is their obligation to familiarize themselves with the cultural background of their students. Little Bear (p 227) points out "There is no such thing as a generic Indian for which a standard Indian history, culture, and language curriculum can be designed." It may be helpful for teachers to think of themselves as students of the new culture. The parents and extended family of the students can be excellent resources for this educational process. The following suggestions are guidelines to help teachers facilitate interaction with the parent population:

1. Familiarize Yourself with the New Environment

Read one or more books written and/or recommended by tribal members or a professional educator in the school system.

Visit with several older people about the local culture. In your search for information focus on traditions, values, and specific ideologies (Little Bear, 1986).

Look for tribal cultural events such as pow-wows or feast days, and ask a tribal member if you will be welcome to attend.

Become aware of tribally-specific differences. Little Bear points out that what is acceptable in one tribe may be taboo in another tribe.

Explore the land in order to create a visual and effective image of the students' environment and resources.

Limit your own vocalization and *listen*.

2. Talk to Local Head Start Personnel

In many Native American communities, Head Start has provided a beginning in parental involvement in the child's classroom. However, since this parental participation component involves pre-school education, many times the parents as well as the educators do not know how to effectively and appropriately transfer this model into the elementary school system. One help for the new teacher might be to talk to the local Head Start personnel to find out what parent activities worked well in that setting. If some of these activities could be transferred to the elementary classroom, this might be a comfortable activity to use for the first parent participation activity.

IMPLEMENTING PARENT PARTICIPATION

Once a teacher has made the commitment to interact with parents the "how to" becomes important. What does parental involvement mean? What should the teacher be striving for? The first step in this process is to recognize that, in spite of cultural differences, the parent and teacher have a common goal. That common goal is to provide the best possible education for the child. Many new teachers get frustrated because they are unrealistic; they expect the same degree and kind of interaction with every parent. Parents are as individual as the students. If a teacher welcomes diversity in parental response, then the teacher's expectations are not as likely to exceed the participation level of most parents. McConkey (1985) suggests that a teacher can interact with the parent on five different levels.

1. Individually, on a one-to-one, face-to-face basis.
2. Individually, at a distance.
3. Group, face-to-face.
4. Group, at a distance.
5. Parent networking: Encourage parents to be involved with other parents.

1. Individually, on a One-to-One, Face-to-Face Basis

Many parents are comfortable interacting in the classroom or as sponsors for class trips. In communities where Head Start was active, parents already understand how important they are in the educational development of their children. They may have developed important interactional skills during their child's pre-school experiences that can be utilized in the elementary and secondary classroom.

One-on-one direct interaction between a parent and a teacher also takes place when the parent attends a parent teacher conference. Parent-teacher, one-on-one interaction can take place outside of the school environment. Out of school contact with the parent may be especially important when the parent did not have a good experience in school as a child. A parent, even though now an adult, may see the teacher in the school setting as an authority figure and remember feeling powerless and helpless. A home visit by the teacher may indirectly address the feeling of powerlessness. The teacher when in the parent environment may seem less threatening.

Casual, unplanned visits with parents take place when the teacher is participating in community activities such as sporting events, shopping, church, and money-making suppers. In these casual settings the parent also has the opportunity to see the teacher as a person in society.

2. Individually, at a Distance

Working with individual parents at a distance might include the following activities:

A telephone conversation with the parent.
Writing a personal letter to the parent.
Sending home a picture of the child interacting in the school setting.
Sending home report cards.
Sending home "home work" assignments.

3. Group, Face-to-Face

Many Native American adults feel uncomfortable when they are in the "minority" in the school building. Consequently, arranging a time when several parents can come to the classroom together to learn about what their children are doing might increase participation. An important consideration when working with parents is to make the school room an emotionally and socially "safe" environment. During group gatherings, the children might serve refreshments and show the parents "their" classroom. Pictures and script depicting Native American roles in today's society can demonstrate that this classroom is dealing with the issue of the relationship of education to the loss or change in Indian identity. The classroom should also reflect the culture of the community and demonstrate in words, pictures, and displays the ways education impacts life.

4. Group, at a Distance

Some suggestions for this mode of parent-teacher interaction include:

A class newsletter edited by the children could provide the parent with information on class activities.

Bulletin boards and class displays in the window of the local store could provide a means of disseminating information to the parents and community.

Parent study groups might also work in select locations.

Perhaps local agencies could also be supportive of parental involvement in the classroom by providing a "get to know the teacher" social occasion. For example, the kindergarten teacher might be invited to participate in several of the spring Head Start activities so that the children and parents could become acquainted with the teacher on the parent and child's "turf." This might also be done by several church or social organizations in the early fall as a way to demonstrate community support for parental involvement in education.

5. Parent Networking

Encourage parents to maintain contacts with other parents and to participate in school board decisions. If success in school is important, then the community, tribe or family needs to address the issue of what can be done to help parents provide active support for their children. Watson et al. (1983) suggested the following guidelines:

1. Parents must have a community support network from which they can draw in carrying out their roles.
2. Parents must perceive their role as "educator" and their children's role as "learner" as important and vital to the functioning of the family.
3. Parents must act on their perceptions that learning is essential for healthy family living.
4. Parents must have an understanding and knowledge of young children.

PARENTAL ATTITUDE

Watson also indicated that many parents believe it is important for children to learn but never actively pursue education for their child. Maynard and Twiss (1970, p. 96) express a similar concern with Indian parents:

Of great importance in the lack of motivation to learn is the indifference or disinterest of Indian parents in the education of their children. Some parents feel that they are obliged to turn over their children to the schools which they regard as alien institutions, completely separate from their home life. What goes on in the school is out of their hands and of no concern to them. Consequently, these parents offer little encouragement to their children to do well in school and show no interest in what they are learning.

Attitudes such as these may need to be addressed by the teacher if, in fact, parents are going to participate in the school setting. Parents from a minority culture need to provide their children with active as opposed to passive support in the educational setting. Active parental support might be facilitated by providing the parent with explicit information on teacher expectations for each parent-teacher contact. Once the parent is comfortable in the school setting, parental expectations and concerns can then be addressed.

REFERENCES FOR FURTHER READING

Herman, J.L. and Yen, J.P. "Some Effects of Parent Involvement in Schools." Paper presented at the American Educational Research Association Meeting, Boston, April, 1980.

Little Bear, D. "Teachers and Parents: Working Together." in J. Reyhner (Ed.), *Teaching the Indian Child: A Bilingual/Multicultural Approach*. Billings, MT: Eastern Montana College, 1986.

Lyons, P., A. Robbins, and A. Smith. *Involving Parents in Schools: A Handbook for Participation*. Ypsilanti, MI: High/Scope, 1983.

Maynard, E. and G. Twiss. *That These People May Live*. DHEW Publication No. HSM 72–508, 1970.

McConkey, R. *Working with Parents: A Practical Guide for Teachers and Therapists*. Cambridge, MA: Brookline, 1985.

Umansky, W. "On Families and the Re-valuing of Children." *Childhood Education*. 59, March/April 1983, pp. 260–266.

U.S. Department of Education. *What Works: Research about Teaching and Learning*. Washington, D.C.: U.S. Department of Education, 1986.

Watson, T., M. Brown, and K.J. Swick. "The Relationship of Parents' Support to children's School Achievement." *Child Welfare*, 62–2, 1983, p. 175–180.

Chapter 8

Learning from the History of Indian Education
by Jon Reyhner

What type of teaching has worked well with Native Americans in the past? Despite the fact that Indian education has been characterized in a congressional report as "a national tragedy" (*Indian*, 1969), there have always been responsive teachers who have worked to meet the special needs of their Native American students. Also, Native Americans were becoming doctors, teachers, and ministers a century ago, and more and more of them are successfully attending universities and colleges today.

Traditional education for Native Americans began with the extended family and taught survival skills which allowed Indian children to learn how to procure food and shelter in an often adverse environment and how to live in harmony with nature and their fellow man (Morey & Gilliam). Native American education produced tribal members fit to survive and prosper in the North American environment. Apprenticeship provided a means of higher education for those seeking to become healers and religious leaders. With the coming of the Europeans, the living conditions of Native Americans changed rapidly through the introduction of guns, horses, Christianity, new diseases, and many other foreign developments.

ORGANIZATION OF SCHOOLS FOR INDIANS

The first Europeans, when they considered Indian education, saw it in religious terms. They felt Indians were uncivilized and needed to be saved by becoming Christians. Dedicated missionaries, both Catholic and Protestant, sought to convert Indians to Christianity. Many missionaries found that the quickest and most logical way to explain Christianity to Indians was to learn their languages and to translate the Bible into those languages, as it had been translated centuries before into the many languages of Europe. In 1637 John Eliot published an Algonquian translation of the Bible (Bowden, 1981). While he used the native language, Eliot did not try to draw any connection between Christianity and traditional culture. Instead he encouraged converts to come together in what proved to be unsuccessful "praying" towns where they were to dress and live like the colonists.

After the American Revolution, the new U.S. government felt it was necessary to civilize Indians living in the country so that they would live in harmony with the settlers who were moving in on their lands. The idea of Indian education was to make yeoman farmers of Indians, thus freeing up the vast Indian hunting grounds for White settlement.

Many Indian missionaries combined their attempts to Christianize Indians with the effort to make them farmers.

The 1802 Trade and Intercourse Acts incorporated a plan to civilize Indians that included providing them with social and educational services. Up to $15,000 per year was authorized "to provide Civilization among the aborigines." The House Committee on Appropriations reported in 1818:

> In the present state of our country one of two things seems to be necessary. Either that those sons of the forest should be moralized or exterminated. . . . Put into the hands of their children the primer and the hoe, and they will naturally, in time, take hold of the plow. . . . (Roessel, 1962, p. 4)

The following year Congress established a civilization fund, which lasted until 1873, to provide financial support to religious groups and others willing to live among and teach Indians.

By 1838, the federal government was operating six manual training schools with eight hundred students and eighty-seven boarding schools with about 2,900 students (Indian Education, 1969, p. 11). In 1839, Commissioner Harley Crawford formalized development of manual labor schools to educate Indian children in farming and homemaking (Report, 1976, pp. 38–39). Pressure by settlers and the federal government led to treaty after treaty being signed with Indian tribes. In return for accepting reservations, tribes were offered annuities and education. An example of the promises made can be found in the Fort Laramie negotiations by President Grant's Peace Commissioners:

> Upon the reservation you select, we propose to build a house for your agent to live in, to build a mill to saw your timber, and a mill to grind your wheat and corn, when you raise any: a blacksmith shop and a house for your farmer, and such other buildings as may be necessary. We also propose to furnish to you homes and cattle, to enable you to begin to raise a supply of stock and with which to support your families when the game has disappeared. We desire to supply you with clothing to make you comfortable and all necessary farming implements so that you can make your living by farming. We will send you teachers for your children. (Prucha, 1985, p. 18)

Protestant missionaries translated religious and educational tracts into Sioux starting in 1834. In 1882, Stephen R. Riggs completed a *Grammar and Dictionary of the Dakota Language* (Wilson, 1983, p. 11). The Santee Normal School was started in 1870 to train Sioux teachers. It received government funding until 1901, when funding for sectarian schools was ended. Wilson reports that,

> Although considered by many people at the time to be one of the best schools of Indian education, the institution received criticism for teaching Indians to read and write in their own language. (1983, p. 27)

Charles Eastman was one of the most famous students who attended Santee Normal School. Eastman, who graduated from Dartmouth and who became a medical doctor, is most famous for his autobiographies describing his transition from "the deep woods to civilization." Eastman, educated by missionaries, became convinced after observing the materialism of late nineteenth-century America that "Christianity and modern civilization are opposed and irreconcilable and that the spirit of Christianity and of our ancient [Sioux] religion is essentially the same" (Eastman, *Soul of the Indian* as quoted in Wilson, 1983, p. 87).

A teacher on the Warm Springs Reservation in Oregon reported in 1862:

Indian children, situated as they are in this reservation, in commencing an education, are placed at a great disadvantage as compared with white children. They are unable to enunciate many of the sounds represented by the letters of the English alphabet, and being ignorant of the meaning of words which they learn and the sentences they read, the exercises do not naturally possess an equal interest to them as to white children. (Report, 1863, p. 295)

This teacher also declared that the textbooks he had were for "advanced scholars" and that more elementary ones were needed (p. 296). Another teacher on the Tulalip Reservation in Washington reported "My scholars complain that they do not understand what they read in English, and, in order to aid them, I am compiling a Snohomish-English and English-Snohomish Dictionary" and that his students "must become as orphans, that is, they must forget their parents as far as possible in order to abandon the habits of the Indians with less difficulty"(*Report,* 1863, p. 406).

In the 1878 *Annual Report of the Commissioner of Indian Affairs,* "education of their children" was seen as the quickest way to civilize Indians and that education could only be given "to children removed from the examples of their parents and the influence of the camps and kept in boarding schools" (*Annual Report,* 1878, pp. xxv-xxvi). In the same report school children were described as "hostages for good behavior of [their] parents" by Lieutenant R.H. Pratt (p. 174).

In 1878 Pratt brought 17 Indian adult prisoners of war from Florida to Hampton Institute and recruited another 40 boys and 9 girls from Dakota Territory (Eastman, 1935, pp. 63 & 67). The children were encouraged to speak English, but were not punished if they did not (p. 68). Two years later Pratt opened the famous Carlisle Indian School in Carlisle, Pennsylvania, after obtaining support from the local community and Congress (pp. 77–78). Initially there were 136 students. Disturbed by the small food allowance provided by the Indian Bureau, Pratt insisted that the students be fed on army rations (p. 82). From then to 1903 Carlisle graduated 158 Indian students and had another 1,060 students who did not graduate (p. 71). The school provided an elementary education to older Indian students, who usually remained away from their families for three years. In the summers students were placed with area families under the "Outing System." The average age of new students at Carlisle was 15 (p. 216).

Pratt argued with missionaries who he felt did not "advocate the disintegration of the tribes, and giving to individual Indians rights and opportunities among civilized people" (p. 113). Pratt wanted his students to merge with the White population.

Carl Schurtz, Secretary of Interior under President Rutherford B. Hayes, felt the alternatives for Indians were extermination or civilization. The object of Indian policy was "unquestionably the gradual absorption of the Indians in the great body American citizenship" (Prucha, 1973, pp. 14–15). Reservations were seen as "socialism" (p. 73), a charge repeated recently by James Watt, Secretary of the Interior during Ronald Reagan's first term as President.

METHODS OF INSTRUCTIONS

Under Schurtz the Indian Bureau issued regulations in 1880 that "all instruction must be in English" (Prucha, 1973, p. 199) in both mission and government schools under threat of loss of government funding. It was felt by J.D.C. Atkins, Commissioner of Indian Affairs from 1885 to 1888 that "to teach Indian school children their native tongue is practically to exclude English, and to prevent them from acquiring it" (Prucha, 1973, p. 203). The ethnocentric attitude of the late nineteenth century is evident in Atkins' 1887 report,

> *Every nation is jealous of its own language, and no nation ought to be more so than ours, which approaches nearer than any other nationality to the perfect protection of its people. True Americans all feel that the Constitution, laws, and institutions of the United States, in their adaptation to the wants and requirements of man, are superior to those of any other country; and they should understand that by the spread of the English language will these laws and institutions be more firmly established and widely disseminate. Nothing so surely and perfectly stamps upon an individual a national characteristic as language.*
> *(Prucha, 1975, p. 175)*

Despite patriotic announcements like the one above, observers in the field like General Oliver O. Howard reported that successful missionary teachers learned the tribal language so that they could understand them (1907, pp. 139–140 & 320).

A number of Indian Service employees who worked in Indian boarding and day schools at the turn of the century have written autobiographies. They reported both good and bad experiences. Janette Woodruff (1939), hired as a matron, found Crow children in 1900 to be "restrained and orderly and never given to outbursts of any kind" (p. 26). She found that to teach the children, "There always had to be a concrete, and objective way of presenting an idea" (p. 65). She observed that teachers who did not demonstrate their lessons found attempts to teach "utterly futile" (p. 97).

Gertrude Golden (1954), who started teaching in Oregon, found her students "excelled in those subjects which required observation, imitation and memory and were more backward in those demanding reasoning and imagination" (p. 8). She found many teachers worked in Indian schools only for the money and had no respect for the "lousy Indians" they taught (p. 10). Estelle Brown (1952), working at Leupp Boarding School, found "no employee was here because of an interest in Indians and their welfare. We were here to make a living" (p. 153).

School principals and inspectors were often more interested in the attractiveness of the bulletin boards then the quality of teaching (Golden, p. 13). Brown (1952) reported that if the students sat quietly with shoes shined and noses wiped, the inspector would send a good report back to Washington about the teacher (p. 88).

In one school Golden worked in she found the educated Indians working in the school segregated from the white employees (p. 70). She found among all the tribes she worked with a universal aversion to learning English, "the language of the despised conquerors" (p. 83). Albert H. Kneale (1950) concluded after a long career in the Indian service which started as a teacher with Sioux in 1899 that,

> *Every tribe with which I have associated is imbued with the idea that it is superior to all other peoples. Its members are thoroughly convinced of their*

*superiority not alone over members of all other tribes but over the whites as well
. . . I have never known an Indian who would consent to being changed into a
white man even were he convinced that such a change would readily be
accomplished. (p. 105)*

On being transferred to a school in Oklahoma, Kneale found the discipline "notoriously
bad." To keep students from running away, windows were barred and doors padlocked, a
common practice. An attempt to restore discipline by force by a "hard-bitten army
sargeant" ended with the sargeant being beaten and sent to the hospital. Kneale refused to
follow recommendations to continue the old policies, and through interpreters secured the
cooperation of the boys by organizing them into companies and letting them choose their
own officers:

> *These officers, with myself, formed a group to enact such rules and regulations as
> it was deemed wise to enforce, to pass judgment on all infractions of these rules
> and outline proper punishments for infractions. Every boy in school pledged
> obedience to the rule of this group.*
> *It worked! (p. 86)*

Estelle Brown replaced a teacher who took one look at the Crow Creek School in 1897 and
left. She found the living and working conditions harsh, crude, and discouraging and
requiring lots of patience (1952, pp. 36 & 42). "Instinctively, [she] felt that, in teaching
Indian children to like and want the things we liked and wanted, we were heading in the
wrong direction" (p. 42). The Indian service bureaucracy was preoccupied with paperwork
and staff morals rather than the first hand views of their field workers or the Indians they
supposedly served (p. 173). "A knowledge of the pupil's environment was not considered
necessary since their education aimed to make the environment unsuitable to them" (p. 204).

Brown found her students to be underfed, forever scrubbing the school, and housed in
unheated dormitories. Corporal punishment was discouraged in favor of depriving students of
playtime or making them work longer hours. Hoke Denetesosie, a Navajo, found as a
boarding school student early in this century that,

> *Conditions at the School were terrible. . . . Food and other supplies were
> not too plentiful. We were underfed; so we were constantly hungry. Clothing was
> not good, and, in winter months, there were epidemics of sickness. Sometimes
> students died, and the school would close the rest of the term.*
>
> *It was run in a military fashion, and rules were very strict. A typical day
> went like this: Early in the morning at 6 o'clock we rose at the sound of bugles.
> We washed and dressed; then we lined up in military formation and drilled in the
> yard. For breakfast, companies formed, and we marched to the dining room, where
> we all stood at attention with long tables before us. We recited grace aloud, and,
> after being seated, we proceeded with our meal. . . .*
>
> *Some teachers and other workers weren't very friendly. When students made
> mistakes they often were slapped or whipped by the disciplinarian who usually
> carried a piece of rope in his hip pocked.*
>
> *At the end of the term in May parents and other visitors would come to the
> school. (Johnson, 1977, pp. 83–85).*

Education in white ways was seen as a way to destroy Indian tribal life and to rid the government of its trust and treaty responsibilities. The General Allotment (Dawes) Act passed by Congress in 1887 was designed to break up Indian reservations by giving Indian families small 160 acre farms and allowing the remaining reservation land to be sold to whites.

The Dawes Act did not lead to assimilation of Indians into the dominant society as planned. Instead, it eroded their land base by 140 million acres and made them more dependent on the federal government. The Meriam Report of 1928 condemned the allotment policy and the poor quality of services provided by the Bureau of Indian Affairs. In discussing education, it pointed out shocking conditions in boarding schools, recommended not sending elementary age children to them, and urged an increase in the number of day (non-boarding) schools.

When Franklin D. Roosevelt was elected president in 1933, he appointed John Collier Commissioner of Indian Affairs. Collier helped reverse the assimilationist policies of the Bureau of Indian Affairs. The Indian Reorganization (Wheeler-Howard) Act of 1934 ended allotment of Indian lands and provided for Indian religious freedom and a measure of tribal self government. Collier also encouraged the teaching of Indian culture and languages in government schools. After World War II the assimilationist trend again gained strength. Under President Dwight D. Eisenhower, several Indian reservations were terminated. However, the new policy to terminate reservations was quickly reversed, and a new policy of Indian tribal self-determination was started which continues to this day.

CONCLUSION

In this chapter a brief look at how Indians have been taught in the past is given. Perceptive teachers of Indian students saw the advantages of using Indian languages and recognized the gap between what Indians wanted and what was forced upon them in mission and government schools. In the last thirty years the civil rights movement has focused attention on the rights of Native Americans. Reports like *Indian Education: A National Tragedy, A National Challenge* (1969) focused attention on schools serving Indian students. Schools serving Indian students were also examined from an anthropological perspective (King, 1967; Wolcott, 1967) and found to be destructive to the identity of the children they served. The cultural discontinuity between home and school (Spindler, 1987) and the fact Indian schools often do not recognize and build upon the heritage of their minority students made them ineffective. The lack of culturally appropriate teaching methods and materials, including instruction and materials in their native language, for cultural minority students in most schools is still acute.

Today there are clear and present dangers on several fronts to culturally appropriate curriculum for minority group children in the United States. The "English Only" movement, as promoted by groups such as *U.S. English,* by advocating the adoption of English as an official language (presumably to be used as the sole language in all official government activities including public schools) jeopardized the early education of non-English speaking American children. The "cultural literacy" movement that has received a lot of media attention with E. D. Hirsch, Jr.'s new book *Cultural Literacy: What Every American Needs to*

Know (1987) jeopardizes the teaching of non-Western, non-European and non-Judeo-Christian, heritages in our schools.

Throughout history, teachers who have been responsive to their students have been more successful than those who have slavishly taught from textbooks and curriculums that may or may not reflect the culture of their students. The results of a study of a successful mission school in Alaska pointed to the teachers and other school staff taking an interest in the lives of their students as the key factor in the school's success (Kleinfeld, 1979). Friendly, informal discussions were a key factor in developing the knowledge of the students. The students from this school did well in college, in spite of the fact they did not perform well on standardized tests.

Perhaps the greatest danger facing Indian education today is the increasing use of standardized tests in all facets of education. Young minority students who do not do well on these tests are put in special education programs rather than culturally appropriate programs. High School students are tracked into non-college bound curriculums based on achievement tests, and college students are denied access to professional programs. In one state only four percent of Native Americans passed the Pre-Professional Skills Test required to get into teacher education. In California the State Supreme Court banned the use of Intelligence Tests (Larry P. V. Wilson Riles, State Board of Education, 1979) as an instrument in placing Black students into special education programs because of their cultural bias.

Today more than ever teachers must become advocates for their minority students, protecting them from culturally insensitive textbooks, curriculums, and tests. The late nineteenth—and early twentieth-century ethnocentrism, cultural chauvinism, and insensitivity to students needs described in this chapter still exists. Students' lives can be changed for the better by individual teachers learning from their students as well as teaching their students.

REFERENCES FOR FURTHER READING

Annual Report of the Commissioner of Indian Affairs to the Secretary of the Interior for the Year 1878 Washington: Government Printing Office, 1878.

Bowden, Henry Warner. *American Indians and Christian Missions.* Chicago: University of Chicago Press, 1981.

Brown, Estelle Aubrey. *Stubborn Fool: A Narrative.* Caldwell, ID: Caxton, 1952.

Eastman, Charles A. (Ohiyesa). *From the Deep Woods to Civilization: Chapters in the Autobiography of an Indian.* Lincoln: University of Nebraska Press, 1977. (First published in 1916).

Eastman, Elaine Goodale. *Pratt: The Red Man's Moses.* Norman: University of Oklahoma Press, 1935.

Golden, Gertrude. *Red Moon Called Me: Memoirs of a School teacher in the Government Indian Service* edited by Cecil Dryden. San Antonio, TX: Naylor, 1954.

Hirsch, Jr., E.D. *Cultural Literacy: What Every American Needs to Know.* Boston: Houghton Mifflin, 1987.

Howard, Oliver O. *My Life and Experiences among our Hostile Indians.* Hartford, CN: A.T. Worthington, 1907. (Reprinted by DeCapo, New York, 1972).

Indian Education: A National Tragedy, A National Challenge (The Kennedy Report). Washington, D.C.: U.S. Government Printing Office, 1969.

Johnson, Brodrick H. (Ed.). *Stories of Traditional Navajo Life and Culture by Twenty-two Navajo Men and Women.* Tsaile, AZ: Navajo Community College Press, 1977.

King, A. Richard. *The School at Mopass: A Problem of Identity.* New York: Holt, Rinehart and Winston, 1967.

Kleinfeld, Judith S. *Eskimo School on the Adreafsky: A Study in Effective Bicultural Education.* New York: Praeger, 1979.

Kneale, Albert H. *Indian Agent.* Caldwell, ID: Caxton, 1950.

Meriam, Lewis (Ed.). *The Problem of Indian Administration.* Baltimore: John Hopkins.

Morey, Sylvester M., & Gilliam, Olivia L. (Eds.). *Respect for Life: The Traditional Upbringing of American Indian Children.* Garden City, NY: Waldorf Press, 1974.

Prucha, Francis Paul (Ed.). *Americanizing the American Indians.* Cambridge, MA: Harvard University Press, 1973).

Prucha, Francis Paul. *Documents of United States Indian Policy.* Lincoln: University of Nebraska Press, 1975.

Report of the Commissioner of Indian Affairs for the year 1862. Washington: Government Printing Office, 1863.

Roessel, Jr., Robert. *Handbook for Indian Education.* Los Angels: Amerindian, 1962.

Spindler, George D. "Why Have Minority Groups in North America Been Disadvantaged in their Schools." In *Education and Cultural Process: Anthropological Approaches* edited by George D. Spindler. Prospect Heights, IL: Waveland, 1987.

Wilson, Raymond. *Ohiyesa—Charles Eastman, Santee Sioux.* Urbana, IL: University of Illinois Press, 1983.

Wolcott, Harry F. *A Kwakiutl Village and School.* Heights, IL: Waveland, 1967.

Woodruff, Janette. *Indian Oasis.* Caldwell, ID: Caxton, 1939.

Chapter 9

Social Studies and Native Americans

by Adrian Heidenreich, Jon Reyhner and Hap Gilliland

"Those who cannot remember the past are condemned to repeat its mistakes."

—George Santayana

Regardless of the culture from which our students come, they need to get a true picture of Native Americans and all other racial and ethnic groups in their Social Studies lessons. Teachers need to learn more about Native Americans both in the past and present so that they can adequately teach their students. Information about the Social Sciences given in this chapter can be used in all classrooms with Native American and non-Native American students because we all need to learn more about each other.

WHAT ARE THE SOCIAL SCIENCES?

In Social Studies lessons, the individual and group behavior of people is studied along with how people relate to the environment in which they live. Modern Social Studies and behavioral sciences include the disciplines of anthropology, economics, geography, history, linguistics, political science, psychology, and sociology. Social Studies refers to the combined use of methods and data from the several social and behavioral sciences to understand and predict our own behavior and the behavior of others.

The overall goal of the study of the social sciences is to understand the social forces and institutions which affect us. They help us understand human and institutional behavior and to establish facts and theories which will provide a basis for more rational management of human affairs in both our personal and group life. This understanding helps to fulfill a major goal of education: to prepare students to be participating citizens in a democratic society.

In teaching the Native Student, there ought to be an emphasis on development of practical knowledge and effective democratic political skills which can be of benefit to the individual and the community. Much of this focuses on becoming freed from institutional and other forms of racism, poverty, economic exploitation, political powerlessness and alienation, and low self-esteem. Key concepts for the Native American that relate to these issues include *culture, tradition,* and *ethnocentrism.*

Culture is the complex totality which is the way of life of a group of people. Each culture is patterned and includes social structure, knowledge, belief, art, environmental adaptation, and other customs learned by people as members of a society. Phrasing this more generally, Vine Deloria, Jr., writes:

Culture, as Indian people understood it, was basically a lifestyle by which a people acted. It was self-expression, but not a conscious self-expression. Rather, it was an expression of the essence of a people. (1969, p. 185)

All cultures are characterized by both persistence and change. They adjust and adapt to changing environmental conditions as well as to the creative thinking of the people who make up the culture. The Laguna Pueblo poet Carol Lee Sanchez writes of Indian identity as creation:

Each tribe adapted various
forms of European beads and
ruffles and braids that
became traditional
ceremonial dress by
the late 1700s—
but—they are Indian!
because: We wear them!
because We put them together
in a certain way. (Hobson, 1981, p. 241)

Culture is characteristic of the unique quality of humanity as defined by N. Scott Momaday (1975), Pulitzer Prize-winning Kiowa Indian and author of *The Way to Rainy Mountain:* the ability—as individuals and as groups—to imagine ourselves into existence.

Tradition is the link with the past which influences our behavior through time-tested and honored ways of living. Sometimes it keeps us from repeating old mistakes, and other times it keeps us from progressing. Whether students accept or reject traditional beliefs, they need to learn about their traditions and respect them.

One of the characteristics of all traditional cultures is ethnocentrism, the feeling by each culture, each group, that they are the chosen ones, the most important people in the world. This idea that the group one is born into is better, and that other groups and cultures are inferior, must be overcome if different cultures are to live together in harmony.

The major goal of multicultural education is to give students an appreciation of other cultures. Ideally children must learn to adapt and be able to live in several cultures, not just their own (which itself changes). It is important for students to learn about their own culture, those of other tribes and groups, and the "mainstream" or national cultures with which they will have to interact as adults. However, a month-long unit, or several month-long units on Indian culture, can only give an introduction to what normally takes a lifetime to learn.

EIGHT SUGGESTIONS FOR IMPROVING SOCIAL STUDIES FOR NATIVE AMERICANS

1. Teach from a Multicultural Viewpoint

Help all students to see multiple points of view. Social Studies is an opportunity for students to learn about both their own culture and others. Studying other cultures and emphasizing the viewpoints of people from other cultures can help overcome ethnocentric attitudes.

Many states and the National Council for Accreditation Teacher Education (NCATE) have multicultural and/or Indian studies requirements.

2. Allow Time for Native American History and Culture

It is important that Native American history and culture be included in the Social Studies curriculum. Both historical and contemporary social, economic, and political issues that affect Indian people should be included. Ignoring Indian history and culture, or the distortion of it, is detrimental to all students. Indian students need to learn about the world they will live in and how it came to be the way it is, and non-Indian students need to be aware of Indian issues. For example non-Indians elect representatives to government that pass laws affecting Indian Reservations. Many non-Indians have mistaken ideas such as the myth that all Indians receive money from the government for being Indian. Education about the relationship between the federal government and tribes can correct such myths.

In a major study of Indian education, Estelle Fuchs and Robert Havighurst (1973, pp. 170 & 187) found that the most common suggestion by parents was that "schools should pay more attention to the Indian heritage" and that Indian community leaders were "overwhelmingly in favor of the school doing something to help Indian students learn about their tribal culture."

The curriculum of the schools in most communities allows for the teaching of a unit on American Indian life and culture only on about three grade levels in the elementary school. Little is said in most textbooks about Native Americans after the time of the Civil War and the "closing of the frontier." Perhaps once in the primary grades when studying the home, and again when studying state or provincial history, and again with national history, some mention of Native Americans is made. However, any school with an appreciable number of Native American students should include at least one unit on Indian life and culture every year. History textbooks need to be supplemented with additional information about Native Americans especially for the period after the Civil War.

Learning is gradual, and one unit every two or three years does not necessarily lead to understanding the complexities of a particular culture or of social relations generally. There should be awareness of the levels of understanding of the information studied; for example a seventh grade class will not be able to comprehend sophisticated knowledge about concepts such as kinship and religion to the degree that a twelfth grade class could. It took Cheyenne priests years to learn the proper knowledge about the Sun Dance, both its performance and theology. A one or two hour interview or a week-long topical unit on the Sun Dance will not be the equivalent. But it will encourage the student and provide entry into the skills and knowledge of Social Studies.

One of the most difficult issues in discussing the findings of the Social Studies regarding Indians and Indian-White relations is the matter of the feelings and anger bought out, on the part of both Indians and non-Indians, for different reasons. This can become quite sensitive when the Indian students appreciate the information or focus and the non-Indians feel that they are being attacked or feel guilty and vulnerable. One of our students wrote in evaluating one of us that "he is so sympathetic to Indian culture that he hates other cultures," an impression that was certainly not intended.

Sensitive topics can be approached from a variety of ways. For example, an overview of Plains Indian history can emphasize the brutality of warfare and the massive number of deaths which occurred in smallpox epidemics. Or it can emphasize the constant heroism of individuals and ultimate survival of the group, and the creativity developed by the tribes in their continual adaptation to new conditions. Or, there can be a balance in presenting both of these issues as they relate to Indian culture and history.

3. Give Native Americans Their Rightful Place

A study of groups in world history should give Native Americans an equal place with other groups from Europe Asia, Africa, and the Islands of the Pacific. Textbooks should not leave the impression that "American" history begins with European settlement. Along with other great leaders, great Indian leaders should be given equal prominence. Pontiac (Ottawa), Tecumseh (Shawnee), Pope (Tewa-San Juan Pueblo), Benito Juarez (Zapotec), Ely Parker (Seneca), and Plenty Coups (Crow) among others should be mentioned in textbooks and included in biographies.

Indians should not be studied just in terms of their relations to the European invaders. Relationships within the Indian society and between tribes should also be studied. When the Indian way of life is discussed, it should be described as the way of life of a particular group at a particular time. In the words of Dick Little Bear (1986), a Northern Cheyenne, "There is no generic Indian."

An eighth grade text on American history used on a Montana Reservation recently was examined for Native American content. In the 400 page textbook, there were three pages on Indian life and culture, beginning with the sentence: "There were savage Indian tribes that hunted the buffalo for food. They made clothes of the hides, and used skins to cover their tents. The Indians often attacked the covered-wagon trains." The Council on Interracial Books for Children (1841 Broadway, New York, N.Y. 10023) publishes a guide for evaluating history books, *Stereotypes, Distortions and Omissions in U.S. History Textbooks,* and *Guidelines for Selecting Bias-Free Textbooks and Storybooks.*

Tribal governments need to be studied as well as state, county, and city governments. Teachers can collect their own materials, or for some of the larger tribes like the Navajo, published material is available. The Navajo Curriculum Center (Rough Rock Demonstration School, Rough Rock, Arizona 86503) publishes a whole series of books including *Our Community—Today and Yesterday* and *Navajo Police.* The Bilingual Materials Development Center (P.O. Box 219, Crow Agency, Montana 59022) published in 1986 a bilingual history of their tribe for the intermediate grades titled *Spsaalooke Bacheeitche.* Many more books like these need to be published. When they are written it is often owing to the dedicated efforts of classroom teachers who recognize the need for such materials.

4. Assure Historical Accuracy

Materials in the classroom need to present a balanced, honest portrayal of Native American history and society. Battles and strange (usually unexplained) customs should not be emphasized. Theories and educated guesses based on incomplete evidence should not be stated as simple facts. Native American traditional views and oral history should have a place in the curriculum along with archeology, historical analysis, and other scientific/humanistic interpretations.

Particular cultural practices of the past should be considered in comparison with contemporary practices in other parts of the world rather than with current practices. For example, writers have made scalping a significant aspect of Indian life and used this as an evidence of savagery. Usually they do not make clear that the Indians of the New England and Southwest areas were encouraged to take scalps by the French, English, and Spanish, who also took scalps and paid bounties to the Indians for scalps of their enemies. Similar "savage" customs in Europe are usually downplayed or ignored.

Native Americans also are portrayed as nomads who did not use the land when in fact many more Native Americans lived in villages growing corn and other crops that they had domesticated over the years than hunted Buffalo on the plains.

5. Teach Native American Contributions

Social Studies is more than battles and political events. It should include the daily life, the ideas, and the values of each group of people studied, as well as their contributions to our thought and well-being. For example the contributions of Native Americans to the field of medicine which are described in Virgil Vogel's *American Indian Medicine* (Norman: University of Oklahoma Press, 1970) should be studied. The contributions of the Mayans, Incas, and Aztecs to the fields of astronomy, genetics, mathematics, and architecture are largely ignored in most history books as well as the political contributions of groups like the Iroquois to our democratic institutions.

John Collier (1947, p. 154–55) believed that Indians had a "power to live . . . the ancient, lost reverence and passion for human personality, joined with the ancient, lost reverence and passion for the earth and its web of life" which they have tended as "a central, sacred fire" and from which modern America had much to learn.

6. Teach Social Studies as On-Going and Dynamic

In addition to having tribal elders come to school and talk about the old ways, the current issues for tribes of self-determination, land and fishing rights, and economic development should be discussed in classes. Tribal councilmen should be invited to talk to classes, and students should go on field trips to tribal offices and might interview tribal officials or other community leaders.

7. Integrate other Subjects into Your Social Studies Unit

A good Social Studies unit will add interest to all the other subjects in the curriculum, and will provide an opportunity for application of the knowledge learned to those subjects. During your unit on Indian life, your language arts time can be used for recording and revising information obtained in committee work and for writing down stories and information acquired from tribal elders, parents, or guest speakers. Music, physical education, science, art, and even a little of your mathematics program can be integral to parts of your Social Studies unit.

8. Learn More about Native Americans

This chapter provides only a starting place for teaching Social Studies to Native Americans. Teachers are encouraged to read more and take classes in Indian history and culture, such as those offered by tribal community colleges and Native American Studies Programs in regional colleges. Below are some suggested sources for more information about native Americans:

A. General Works on Native American History and Culture

America's Fascinating Indian Heritage. (1978). Pleasantville, NY: Reader's Digest.

Debo, Angie (1970). *A History of the Indians of the United States.* Norman: University of Oklahoma.

Kehoe, Alice B. (1981). *North American Indians: A Comprehensive Account.* Englewood Cliffs, NJ: Prentice-Hall.

Schneider, Mary J. (1986). *North Dakota Indians: An Introduction.* Dubuque, IA: Kendall/Hunt.

Smithsonian Institution. (1978-ongoing). *Handbook of North American Indians.* William C. Sturtevant, General Editor. (Will be 20 volumes on various regions and topics)

Utley, R.M. (1984). *The Indian Frontier of the American West 1846–1890.* Albuquerque, University of New Mexico.

Vogel, Virgil. (1972). *This Country Was Ours: A Documentary History of the American Indian.* New York: Harper & Row. (Contains a list of famous Americans of Native American Descent).

Wissler, Clark. (1966). *Indians of the United States.* Garden City, NY: Anchor Books. (Revised American Museum of Natural History edition).

B. Specific Works on Particular Tribes Abound. Only a sample list is given here:

Ewers, John C. (1982). *Blackfeet: Raiders of the Northwestern Plains.* Norman: University of Oklahoma.

Underhill, Ruth. (1983). *The Navajos.* Norman: University of Oklahoma Press.

Weist, Tom. (1984). *A History of the Cheyenne People,* Revised Edition. Billings, MT: Council for Indian Education.

C. Reading Material (Stories) for Students

The Buffalo of the Flathead (1981) and other books in the *Indian Reading Series.* Portland, Or: Northwest Regional Educational Laboratory.

The Council for Indian Education (Box 31215, Billings, MT 59107) has a number of booklets containing stories about Native Americans.

Gerrard Publishing Company (1607 North Market Street, Champagne, IL 61820) has a series of ten Indian biographies at the third grade level as well as two books on "Indian Patriots."

Grandfather Stories of the Navahos. (1968). Rough Rock, AZ: Navaho Curriculum Center.

Kleitsch, Christel, & Stephens, Paul (1985). *Dancing Feathers.* Toronto, Canada: Annick.

Linderman, Frank B. (1972). *Pretty Shield, Medicine Woman of the Crows.* Lincoln, University of Nebraska.

McDermott, Gerald (1977). Arrow to the Sun: A Pueblo Indian Tale. New York: Puffin.

Ryniker, Alice D. (1980). *Eagle Feather for a Crow.* Kansas City, MO: Lowell.

Sandoz, Mari. (1985). *These Were the Sioux.* Lincoln: University of Nebraska Press. (First published in 1961).

D. Directories, Catalogs, and Lists

Canyon Records (catalog). Major producer of Indian records, 4143 No. 16th St, Phoenix, AZ 85016; (602) 266-4823.

Native American Directory. (1982). San Carlos, AZ: National Native American Cooperative. (Includes tribes, museums, organizations, events, stores, and so forth.)

Newberry Library Center for the History of the American Indian. Bibliographic Series. Francis Jennings, General Editor. Chicago, IL (Includes tribes, regions, and special topics.)

Weatherford, Elizabeth (1981). *Native Americans on Film and Video.* New York: Museum of the American Indian (Broadway at 155th Street, NY, NY 10032). A listing with descriptions of about 400 films and videotapes.

E. Teaching Guides

American Indian Education Handbook. (1982). Sacramento: California State Department of Education.

Oklahoma's Indian People: Images of Yesterday, Today, and Tomorrow. (1983). Oklahoma City: Oklahoma State Department of Education.

SUMMARY

James Banks (1987) has declared that developing "the ability to make reflective decisions" should be the main goal of multiethnic education. Native American and non-Native American students need to be exposed to the truth about the history of the United States, including unpleasant truths about slavery and discrimination and more pleasant truths about the cultural strengths of the native tribes and the various immigrant groups. Only when armed with the truth, can students make realistic decisions, both personal and political. Teachers of Native Americans need to allow students to explore their past and present and facilitate that exploration by being knowledgeable about Native Americans in general and the specific groups near their schools in particular. Teachers must be advocates for their students by searching out culturally related materials and by encouraging their schools to procure books and other materials on native history and culture.

REFERENCES FOR FURTHER READING

Antes, J.M., & B.J. Boseker. "Using an Indian Community in Social Studies Education." *Journal of American Indian Education,* 22, January 1983, pp. 28–32.

Banks, James A. *Teaching Strategies for Ethnic Studies: Fourth Edition.* Boston: Allyn & Bacon, 1987. (Chapter 5 is a good introduction to American Indians and chapter 6 is a good introduction to Native Hawaiians).

Burnes, B. "Teaching about Native American Families." *Social Education,* 50, January 1986, pp. 28–30.

Cohen, Felix S. "Americanizing the White Man." In *The Indian in the Classroom: Readings for the Teacher with Indian Students* (pp. 2–13). Helena, MT: Office of Public Instruction, n.d.

Collier, John. *The Indians of the Americas.* New York: Norton, 1947.

Deloria, Vine. *Custer Died for your Sins: An Indian Manifesto.* New York: Macmillan, 1969.

Fox, Sandra. *Indian Culture Unit; American Indians and their Foods.* Washington. 1411 K. Street, NW, Washington, D.C.: Indian Education Act Resource and Evaluation, Center one, n.d.

Fuchs, Estelle & Robert Havighurst. *To Live on This Earth: American Indian Education.* Garden City, NY: Anchor, 1973. (Reprinted by the University of New Mexico, 1983).

Gearing, Frederick D. *The Face of the Fox.* Chicago: Aldine-Atherton, 1970. (Contains an excellent discussion of the process of cultural description, understanding, and intercultural attitudes and perspectives)

Hobson, G. (Ed.). *The Remembered Earth.* Albuquerque: University of New Mexico, 1976.

Jennings, F. "Growing Partnership: Historians, Anthropologists, and American Indian History." *History Teacher,* 14, November 1980, pp. 87–104.

LeBrasseur, Margot, & Ellen Freark. "Touch a Child–They are my People: Ways to Teach American Indian Children." *Journal of American Indian Education,* 21, May 1982, pp. 6–12.

Little Bear, Dick. "Teachers and Parents: Working Together." In Jon Reyhner (Ed.), *Teaching the Indian Child* (pp. 222–231). Billings, MT: Eastern Montana College, 1986.

Momaday, N. Scott. "The Man made of Words." In A. Chapman (Ed.), *Literature of the American Indians* (pp. 96–110). New York: New American Library, 1975.

Noley, G.B. "Historical Research and American Indian Education." *Journal of American Indian Education,* 20, January 1981), pp. 13–18.

Turvey, J.S. "Investigate a Culture: Map, Research, Present, and Write." *English Journal,* 75, January 1986, pp. 82–83.

Chapter 10

Selecting and Producing Valid Material for Reading and Social Studies

by Hap Gilliland

Children learn about cultures and values, their own and others, through the things they read. Most of the culturally related reading in your classroom will be in Reading and Social Studies. It will require time and effort for you to find an adequate amount of materials and separate them from those which could be damaging to self-concepts and inter-group relationships. There are many ways in which you can also produce some locally relevant materials to meet the needs of your students, but you will have to be creative and alert to the possibilities. However, the difference in achievement and attitude that good materials make will be well worth the effort.

SELECTING MULTICULTURAL MATERIALS

If Native American students are to build self-esteem, a feeling of personal worth, and a sense of their place in history, their reading must include adequate culturally and historically accurate material about their own people.

It is not necessary that all reading be culturally related. To have a well-rounded and complete instructional program in Reading and Social Studies, the school will need to use other materials also, but it is necessary that enough cultural materials be included to give the students a feeling of their place in history, of the importance of their people in American culture, and to provide a reading program that is relevant to the lives of the students. As teachers, we must be aware of student backgrounds and interests and be on the alert to obtain as much relevant material as possible.

All students should be exposed to other cultures and new ideas. However, the way in which those cultures and values are presented is important. If they portray urban, middle class values, do they imply that the culture and values of other groups are wrong, or even that they are less worthwhile? If so, they may do great harm to the self concept of the Indian or other minority students in addition to causing them to develop a dislike for reading and the study of history. Therefore, you must have an understanding attitude toward all cultures to guide you in selecting materials and in guiding class discussions on any culture. Whenever possible, local community members and tribal cultural committees should aid teachers in producing, examining, and choosing cultural materials to be used in the school.

There is now so much good material that there is no longer any excuse for using inaccurate materials. However, we must select carefully. Keep in mind the seven criteria listed below. These criteria will apply whether your students are Indian or non-Indian, and whether the material is to be used as a part of a lesson in social studies, reading, literature, or for recreational reading. These same criteria should be considered by parents, librarians, editors, and anyone else who influences the selection of books for children's reading.

1. Is It Accurate?

There are inaccuracies regarding Indian life and culture in many historical materials. There are many more in "historical" fiction. Do the Indians portrayed live and act according to the Indian customs and habits of the particular area at the time the story takes place? Does the material over-emphasize one particular aspect of the culture to the point that it gives a false concept of a way of life?

If the non-Native child is to develop an appreciation for the Native culture and its contributions, and is to learn to accept his Indian neighbors as friends and equals, then the books he reads must be culturally and historically accurate, and they must be realistic enough so that he can see the relationship to the Native people with whom he is acquainted.

There is a great contrast between the reading material dealing with Native people that is being written now, and that which was written a few years ago. Most editors, too, are refusing to accept material that is misleading or derogatory to any minority group. However, some authors and editors do not have adequate knowledge of the Native culture to be able to identify false or biased information.

In 1965, a committee from the American Indian Historical Society, an all-indian organization, appeared before the California State Curriculum Commission choosing textbooks for use in California Schools. They wrote:

"We have studied many textbooks now in use, as well as those being submitted today. Our examination discloses that not one book is free from error as to the role of the Indian in state and national history. We Indians believe everyone has the right to his opinion. A person also has the right to be wrong. But a textbook has no right to be wrong, or to lie, hide the truth, or falsify history, or insult or malign a whole race of people. That is what these textbooks do. . . . A true picture of the American Indian is entirely lacking." (Costo, 1970, p. 7)

What was true of textbooks was just as true of fiction. Most of the Indians portrayed were stereotyped. Battles between Indians and whites were emphasized, with Indians usually in the wrong, and having no right to protect their land from the invaders. Indians were either described as savage beasts, nomads, or drunks; or noble savages living in an ideal world. Neither made them appear as real people with faults and virtues, people with whom a child could relate.

There is a great change in the books published recently. However, a book cannot be judged by date alone. A few excellent books on Indian life were published long ago, and some publishers still accept very biased material. While less *distortion* of facts occurs in present-day writing, the *omission* of facts remains a serious fault of much of the literature. The treatment Indians received is usually omitted from children's literature, as are Indian contributions to agriculture, medicine, architecture, biological science, and other aspects of modern life.

Writers seem unaware of the Indian's philosophical thought, close family ties, emphasis on cooperation and sharing with others, respect for the land and all of nature, hospitality and generosity, and the relation of all of these to the Indian's spiritual life.

Do your history books ignore Indian history and culture, or present distorted views of it? Do they treat Indian people as the original Americans and study their civilization, then bring in the arrival and contributions of each group of people, including Asians? Or do they sound as if all history began in Europe and nothing important happened unless the European-Americans did it? The book from which I had to teach California history stated, "The history of California begins with the Spanish settlement"!

2. What Are the Author's Attitudes toward Native American People?

Authors may be very accurate in the historical facts they present, yet reveal attitudes toward the Indian of which they may not even be aware. Even though unintentional, if the author shows prejudicial feelings, or attitudes of superiority, the material will be damaging to the child who reads it.

Authors' attitudes show through their writings in many ways. Books, both old and new, should be checked for stereotypes, prejudices, and loaded vocabulary. It is the little inuendos which are often missed by the non-Indian reader that may do the most harm to the self concept of the Indian child, or develop lifelong prejudices in the non-Indian. Often the author who intends to say something good is actually, because of his own inner feelings, downgrading the Indian. Consider this statement: "He was an Indian, but he was a very smart man."

It is the vocabulary used which often brings out the writer's attitudes. Battles won by soldiers are called "victories" while Indian victories are "massacres" even when they resulted from surprise attacks by the whites. Settlers who protected their homes were "patriots" Indians who did the same were "murderers". Indians who did not disclose their military plans to the white man were "treacherous", but the word is not used for the generals who made treaties, then broke them, or who attacked the Indians who were abiding by these treaties. Modern workers who must move with their jobs, are not termed "nomads", but an Indian who only changes location from summer to winter is "nomadic". All Indians are called "primitive", even those who were creative artists, skilled architects, or who built great irrigation systems!

Do the Indians in the books in your school follow the stereotypes of the Indian still believed by many readers who have no contact with Indians? Do they have many faults, but few, if any, virtues? Do they emphasize battles, in which the Indians are always in the wrong? Do they give the feeling that the Indians had no right to protect their lands from the invaders? Are the only Indian heroes the ones who were traitors to their own people?

Are people from minority groups depicted as "different" in such a way that they seem inferior to white middle-class suburbia? Are there value judgments on their behavior? If a culture is depicted, do they include genuine insights into the life-style, or do they over-simplify?

Not only were many authors of the past misinformed, editors chose the stories which perpetuated the stereotypes because "that's what the readers want." In 1955, I wrote a short story which included an Indian who I thought was very realistic. The editor's first comment was, "Your Indian character speaks English as well as your other characters. Indians don't talk like that. Make him talk like an Indian."

3. Does It Portray Indian Values?

Are values interpreted in terms of an Indian or non-Indian point of view? How is success described? Is a person respected only if he gets ahead in White society? To gain acceptance, does he have to get A's, excel in sports, and make money?

Many stories which accurately portray historical events and the physical environment of the Indian completely misinterpret Indian values. The concepts of sharing and cooperative living are missed, along with the differences in feelings about property, time, family relationships, the significance of nature, and the importance of spiritual life. Authors who have not lived among Indian people are prone to give their Indian characters the same motivations and values as their non-Indian friends. Watch for these fallacies. If you must use these books, discuss the misconceptions as you read with your students.

Watch also for the attitudes in stories about non-Indians. Reading materials which portray urban, middle class life often imply that the culture and values of other groups are wrong or less worthwhile. A class of Indian students was reading a story in their basic readers. The main character of the story entered a contest to try to win a cash prize. He competed against all his friends, refusing to help them because it was important to him to win. He not only won the cash prize, but put the prize money in the bank to save it for a bicycle he wanted to get for himself. The teacher of the class could not understand why her Indian pupils disliked the story and the main character. She did not see that everything the "hero" did was wrong. If the teacher had known more of the Indian culture, she could have discussed the story more meaningfully with the students, reinforcing their concept of sharing and helping, or else she could have omitted the story from the reading program.

Check the textbooks from which you are expected to teach. Do they represent fully the viewpoints, achievements, cultures, heritage, contributions and experiences of Native Americans, Mexican Americans, Asian Americans, and Afro-Americans? Is information about these groups stereotyped or biased? Does it judge all groups by white middle class standards? If so, the information the children learn from these books will be distorted and incorrect. Worse yet, it will lower the self-image of some students, and make acceptance of all people as equals unlikely for others.

Compare the values by which Native American characters in your book live with those described in Chapters 3, 4, and 5. Unless the majority of them are similar, perhaps you should study the book carefully before you recommend it to your students.

4. Does It Portray Indian People in a Positive Way?

In the majority of basic readers, the only Indians are Indians of the past. Modern Native American children see no relationship between the feathered warriors of the plains and the people of their own neighborhood. If they look for it, they find only fighting warriors, not loving families with close relationships and concern for each other. Then they read about the ideal family of the basic reader; about happy children living in ideal homes and ideal neighborhoods where there is no poverty, and they are never told that loving families are better than expensive toys, or that helping others is better than driving fancy cars. Will the book you use help your Indian students identify with and be proud of their heritage? Will it foster a positive image of present day Indian people? Will it encourage Indian students to want to achieve?

5. Do the Illustrations Authentically Depict Indians of the Time and Location?

Books as well as motion pictures sometimes depict Indians of the Southwest wearing Plains Indian Headdresses, New England Woodland Indians living in teepees, or Navajos living among Saguaro cactus. These errors do not necessarily reflect upon the knowledge of the writer, as the author does not always see the illustrations that the publisher will use, but it does indicate that all of the content needs to be checked for accuracy. The illustrations themselves can teach misinformation regarding the history and culture of the people depicted.

6. Is It Interesting?

High interest materials that promote a desire to read are even more important for Indian children than for other children because many of them have had less exposure to reading in their homes and have less feeling of a need for reading. Stories should be fast starting and short. Even the top Indian students will often state that they are "turned off" by thick books and small print.

The materials should be relevant to the particular needs and interests of the Indian children of your community. These are often very different from the needs and interests of middle class urban children. Children from upper economic urban levels are more likely to be interested in geography, history, and true science, while Native Americans have more interest in reading books about people. Television has had some effect in broadening the interest and the background for understanding of other geographic areas of some children, but the main interest still has to be people.

7. Is the Readability Level Appropriate?

Can the students for whom the material is intended read it easily enough to understand it and enjoy it?

The material which is used must be at a reading level appropriate to the individual student. A child will not develop an interest in reading and read enough to become a good reader unless he enjoys what he reads. He cannot enjoy reading if the vocabulary or comprehension level are such that he has to struggle to read or understand it. If the vocabulary level is too difficult, he may lose both self-confidence and interest in reading. He will also make little if any progress in reading skills, because, faced with too many unknown words, it will be difficult for him to remember any of them, and he will not read enough material to get adequate practice.

There are numerous readability formulas available that will give you an approximate reading level of books that you want to evaluate. Formulas such as Fry's, which are based on sentence length and number of syllables give a quick estimate. However, for books written with a high interest and mature format, but easy vocabulary, intended for remedial readers, the estimate will be much too high. For these you need a formula based on word lists of common words, but analysis with these formulas takes longer. There are also computer programs available that will quickly give you readabilities from several different formulas.

97

Readability, however, is more than sentence length and difficulty of vocabulary. It is also how well the sentence construction, vocabulary, and means of expression match that of the reader, and how the content fits the student's background, and his desire to read. For this reason, although formulas will give you some indication, and help you eliminate some very inappropriate material, they will not accurately tell you how difficult the material will be for the Indian students in your class.

DEVELOPING LOCALLY RELEVANT MATERIAL

Although there are many good books on Indian life and culture, many of these will be only slightly relevant to any one group of Indian students. Penobscot children of Maine or Abnaki children of Quebec may prefer stories of the Navajo and Apache in Arizona to stories of the dominant society since Indian children are usually interested in how other Indian children live, but to really build interest in reading and the self concept that comes from knowing of the importance of your own group, children need reading material that is about them, their people, material that is "real." Many different groups have worked on developing their own materials, so some may be available, but there are almost never enough of these to adequately supplement the commercially available materials. Therefore, most teachers find it necessary to, somehow, supplement these with locally developed materials. Below are descriptions of seven ways that some of us have produced materials for our own classes. Perhaps you will find some of them applicable to your classroom and your school.

1. Record Children's Experiences

Recording of children's own experiences can begin very early in the first grade, and continue at all levels. If the stories are typed, bound, and kept on file they can provide much good reading material for other children as well as those who write or tell them.

These stories have the advantage of being about local people and typical local experiences. They emphasize that the children's own experiences are worth writing about, reading about, and keeping. They have the further advantage of being in the local language or dialect, the vocabulary and way of speaking of the children themselves.

The writing of "language experience" stories is not just an activity for the beginning reader. It is equally appropriate for older students. In the Reading Clinic at Eastern Montana College they have been an essential part of the reading instruction for remedial students of all ethnic groups and all ages from primary students to adults. They have been especially valuable for Indian adult beginning readers.

A more thorough discussion of language experience for Native American children is included in the chapters on teaching reading skills and the whole language approach.

2. Produce a School Newspaper

In Arctic Village, a small Athapascan village in Northern Alaska, the little two teacher school published the Arctic Village News, about four dittoed pages, that came out every two weeks and was distributed to everyone in the village. The children all wrote new items, and parents also contributed news. The whole village was always anxious to read it, so it gave the children a real incentive to write, as well as providing reading material of importance to them.

The same idea could be adapted to many situations. In a larger school the paper could be distributed just to the students, or it could be for the members of one class and their parents.

As part of this, a teacher can take pictures of students and their activities, as well as other activities around the school and community. Young children can write captions for the pictures. Older ones can write news articles about them. The children are usually very enthusiastic when their pictures are included. Although it is not a recommended method of copying photos, copies made on the school's copy machine are usually adequate for school use.

3. Let Students Conduct Interviews

Students on the Pima reservation interviewed their parents, grandparents, and other elders, and collected stories. Some were old folk stories or legends. Others were the experiences of the people interviewed. The students then wrote the stories. When they had difficulty expressing Pima ideas in English they talked them over with each other or with a bilingual teacher aide and tried to agree on a translation. When the stories were completed they were typed. Most were one or two pages long. "Reader's Digest type" blurbs to interest the reader were put at the top of each story. any words that other children reading the story might not know were defined or used in a defining sentence in the wide right hand margin. Each story was then put into a bright colored cover which included the title and illustration. A number of copies of each story were made and put into the school library so that any teacher could check out enough copies for a reading group or a whole class. They became an important supplement to the reading program, as well as preserving much information that could have soon been lost as the elders passed on.

In a similar project at Tuba City, Navajo and Hopi students and parents produced a book called *Desert Wind*. The school at Craig, Alaska, published *Kil-Kass-git*, a small magazine that included stories and photos about their Haida community. Similar projects have been found practical and have benefited many schools and communities since Elliot Wigginton and his Apachian students made the idea popular with their book *Foxfire* in 1972.

4. Develop Local Culturally Related Books

Northern Cheyenne teachers, tribal council leaders, parents, and other elders formed a committee under the chairmanship of John Woodenlegs, who was the tribal president, to produce a series of small books from which Northern Cheyenne children could learn to read using material relevant to their own lives. After several books were printed the group felt that their books should be shared with other tribes and others should share with them, so the non-profit council for Indian Education was formed to continue and expand the project. They have now published over 100 of these small books about Indian people throughout the U.S. and Canada. (Gilliland 1970-)

Others have developed similar materials. Crow teachers and teacher aides have developed a Crow Easy Reading series for their library. The menominee have produced folk stories and even a science book. Consultants working with Winslow teachers and parents at Kayenta developed some small humorous books about local present day Navajo life. This kind of project is a good opportunity for teachers and parents to work together and get parents interested and involved in the school. If all such projects would share and make their materials available to the others, there would be more than adequate material to carry on a complete culturally related reading program.

5. Invite Local Story Tellers

The interest, and knowledge, of any class can be enhanced by inviting local story tellers to come to the class to talk and tell stories. If they do this, ask the story tellers to allow you to turn on the tape recorder while they are there, and to write the stories out later. If they are telling the stories to the grade level for which you intend to use them, most of them will naturally, without being told, adjust the vocabulary and language structure to the maturity of the students. If they tell the stories to you, you will have much more adaptation to do.

If your guest story tellers speak the native language, record at least half of the material in their language so the children can use it for listening. Feelings cannot be expressed as well in English, and there is much description and humor that is lost in translation.

Guest story tellers can also be a good way of getting children interested in storytelling, and this can greatly improve the program in oral English. A relaxed story telling time at least once a week could do more for students' oral English than many standard uninteresting drills.

6. Inspire the Writing of Creative Stories and Poems

Both the recording of stories from interviews, and writing their own experiences can lead children into writing purely creative stories and poems. Many Indian children have great ideas for creative fiction and they love to write poetry if they can be inspired. As Mick Fedulo travels to various Indian schools teaching poetry, he has every student writing with enthusiasm. Try out the ideas in Perie Longo's chapter on inspiring creative writing and you may end up with much good material that can supplement your reading program.

If you teach remedial reading and work with high school children who are reading at a low elementary level, they may hesitate to write because they think they cannot write well enough. Explain to them that you need material for your first and second grade students to read and want them to write about their experiences, but to be sure to write it in easy words that these children can read. It may work wonders for you—it did for me.

7. Rewrite Material at an Easier Level

Tribal information material, occupational, consumer information, adult education, and other materials written for adult use are often more appropriate for high school students than those provided for their use, as the students can see more relevance to their own use. Some teachers have provided material by rewriting these at the reading level of their students, with terms not familiar to the students paraphrased to aid understanding and vocabulary building.

SUMMARY

If Native American children are to build reading skills and a good self-concept, if they are to be interested and gain an adequate understanding of the history of both their own people and society in general, they must have a wealth of culturally and historically accurate materials. As teachers we must select carefully the materials we will use to separate truth from untruth and the biased from the unbiased. Are the materials accurate, complete, and informative? Do they portray Native values positively? Are the characters and the illustrations true to the way of life of the particular group at the time depicted?

When adequate materials relevant to the local way of life are not available they can be supplemented with materials developed in the classroom through children writing about their own experiences, their creative ideas, and material that has been told to them by local people. Parents and elders can help to produce additional relevant material.

REFERENCES FOR FURTHER READING

Costo, R. Ed. *Textbooks and the American Indian.* Indian Historian, 1970.

Gilliland, Hap. *Indian Childrens Books.* Council for Indian Education, 1980.

Gilliland, Hap, Editor. *Indian Culture Series.* 103 small books for Indian children, published by the Council for Indian Education, Box 31215, Billings, MT. 1970 to present.

Gilliland, Hap. "The New View of Native Americans in Children's Books." *The Reading Teacher* 35, May 1982, p 799–803.

Gilliland, Hap. "Selecting Reading Materials for Indian Children." in J. Reyhner, *Teaching the Indian Child.* Eastern Montana College, 1986, pp 83–90.

Indian Reading Series, many small books of stories and legends of Northwest, Plateau, and Northern Plains Indians. Northwest Regional Educational Laboratory, Portland, Ore.

Reyhner, Jon. "Native Americans in Basal Reading Text Books: Are There Enough?" *Journal of American Indian Education,* 26–1, Oct. 1986, pp. 14–22.

Reitz, Sandra and Norma Livo. *Storytelling: Process and Procedures.* Libraries Unlimited, 1986.

Rig, Pat. *"Desert Wind:* A Fresh Breeze in Indian Education," *Journal of Reading,* Feb. 1985, pp 393–397.

Saucerman, James R. "Teaching Native American Literature." in Reyhner, *Teaching The Indian Child,* Eastern Montana College, 1986.

Unlearning "Indian" Stereotypes: A Teaching Unit for Elementary Teachers and Children's Librarians. Council on Interracial Books for Children, 1977.

Wigginton, Eliot, *Foxfire.* Doubleday, 1972.

Chapter 11

A Whole Language Approach to the Communication Skills

by Sandra J. Fox

The instructional philosophy called the "whole language" approach is the natural way to teach language. It incorporates oral language practice, reading, listening, and writing activities, and the use of culturally relevant materials.

The majority of Indian students are "holistic" learners. They learn more easily if they see the whole picture first, then learn the details as a part of the whole. This holistic method is preferable for Indian students as it provides for the practice of language skills in a meaningful way as interrelated and useful tools. It allows students to explore life experiences, then to look at language in relation to those experiences rather than doing meaningless workbook pages, spelling and vocabulary lessons which are isolated parts of language and have no experiential basis. Whole language instruction includes the language-experience approach for communication skills.

PRINCIPLES OF WHOLE LANGUAGE

The principles of whole language instruction include:

- It is student-centered. Much of the content of instruction comes from the student's own language and experience.
- It is comprehension-centered. Aspects of language are learned as parts of a "whole" language rather than being learned as isolated parts. For example, words are learned in the context of meaningful language experiences. Sound/symbol correspondence (phonics) is learned from sounds within words which students know and use.
- Instruction is based upon active learning, hands-on strategies.
- Communication skills are not taught in isolation. Students learn to read from writing and vice-versa. Programs, therefore, include reading, writing, speaking and listening activities.
- Students are taught to enjoy and appreciate literature—the written works of others.
- Students are involved in planning activities based upon a selected theme for the whole language lessons.

STRATEGIES FOR TEACHING

Nine strategies for teaching language as an integrated whole to Indian students are recommended.

1. Begin with Language Experience and Continue at All Levels

A basic activity of the whole language approach is writing a language-experience story. Basal reader stories are usually far removed from any of the experiences of the Native American child. Language experience is based on each child's own experiences. Therefore, the instruction relates to his background, his interests, and his culture.

You can begin language experience instruction by providing a group experience such as doing a project, seeing a movie, going on a field trip. After the experience, the class discusses what they did and you ask the students to "summarize" the experience so they can write a story about it. As they summarize, you initially lead the students with questions such as "What did we do?", "What did we see?" Later on, the students will give summary information on their own. Write the story on the board while students give you the information. When writing the language-experience story, you are modeling writing for the students. The finished story is used for reading instruction. The students see their own words written down and practice reading words from their own experience. They have practiced speaking when discussing the experience and when providing the summary information for the story. Illustrating the stories provides for students' visualization and reinforcement of concepts. Thus, the language-experience story involves students in reading, writing, speaking and listening, all in the same lesson, and all related to the students' own experiences.

For students at higher grade levels, the language-experience story technique is usually adjusted so that students write their own individual stories from their group experiences. Language-experience stories, both group and individual, can be "published" as books the students have written. These books are then available for others to read. Language experience stories are often illustrated, thus providing for visualization which many students need.

The idea of the language-experience story can be extended to activities such as the writing of a daily class newspaper (including the date, weather and news items about the class, school, or activities in the community), the writing of real get-well cards or thank you notes, and the writing of plans for class activities. In this manner, children learn communications skills from language which is within the realm of their own experience and communication needs.

The procedure for writing language-experience stories (experience, discussion, summarizing, and writing) can be used with older students to help them keep class notes in notebooks. This is an especially good technique for classes such as Indian culture classes in which there are no single textbooks for use, but the technique can also be useful in all academic areas. Students can refer to their notebooks for purposes of reviewing the material; they are simultaneously practicing language skills and the actual process of notetaking.

2. Bring Familiar Language to the Classroom

The language-experience story allows students to read and write their own language. In addition, students can bring jingles and words from their favorite television shows and commercials, words of rhymes they know, words of their favorite popular songs and words relating to sports or other activities in which they are especially involved. Students can also examine words which are the names of things within the classroom, within the school building, and in the community. They can examine their own slang, popular expressions or terms. These words, this familiar language which students bring to the classroom, then become word lists for you to use in reading and writing instruction.

Students can make word lists based upon the theme of the whole language lessons. For example, if the theme is "grandmothers," the students can give words they use to describe grandmothers. You, the teacher, can write the words on the board or flip chart. The meanings and spellings and grammatical usage of the words can be discussed. These words are from the students' oral vocabulary, words they know and use but may never have seen written down. These words can then be used by the student to write short stories and essays.

3. Incorporate Instruction in the Reading Strategies

The words in the language experience story and in other language brought to the classroom by the students are the primary medium for teaching word attack skills—the skills involved in sounding out or pronouncing words. In addition, words encountered in literature being read and in experiences taking place are used for word attack instruction.

When stories or words are on the board or flip chart, you have an opportunity to point out words with sound/symbol correlations or examples of the phonetic analysis which you want to stress.

You thus build upon certain things which the students already know about phonics and also use words which they already know for examples.

Students can write words from language-experience stories and other activities on word cards. These cards should then be kept in the students' banks of words (the collection of words they already know how to read). Each student should have his own box or bank. Other students may prefer to write in word notebooks the new words which they encounter.

The words from these word banks can be used by students in several ways:

1. The words can be put in alphabetical order.
2. The student can make new sentences with them.
3. Students can identify words with the same beginning sounds, etc.
4. Students can review the words as flashcards.
5. The words can be analyzed for spelling and word attack information.

It is important that you include all the important phonetic and structural analysis skills. Some teachers are very adept at pointing out aspects of phonics and structural analysis in words as they arise. Others choose to rely on some guide to be sure all skills are included.

It is also important that all the comprehension skills (word meaning, main ideas, exploring details, retelling, searching for answers to questions, predicting happenings, etc.) are practiced both with student-written and published culturally relevant material. Concept

105

mapping and semantic webbing are helpful for assisting Indian students in improving comprehension skills.

4. Read to Your Students Every Day

Students who become good readers usually have been read to when they were preschoolers. They got the idea of what reading is. They learned there were words on the pages and often memorized the book so they knew exactly which words were on a page. The reader dared not skip a word or a page. These students learned to enjoy a book. They also saw adults "model" reading behaviors. Reading to students is important at school for these same reasons and students never get too old for this activity. This is especially important for Native American students, as many of them have never been read to at home and some have never seen anyone read until they entered school. It is an important learning activity.

Students who are being read to are practicing comprehension and the important communication skill of listening, which is not stressed enough in our schools. Students learn how to listen for information and they hear new words which can increase their vocabularies. When reading to students, you can help them practice good reading habits. Help students relate happenings to their own experiences. Stop to examine meanings and spelling of words encountered and include comprehension questions and higher level critical thinking questions to promote analysis.

Reading to students is the perfect time to include good culturally relevant Indian materials. Often good Indian literature is left on school shelves or only a few students read it. Here is an opportunity for many to share in it. In any case, the material read to students should be something in which the group of students is interested. For kindergarten and first grade, favorite books or poetry can be read over and over again.

Groups of all ages can be read to, or tutors or older students can read to individual students. Older students can listen individually to books or other materials which have been taped by tutors and they can follow along in the book while listening.

The idea of the importance of reading to students, especially in the primary grades, should be extended to the home. Parents should be urged to read to their children, and vice versa. If there is any one way Indian parents can help their children with reading it is by reading to them.

5. Have Students Do Much Independent Reading

Time should be spent having students read silently. Allow students some selection of their reading material.

There may be a range of reading ability within a group. Independent reading level is usually two grade levels below the student's grade level test score. Once the independent reading levels of students are determined, books and other materials at those levels need to be identified. Sometimes books include an indication of their reading levels. Otherwise, one can use a readability formula to determine readability levels of books and other materials.

A variety of reading materials should be made available. although students may not choose books at their independent reading levels, they should be available. Steer poor and insecure readers away from books that will only frustrate them. The books they do choose should also be of special interest to them. Although reading of entire books should be encouraged, many Native students, even the best high school students, hesitate to attack a full sized book. Supply plenty of poetry, short stories, and materials such as *Reader's Digest Reading Skill Builders* so students can choose shorter selections which may help to build their confidence. Guide each student to materials with his interests in mind and at his independent reading level. Record students' special interests for this purpose. The available materials should include Indian culture materials and also books and magazines on subjects being studied in social studies and science, and materials on themes being used for other language activities. For older students who do not read well, high interest-low readability level materials should be made available. There are now many of this type on the market.

When students read silently, you should read silently as well. This can be sustained silent reading time. Some term it DEAR time: Drop everything And Read. Students at Wingate Elementary School on the Navajo Reservation surpassed their goal of reading 1,250,000 minutes in the dormitories during the 1985–86 school year through the whole language program.

6. Encourage Students to Share the Literature They Enjoy

There should be time when students and the teacher or tutor share poetry, stories or books that they especially like. The sharing can simply be showing books and recommending them, giving short oral book "sales talks" which entice others to read the books, or actually reading aloud the poetry, short story, book or a portion of a book. When sharing literature,the sharer should stress the name of the author and illustrator so students begin to recognize their names and importance. Written book reports which are displayed can also be a form of sharing literature, but don't force students to quit reading by telling them they must write a report when they finish.

Older students who have difficulty with reading can read lower readability books to younger students, or make tapes for them. Younger students can listen to or read along with these tapes. The older students are practicing their reading and helping younger students with reading at the same time. This is a great self-image booster for all involved.

7. Have Students Write Every Day

Students should write every day. Writing should be made a very important activity. Students should have writing folders or large envelopes in which to keep their written work. Classroom rules should emphasize the importance of silence when people are writing. the cooperative effort and sharing which are essential parts of the Indian culture can be utilized by having students help each other with "editing." This helps to prevent the discouragement from writing that usually results from the correcting process. Thus, students also regularly get helpful suggestions from other students about their writing. Students should often work in pairs.

There are two kinds of writing to be done in school: controlled writing and independent writing. These lead to the two kinds of writing which are necessary for life's communication needs: exact writing and imaginative writing.

Controlled Writing Controlled writing is that in which you, the instructor, control the topic and the form of the writing. this is useful for beginning writers and for older students who need to improve their exact writing skills.

One form of controlled writing is to simply have students copy written works. In the early grades, students copy poetry, songs, language-experience stories, and other short works. The best materials to copy are things already familiar to the students, things that they have learned memorized, or at least have heard.

Dictate sentences for your students to write. The length and number of the sentences depend upon the level of the student. The sentences can include students' spelling or vocabulary words or can be from an experience which the class or student has had. After each sentence is written by the students, you can write it correctly on the chalkboard for the students to compare with theirs. This provides immediate feedback as to their success at writing, correct spelling, punctuation, and capitalization. Then, direct students to check to make sure they have capitalized, put a period, and so forth—one aspect at a time, stressing the things with which students are having difficulty. More advanced students can have short paragraphs dictated to them. No hints are given, such as "end of sentence," only the words are dictated. Students then have to check to see if they have divided the materials into sentences correctly, whether they have properly indented the first line, and have correct spelling, capitalization, and punctuation. Remember, however, that there can sometimes be more than one correct form. Short papers can be dictated to see if students can divide ideas into paragraphs, as well as checking on other skills. Teaching these skills this way means that you will not need to block creative writing by emphasizing them at that time.

Another method of controlled writing is converting questions into statements. After you explain or review the difference between questions and statements, students can be directed to write a paragraph of statements in which they use sentences to answer questions such as:

What is your name? What school do you attend? What grade are you in? What is your teacher's name? How many students are in your class? Is your school work easy or hard?

The length of the sentences and the paragraph will depend, of course, upon the level of the student or group.

Another type of practice is having students write sentences using their spelling or vocabulary words. A simple record of types of errors being made should be kept and the teacher should discuss the types of errors being made with each student. This technique worked very well with high school remedial students on a South Dakota reservation. Students saw, after writing the same number of sentences each week, that they were making fewer and fewer errors.

Controlled writing should be done as long as needed and the content of it should depend upon the types of errors being made by students.

Independent Writing Students should be encouraged to put their thoughts and ideas on paper. It should be stressed that their ideas are important. Writing should be viewed as the ability to write one's own ideas and present them in a form for others to read. The ideas can provide real or imaginary information—fiction or non-fiction.

Independent writing should be stressed from the first day of school. Children want to write, as evidenced by their crayon marks and scribbles. They should be encouraged to write in kindergarten, because from the beginning, they must believe that they can write. So they are allowed to scribble, draw pictures, or even write alphabet letters if they know them. Ask what they have written and praise them for what they have done.

Even in kindergarten, children can begin expressing their ideas on paper through drawing or painting pictures. Each artist can tell about his picture, and you can extract two or three sentences that will describe the picture or tell the story. By the next day, attach a story strip to the bottom of the child's picture with the two or three sentences on it. The class can then share the pictures again and read the "stories" that go with them. Later on, students can write their own stories for their pictures.

First grade children often have limited spelling-usage vocabularies. If their flow of thought is interrupted by idea gaps and spelling problems, students may feel frustrated about writing—putting their own ideas down on paper. As a transition from controlled writing, a set of completion blanks is sometimes desirable in initial writing lessons to get students started writing, and so that they can see completed selections more quickly. Be sure to leave an open sentence or two at the end that allow students to write as much or little as they like.

I have a pet and its name is _____. It has _____ fur. It likes to _____. It sleeps in the _____. One day it _____.

ME

My name is _____. I live in _____. I am _____ years old. My dad's name is _____. My mother's name is _____. I have _____ sisters and _____ brothers. My tribe is _____. I like myself because _____ (or One day I _____ or, My friends and I _____.

After the students fill in the blanks they may want to copy the entire paragraph to make it their writing. For older students who need this kind of motivation to get anything written, take a story but leave out the adjectives or the verbs so they can be creative by filling it in and making the story their own.

Sometimes you can provide the beginning of incomplete sentences or the ending of sentences in order to get students started.

Before the students begin writing, stress that they must work quietly so all can think. Music may be played if it is soft music with no words. Tell the students that if they come to a word that they want to use but can't spell, they can put the first sound down and leave a blank so they can ask you or their writing partner later. For the time being, they shouldn't disturb anyone.

Written works should be illustrated regularly. This reinforces the ideas which were used in the writing as well as the skills which were practiced. Students can also write captions for cartoons.

Modeling, rather than just telling, is important for Indian students, so demonstrate writing for them. After you choose a topic, or the class helps choose a topic, you can show the class how you gather your thoughts and organize your writing. You should actually write short papers on the chalkboard, making corrections and reorganizing ideas as you go along. As student's writing becomes more complex, there will be a need for outlining and other higher level writing skills which you should also model for students.

Making corrections in independent writing should be viewed as "editing." Editing should start out simply, with all students turned into editors after being writers. They can edit their own work or they can edit each other's work. At first, they should simply read the work to see if it makes sense. Later, they can check for capitalization, punctuation, correct writing of the title, spelling and paragraphing, etc. Older students might have a checklist of things to look for.

You can be available to help students edit. Some papers may be edited by you as examples of how to edit. Copies can be made of one paper for all to see as you point out the things to be changed, or sentences from many papers can be extracted for the teacher to use as examples. For this purpose, you should be careful to choose papers written by the students who are better writers so as not to squelch the creativity of those who are less confident about their writing.

Some materials should be "published.' Sometimes students' works are displayed on bulletin boards or compiled and actually bound into books to be read by others. Students can write individual books also. The teacher is the "senior editor" in these cases and reviews "drafts" for final copies with students. They do not necessarily have to be perfect. It depends upon the level of the students and the teacher's expectations of students and their levels.

A project for older students is based on the Foxfire concept of gathering information about the local community. The students' writing is then made into a book. Students can also write articles on any topic for local and school newspapers, or their own class newspaper.

Poetry adds spice to the writing program. For early writers, rhyming words—after the first one—can be left out of poetry so that students can fill in the blanks. Later, students can write their own poetry. They get to feel and use a lot of langauge when they write poetry.

The classroom should have many opportunities for writing. Students can keep journals and write in them every day. In the early grades, the teacher can provide the topics. They can be as simple as: Tell how you feel today. Describe your shoe. Journal notes are not "corrected" or edited. You may, however, review them and make comments like "me too" or "I agree" or "nice," etc. Older students may not want their teachers to review their journals. Or journals can actually be written dialog back and forth between teacher and student, and they prove to serve useful as a counseling technique. The classroom could have a message box where students can answer and send messages to the teacher.

8. Provide Oral Language Practice

Oral language practice is involved when students write language-experience stories, bring familiar language to the classroom and share literature. There should, however, be other opportunities for practicing oral language. Reciting of poetry, participating in skits or plays, giving short oral reports, speaking into tape recorders, sharing experiences and discussions—all these things should be included in the whole langauge program. Two-thirds of the students at Wingate Elementary School on the Navajo Reservation tried out for the all-school Christmas play after having gained confidence in themselves through the school's whole langauge program.

9. Organize Your Language Program Around a Theme

The ideas presented in this chapter are just a few of the ideas you could use in a whole language program. There are many others. There is no set way to organize them. To provide some structure to a whole langauge program, we suggest a thematic approach. A language unit can be based on a topic being studied in social studies or science, a book or a special happening of interest to your students. If the topic is chosen with student interests in mind, the students will have many ideas for activities. Use them.

For example, suppose you choose the theme "pets" for students at about the third grade level.

1. *Oral langauge practice.* Students can tell about their pets or pets they know. they can tell the kind of pet, describe the pet and tell something funny the pet does.
2. *Reading to students.* Read the book *Dog story* by Oren Lyons to the group. It is culturally relevant to some tribes and is by an Onondaga author.
3. *Reading Strategy.* Pick out words encountered in reading *Dog Story* for meaning analysis and word attack instruction. The students do a concept mapping of the story.
4. *Language-experience story.* The students can research various kinds of dogs and summarize their findings in a language-experience story format.
5. *Students reading to themselves.* At their independent reading levels, the students can read stories about pets.
6. *Sharing literature.* Some students can tell about stories or books on pets which they have read and especially enjoyed.
7. *Students bringing familiar language to the classroom.* Students can tell about dog foods or dog food commercials they know about. Write and discuss the words in dog food brands or words of commercials.
8. *Writing every day.* Students can write papers on "Why Pets are Important." They can work together in groups to edit these. They may keep daily journals. They may have some controlled writing also.

Students will come up with other activities based on the theme. AS the group plans activities, they may outline them in the form of a concept map or web so they see a picture of their plan. Students may be allowed to choose from proposed activities.

The various activities of the whole langauge approach don't have to be in any particular order. Concepts from other academic areas, such as math or science, should be included if they relate to the topic. Whole language promotes the idea of the teachable moment—teaching a concept or exploring an idea if it relates and if the students seem ready for it. Students learn to do research to learn more about topics they are interested in.

The whole language classroom should be full of stimuli for reading, writing, speaking and listening. some whole language classrooms have reading, writing, speaking and listening centers.

The whole language approach is a much more exciting way to teach than just following textbooks. You will find many more ideas in the books listed at the end of this chapter.

The procedures of the whole language approach can also be used in content areas such as science and social studies. You and your students would plan your reading, writing, speaking and listening activities on the topic being studied. The procedures of the whole language approach can also be used for bilingual programs using the native langauge.

In a culturally appropriate way, the whole language approach stresses the importance of the individual, his langauge, his experiences and his interests. One whole language teacher I know has a mirror in her classroom. Above the mirror are the words *"I AM SPECIAL"*.

REFERENCES FOR FURTHER READING

Allen, Roach Van and Claryce Allen. *Language Experience Activities.* Houghton Mifflin Co. 1982.

Brazee, Phyllis E. and Janice V. Kristo. "Creating a Whole Language Classroom with Future Teachers." *The Reading Teacher,* Jan. 1986.

Cramer, Ward and Suzanne Dorsey. *Read-Ability Books.* (A bibliography of 1850 high interest, low vocabulary books for teenagers.) J. Weston Walch, Portland, ME.

Fletcher, J. D. "What problems do American Indians have with English?" *Journal of American Indian Education, 23, Oct. 1983.*

Graves, Donald H. *Writing: Teachers and Children at Work.* Heinemann Educational Books, 1983.

Grobe, Edwin P. *300 Creative Writing Activities for Composition Classes.* J. Weston Walch, Portland, ME.

Indian Culture Series. Council for Indian Education, Box 31215,Billings, MT 59107. many small books of Indian stories.

Indian Reading Series: Stories and Legends of the Northwest. Educational Systems, Inc., 2360 Southwest 170th Ave, Beverton, Oregon 97005. Contains good discussion of language-experience approach.

Pacific Northwest Reading and Language Development Program. Northwest Regional educational Laboratory. Contains many oral language activities.

Rich, Sharon J. "Restoring Power to Teachers: The Impact of whole Language." *Language Arts,*Nov. 1985.

Stauffer, Russel G. *The Language-Experience Approach to the Teaching of Reading.* Harper and Row, 1970.

Zintz, Miles V. *The Reading Process: The Teacher and the Learner.* Wm. C. Brown Co. 1980.

Excerpts from this chapter have been printed in *Whole Langauge Approach to Improving Reading and Other Communication Skills.* IEA Resource and Evaluation Center One, NAR/ORBIS.

Chapter 12

Developing Reading Skills

by Daniel L. Pearce and Hap Gilliland

Reading is a tool that is essential for Native American students to develop because it enables them to break down the walls between poverty and full membership in society. Reading is a process by which people not only obtain knowledge, but learn how to design and control it.

There are four essentials to be kept in mind in reading instruction for Native American children. First, reading is comprehension. Instruction in reading must be aimed toward reading for meaning. This is especially important for Indian students because their backgrounds, vocabulary, and language are frequently different from those "middle class" children for whom most textbooks are written. Second, Native students must have an opportunity to read, not just school books but also books for fun. Third, reading is something that is not just taught during reading instruction: It must be developed in all subjects and cannot be viewed as just being the responsibility of the reading teacher. Fourth, students need an opportunity to practice active reading techniques.

If the ability to read is going to be successfully developed in Native American children, then teachers must be willing to be flexible and innovative. Native American children can develop reading proficiency, but in order for this to happen, teachers must be willing to adapt their instruction to meet the needs of the children. This means that teachers must go beyond "canned" basal reading programs. Although some teachers may feel most secure when using a basal reading series, it alone will not provide an adequate program for Indian students.

HOW SHOULD READING INSTRUCTION BEGIN?

Teachers who have taught in middle class communities assume that their pupils will begin school with some knowledge of reading, that they have seen parents reading and have been read to, and that they already have a desire to learn how to read. This will be true for some Native American students but not for all. For instance, one teacher on a Montana reservation had 22 students beginning school, 21 of whom had never seen a book or newspaper, or held a pencil in their hands. These students needed a great deal of readiness before formal reading instruction could begin.

One of the ways that children can be prepared for reading is through being read to. Reading to children is probably the most important thing either a parent or teacher can do to prepare a child for reading. While it teaches them what reading is, it also develops an interest in reading and learning to read.

Teachers should read a variety of stories to children. It is usually beneficial for as many stories as possible to be about the children's own people, their tribe, and the life they know. Such reading sessions should be made as comfortable as possible. One way this can be achieved is to sit on the floor with the children, letting the children see the pictures that go with the story, and if possible, letting them see the pictures as they are being read to. During the reading, children should be encouraged to talk about the stories, express their ideas, ask questions, and to tell of their own experiences. Such sessions serve to help develop print awareness, introduce children to aspects of print stories, develop listening skills, and promote language development, all of which are important aspects for success in reading.

Development of fluency in speaking, along with an adequate listening and speaking vocabulary, is a must in preparing Native American children to read. In a study of the Crow and Northern Cheyenne first graders, Simpson (1975) found that these children used less than one fourth of the vocabulary of middle-class urban children in describing the same pictures and objects. As part of their beginning reading experiences, Indian children must be given opportunities to develop their language ability. This means that children must be exposed to language, encouraged to speak, and have their speech accepted without being corrected.

Language Experience

Language experience is an approach which has proved successful with Native American students (Feeley, 1979; Mallett, 1977). We have found that while language experience is used occasionally with Native American students, it needs to be used much more frequently, especially in reservation schools.

A good way to begin is to turn a classroom into a print environment. Make captions for pictures the children have drawn, labels for things they have made, and have books (children's books with pictures and words) out and available for children. This is a crucial point, reading and print must be personal. One way to achieve this is for children to be immersed in print from the very beginning.

An excellent way to begin reading is to let children select key vocabulary words. A key word is a word which has special meaning for that child and is chosen by him or her. Once a child chooses his or her word, the teacher writes it on a piece of paper (tag board is preferable) and gives it to the child to take home, show to people, and bring back to school the next day. The next day, children normally return with "crumpled" words, words which will be remembered. Children's words can be kept and reviewed periodically (say twice a week). This review should be a "fun" activity. If a child does not remember a word "instantly," then that word is filed away without criticism and a new word takes its place. Known words can be used to construct sentences and stories. This approach, known as the "Key Word Approach," was first made famous by Sylvia Ashton-Warner (1963) with the Maori children in New Zealand and is an excellent technique for Native students. For a detailed description of key words see J. Veatch, et. al. (1979).

Gradually working into the language experience type of reading instruction through the key word approach shows the child the relationship of speaking, writing, and reading. It lets students read in their home language and lets them see that their ideas are worthwhile.

114

Most early language experience sessions will be group projects ending with a story which the teacher puts on a large chart which the class can read together. The session usually begins with a conversation between the teacher and a group of students about a topic in which they are interested. Students should be encouraged to change the subject of the discussion as much as they desire. Field trips, an incident at home, the weather, or a television show may provide the beginnings for a discussion. When enthusiasm for a topic is apparent, the teacher suggests that the children tell about the experience and make up a story about it. The teacher records their story on the chart.

Stories should be kept short for beginning readers, who are unsure of their reading ability, and lengthened as they grow in confidence. The stories should be recorded in the exact words of the children. This is what makes it their story. Changing the language to make it "correct" not only decreases children's motivation, it may also make them feel they are being criticized, instead of boosting their self-concepts as the experience should do.

Individual language experience stories begin with the same type of motivation; then the students dictate the story and illustrate it afterwards. The usual method is to write (dictate) the story and illustrate it afterwards. With Indian children it usually works much better to ask them to draw their story, then tell about the drawing. When working with a group, this has the added advantage of letting all the students start at once, and the teacher listens to each student and writes his or her story as the drawing is completed. Start with one or two of the more willing students and let them start telling their stories. Write these stories while the rest of the children are getting started with their drawings, thus spreading the dictation of stories throughout the whole drawing-writing period.

Whether individual or group products, the langauge experience stories can be used for practice in oral reading, for work on sight vocabulary, and for practice in word analysis. The more important words can be analyzed and discussed to aid word recognition, but students must realize that they are not expected to recognize every word. The stories can be bound into individual scrapbooks or into anthologies; they may also be used on bulletin boards made by the class members, or they may be combined into class newspapers. After a student has read a story several times, he or she may wish to take it home to read to others.

When students feel confident enough in their writing abilities so that they want to, they can begin to take the responsibility for writing their own stories. If a child feels more comfortable recording stories on tape, this is possible too. One teacher created a recording booth from a refrigerator box and put a cassette tape recorder inside. Whenever children had a story to record, they would go into the recording booth, turn on the recorder, and tape their stories. A volunteer teacher's aide typed these stories and had them ready for the next day's reading. It is a good idea to keep many of the stories or copies of them in class anthologies, to be used as reading material for students later in the year and for future classes.

The language experience method is especially appropriate for Indian children because it uses the English spoken by the children, not textbook English, which may be very different from the language and vocabulary with which the children are familiar. Also, the subjects of the stories are familiar and understandable, which is an important aspect in promoting fluency, ease of reading, and comprehension. It is, however, important that children read each other's material as well as their own stories. Otherwise, they may not have the inspiration which comes from reading new material and learning through reading.

Too often, language experience activities are assumed to be appropriate only for the beginning reader. This is unfortunate since they can be used equally well with older students. Older students can benefit from studying a topic and constructing "stories" about that topic. These stories are shared with the other students in the class. Langauge experience activities are also an essential part of the reading instruction for remedial students of all ages.

HOW WILL WE TEACH WORD RECOGNITION?

Word recognition is an important facet of reading. While recognizing and being able to "say" the words will not guarantee success in reading, the child with a large sight vocabulary has a better chance of being a successful reader.

1. Learn the Children's Strengths and Match Their Learning Styles

To be effective at recognizing words while reading, students must have a large number of words which are recognized at sight. They must also have a means of identifying words not seen in print frequently enough to be remembered. This requires the combined use of the meaning of the word in the sentence and the sounds represented by the letters. Most Indian children are better at holistic learning than analytic learning. That is, they learn more easily by looking at the whole picture, then analyzing the parts, studying the details, and putting them back together to make the whole picture. Therefore, more of them are better at sight word recognition than at phonics. Of course it is essential that every child learn both to become a really effective reader, but we find it easier for most Native Americans to begin by learning some words through langauge experience, then begin to use other clues for the words they don't recognize through recall and context.

As you work with children's reading experience charts, you can point out letters and name them, then begin finding words that begin with the same letter and same sound. As students progress, they can begin finding words that begin alike, that begin like their names, that end alike, that have letters in the middle that they have learned as beginning sounds.

Flash cards can be made from words in their experience stories and these can be used for comparison of beginning sounds.

Before students can use phonetic analysis they need to recognize small differences in the sounds within words. This is difficult for many Native American students, who are either visual learners or have a native language as their first language. Furthermore, Native Americans (or any students for whom English is a second language) may have problems hearing the sounds of English. This is because the number of phonemes or sounds in languages differ. English has 44 sounds or phonemes in it. In comparison, Kuchi, an Alaskan Indian language has 95 phonemes: 75 consonants and 20 vowels.

Intensive work in phonics may not be appropriate for a child who cannot distinguish between the sounds in English. Furthermore, later direct instruction in synthetic phonics might also not be successful because after 9 or 10 years of age, most people's "sound system" is set and they can recognize or learn to speak new phonemes only with great difficulty.

Children who have difficulty with sight recognition can learn the letters or words that cause them particular trouble by practicing them kinesthetically. They can draw the letters in salt on a cookie sheet, or they can close their eyes and write large letters on the chalkboard using both hands together.

It is important that we teach all the skills through all possible mediums so that all children, regardless of their particular learning style, can learn them. If a child has difficulty with a particular kind of learning and you spend additional time trying to teach him to read through that mode, you will probably condemn that child to frustration and poor reading. It is much more advantageous to emphasize and reinforce strengths, and let children learn to read through them.

2. Try Oral Impress

Most Native American children are especially good at learning through demonstration. One of the best ways to improve word recognition, and one which makes use of this ability, is the oral impress method. It is particularly applicable to Indian students since it is a whole word approach, focuses the child's attention, and culturally related material can be used. It is, however, an individual approach so it cannot be used in its pure format in a large class if there is no outside assistance. But it can be taught to parent volunteers or a teacher aide, and may very well be the best possible use of a volunteer's time.

When using oral impress, sit behind the student, close enough so that you are speaking almost into his or her ear. The child holds the book from which you are both reading. As you read point to the words with your right hand. Read aloud and the child reads aloud with you. Read at a slow-normal oral reading speed, not hesitating or waiting for him. At first, if there are unfamiliar words, a child is likely to be half a word behind, but assure him that is alright. The child's job is to try to stay with you, saying every word if possible. Be sure to move your finger smoothly along, keeping it directly under the word being said; the child will follow your finger, and must be looking at the word he is saying. Read slowly and clearly with good emphasis and rhythm, since the oral reading of the student will be patterned after yours.

Each daily oral impress session should last from 5 to 10 minutes—never longer since it requires a child's concerted, unwavering attention. With most children, you can expect to see a change in their vocabulary, speed of recognition, phrasing, and fluency within the first two hours (three weeks) of instruction.

There are several other activities which use some of the principles of the oral impress method and obtain some of the benefits, but not all of them. One is the use of an overhead projector with a group of children, with the teacher sitting behind the projector pointing to the words as they are read. This works best if there is "language lab" equipment so the teacher reads into a microphone and the children have headphones; a child should hear the teacher more clearly than he hears himself or the other children.

Another method, which includes the sharing that Native children enjoy, is pairing the children. Children are put with either an older child or a better reader, who reads aloud, pointing to the words, as the partner listens.

The cassette tapes of the stories that are available with some of the supplementary reading materials are useful if the children will make an effort to watch the words closely and read with the tape.

One reservation teacher reads a story every Monday morning from a supplemental basal reader. The children watch in their copies as she reads, then she tells them they may read the story as many times as they like, but they must all read it at least once that week.

Many Indian children enjoy poetry; they enjoy its rhythm, its rhyme, its vivid pictures, and they enjoy reading it together. Choral reading of poetry is an excellent way of practicing smooth rhythmic reading and learning new vocabulary. It is a group activity that Native children seem to enjoy. Here, however, it needs to be stressed that in any choral reading situation children should be given a chance to practice and prepare before being called upon to perform.

All of these methods allow students to work cooperatively with the group, to practice reading aloud, to learn new words, and to be corrected when they make mistakes without anyone being aware of their errors.

HOW SHOULD WE DEVELOP COMPREHENSION?

The answer to this question is neither easy nor simple. Reading comprehension is an interaction between various factors, during which a reader constructs meaning. Some of the factors which affect comprehension by Native students include prior knowledge about a topic, motivation, language facility, and familiarity with how to read different kinds of print materials.

Reading means comprehension and reading comprehension involves more than successful decoding, fluent oral reading, or ability to recall information. While the ability to recall information is an important aspect of comprehension, developing the comprehension ability of Native students involves more than students answering questions over material they have read.

1. Adapt to the Children's Background

In comprehending a passage, a reader's mind does not just record the information in the passage and then give it back. A reader is not a passive recipient of knowledge. Instead, a reader constructs meaning by taking ideas from the page and relating them to ideas already in his mind (schemata). The text serves as a sort of 'blueprint' that guides the reader in building a mental model of what is meant through supplying clues to what the author intended (or what the reader thinks the author intended). During this "building" a reader fills in points and makes inferences; after all, no text can explicitly give all of the information, underlying concepts, and relationships necessary to understand what the author is talking about. Consequently, comprehension requires a reader to play a very active role in constructing meaning. The act of constructing meaning is referred to as the comprehension process.

Good comprehension, then, depends upon the reader having the necessary background information *and* being able to relate that background information to what is being read. It is fair to say that "reading is caught through books that fit." The subjects, topics, locale, and activities of characters must be such that the students can relate to them. Stories with exotic and difficult language, or about strange situations or far away places, are for good readers who have read enough to expand their backgrounds. The Native American student who is just trying to learn how to get some understanding from the material is not yet ready for strange and far away places, which may include urban or suburban locations.

Prior knowledge is important in helping a student come up with "acceptable" comprehension. The more a person knows about a subject in a passage, the easier that passage will be to read and understand. Whether one is talking about reading a basal story or a chapter from a social studies book, in order to be successful students must have some knowledge about the topic they are reading about. Not only must the students have some knowledge about a topic, they must also be able to identify the right memories and be able to relate what is being read to what they know.

Prereading activities prepare readers for the material to be read through introducing and building background knowledge. They are especially important when students are asked to read something outside of their normal experiences. Prereading preparation involves introducing a topic, students relating to that topic, and students forming a purpose for reading. It might sound strange, but readers are more likely to be successful if they talk about the subject before reading—rather than after reading.

Among the prereading activities which have proved successful with Native American children are brainstorming and mapping. In mapping, the teacher records the information on a board, so the students can see the results. This helps the students identify what they know and what they might not know about a reading selection.

Another useful activity involves "free" independent reading. In this approach, common "trade" books on a topic are identified and made available before a selection is read. These books are put out for the students to see and the teacher holds a conversation with the students about the subject, idea, or topic. During this conversation, different questions are raised. The teacher then lets the students come up to look at the books. The students get to choose a book (at any level) and may read that book *before* reading a more difficult piece. One fourth grade teacher of the Northern Cheyenne found several books about birds (picture, story, and so forth). The students read one or more books (students chose which books they would read) and were then paired up to cooperatively answer a set of questions the teacher passed out. Since every student had read a different book, each had something to contribute. Obviously, all of the questions could not be answered, but they were told to try! Then, the students went into the science book and read about birds.

2. Use Active Reading Strategies

Children need help in becoming active readers. An active reader interacts with the print and tries to make sense of what is being read. In order for students to become active readers, they need to be exposed to and have an opportunity to practice different strategies. These include previewing difficult material before reading, using cues within the text to make predictions about what is likely to occur next (and reading to confirm those predictions), and switching the rate of reading to fit the material.

An active reading technique which has proved very successful with Native American students is Stauffer's (1976) Directed Reading Thinking Activity. This activity involves predictive reading: the students guess or predict what will happen and read to confirm their predictions. The steps are simple and this procedure can be used with students of any age.

First, read the title and let students guess what the story or chapter will be about. Let them read a page to confirm. Then, let them guess what will happen next. Give them hints, not of the content, but how they should think: "What did the author mean by . . ." or "What do you already know that will give you an idea what will happen?" Be sure to make it a fun activity, help them laugh about the surprises they did not predict so that they will not feel embarrassed about making a wrong guess.

Two observations about this strategy. First, teachers must model the process. Show the students how you do it, then work together by having students tell you their predictions. Second, it takes use and repeated practice before children will use this technique for improving comprehension in independent silent reading.

Another active reading strategy is ReQuest (Manzo, 1969). ReQuest is a form of reciprocal questioning which helps students ask questions about what is being read. This strategy involves students and teachers taking turns asking each other questions about the material being read.

Introduce the lesson by telling the students that they are going to have an opportunity to be the teacher and ask you questions. Then, the students and the teacher read the first paragraph silently. The teacher closes the book and urges the class to ask any questions they want over what has been read. After the students' questions stop, the teacher switches roles and asks the students questions. The process is then repeated with the next paragraph.

Two points about Request: first, the teacher needs to be honest. If the teacher cannot answer a question, then she should admit it. In relation to this, if a question is asked which cannot be answered from the print, then tell the class, "I have to guess since the book doesn't tell me; however, in reading it's alright to guess. My guess is. . . . " Second, this game is also introducing students to higher level thought processes. Initially, many of the students' questions will be literal. Model higher level questions for the students by asking them questions which are not explicitly given in the book, and ask for an explanation ("What in the book makes you think. . ."). For additional active reading techniques see, J. David Cooper, *Improving Reading Comprehension* (Boston, Houghton Mifflin Company, 1986) and John D. McNeil, *Reading Comprehension: New Directions for Classroom Practice,* second edition (Glenview. IL.: Scott, Foresman and Company, 1987).

HOW DO WE ASSURE ADEQUATE PRACTICE?

This is done by making actual reading an important part of the instructional time every day. It is safe to say that if teachers want their students' reading to improve then students should spend more time actually reading than in related exercises or listening to someone tell them how to read.

Where can teachers find the time for reading? One way is by cutting out the unnecessary. A prime example of the unnecessary is workbooks. Instead of having students practice unnecessary and frequently unproductive workbook lessons, have students become involved in more independent reading and writing. Remember, reading comes *first* and students learn to read by reading.

As a general rule of thumb, every reading lesson should include twenty or more minutes of reading. To this, teachers often say, "But their aren't enough reading materials available at the primary levels for this much reading." Yes, there are sufficient materials available. The trick is finding them. Be innovative, ask parents if those with children's books at home could send some to school to be shared with other students. If you are teaching in a Native community in which there are no materials in the home, then ask other teachers, officials, and people you meet if they can help you to find some books for your classroom. One teacher did this and was "adopted" by a church in a city. The members of this church sent books and the children wrote thank you letters. Another sixth grade teacher, on a Montana reservation, went to a paperback wholesaler and was given a pickup load of unsold books.

Reading is FUNdamental is a national program to aid parents and local groups in giving books to children so that all of the children can own books that they can read and enjoy. They give special help to Indian schools. For information, write to Reading is FUNdamental, 600 Maryland Avenue S.W., Room 500, Smithsonian Institution, Washington, D.C. 20560.

Materials are important reading is enhanced by materials which are available and varied. Every classroom should have culturally relevant materials, humorous materials, and serious materials available for all the students, not just the "good" readers. For more information on the development of reading materials see the chapter on "Choosing and Producing Valid Material for Reading and Social Studies."

CONCLUSION

Improving and developing the reading ability of Native American students is facilitated by teachers who are willing to teach to a child's strengths and enthusiastic enough to make reading an enjoyable experience. Reading can be fun, both because of the content and because of the environment. If reading is approached as a meaning-based function, students will be more likely to have a positive attitude and grow in ability when we let them read.

REFERENCES FOR FURTHER READING

Ashton-Warner, Sylvia. *Teacher.* New York: Simon and Schuster, 1963.

Dubois, Diane M. "Getting Meaning from Print: Four Navajo Students." *The Reading Teacher,* 32, March 1979, pp. 691–695.

Feeley, Joan T. "A Workshop Tried and True; Language Experience for Bilinguals." *The Reading Teacher,* 33, 1979, pp. 25–27.

Gilliland, Hap. *A Practical Guide to Remedial Reading,* second edition. Charles E. Merrill, 1978.

Mallett, G. "Using Language Experience with Junior High Native Indian Students." *Journal of Reading,* 21, 1977, pp. 25–28.

Manzo, Anthony V. "The ReQuest Procedure." *Journal of Reading,* 11, 1969, pp. 123–126.

McCarty, T.L. "Language Use by Yavapai-Apache Students: With Recommendations for Curriculum Design", *Journal of American Indian Education, 20, October 1980, pp. 1–9.*

Pearce, Daniel L. "Improving Reading Comprehension of Indian Students." In Jon Reyhner (Ed.) *Teaching the Indian Child: A Bilingual/Multicultural Approach,* pp. 70–82. Billings: Eastern Montana College, 1986.

Simpson, Audrey Koeler. *Oral English Usage of Six-year old Crow and Northern Cheyenne Indian children.* Doctoral Dissertation, University of Maine, 1975.

Simpson-Tyson, Audrey K. "Are Native American First Graders Ready to Read?" *The Reading Teacher,* 31, April 1978, pp. 798–801.

Stauffer, Russell G. *Teaching Reading as a Thinking Process.* New York: Harper and Row, 1976.

Veatch, Jeannette; Florence Sawicki; Geraldine Elliott; Elanor Falek; and Janis Blakey. *Key Words to Reading: The Language Experience Approach Begins,* second edition. Columbus, OH: Charles Merrill, 1973.

Chapter 13

Inspiring Creative Writing

by Perie Longo

Creativity shines in the wondrous expression of each one of us. As teachers, we are entrusted with a sacred duty; to honor each child's special vision of life and manner of expression. When we openly value the uniqueness of children, only then will they be inspired to open up and write creatively.

1. Use Inspiration, Not Criticism

In teaching creative writing to children of all ages and diverse cultures, I have learned that the incentive most children need is a teacher who will say how special their art or writing is, giving them a specific example. I was fortunate to have such a teacher in fourth grade. One day she passed my desk, looked over my shoulder and commented, "You have a wonderful way with words." I felt as if I had just come alive from a long sleep, and have been writing ever since. My art, however, was planted with an F by a seventh grade teacher, and I have never learned to draw.

Children want to please adults so very much, but in the process of "getting it right," they are stifled with the feeling "I'm no good," when their creative endeavors are graded. When they are free to express themselves in their natural speech, there is no stopping what children can create. All they need are a few ideas, permission to play with words, and an eager teacher anxious to learn as much about them as they are to teach the necessary material.

The beauty of creative writing is that it can be integrated with whatever else is going on in the classroom. The difference between creative writing and any other kind, is that the child moves the facts from the heart rather than the head. He describes his feelings about the subject addressed rather than the "correct" facts. I have found the more I open up to children, sharing what I write and feel and think, the more they open to themselves. If we are not afraid to fail, they will not. Teachers are a child's primary inspiration. If our students see us as creative, they will be also.

2. Inspire with the Poetry of the Drum

I love poetry and the drum. When I began teaching poetry writing to young children, I wondered how I could get them to appreciate their natural rhythms of language and the playful way they have of putting words together. Poetic by nature, they have all that is needed to write creatively: Natural rhythm and a sense of play. One day I decided to take my drum to class. What would happen if I played it in a certain rhythm while they wrote? The last thing I wanted to do was bore them with the definition of poetry or lecture about the names of burdensome terms like iambic pentameter.

We talked about how the drum was made, that it was the first instrument used to communicate feelings from the heart. Actually, poetry is the language of the heart. Each child beat out the rhythm of his name and shared the image or picture that came to him with that rhythm. (In later classes, students wrote poems about the many meanings of their names based on these images.) In ceremony, words chanted to the beating drum are magic in that they heal people or turn unpleasant happenings into ones that could teach us important lessons we cannot learn from books. I read them native American chants to inspire them with the understanding that when we use words set in a pattern in our own special way, we find our own music. Anything can happen.

3. Discover the Poem within a Word

Another way I use the drum is to introduce children to rhythm and repetition, the main elements of poetry. Contemporary poetry rarely rhymes. Rather than rhyming, we can repeat individual sounds such as ran/rain, wheel/well, feel/feather, and we can also repeat words themselves and even complete lines. These can appear anywhere, not just at the end of lines.

To get them used to the idea, I put one word on the chalkboard, such as the word eagle. I circled the word and then they think of as many words as possible that have the same sounds; ee words, g words, and l words. Each word is circled, using the clustering technique described in Rico (1983). Then they free associate sounds from these words until the board is filled. As a sort of game, they may write a short poem using as many of these words as possible. To free their creative spirits, I give only two rules: that the poems may not make sense and that they write in short lines, no more than five words in length.

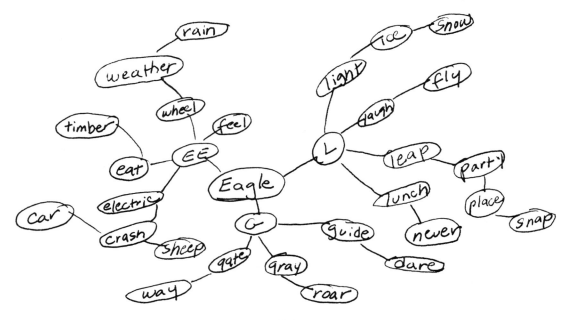

After that, I have them write any word they choose in the middle of their paper, and repeat the procedure. Ralph Waldo Emerson wrote, "every word was once a poem." Walt Whitman said words have become empty and we are here to fill them with meaning again, by writing what these words mean to us. The more fun students have with this, the better, because creative writing comes from setting aside the rigid structures we are trying so hard to emulate. Children learn to love language and use it well by writing it often, not by analyzing it.

During the initial writing, it is very important we do not criticize or correct spelling or punctuation. It is impossible to create and craft at the same time. Many modern poets never bother with periods or commas. Sometimes I say, "Every time you pause to think, begin a new line. Poems often have uneven line lengths."

When the children do their own clusters from a word, they may free associate not only repeated sounds, but any words or ideas that occur to them. A poem follows, written by a fourth grader from the words on the board after a trip to the natural history museum.

One day I saw astronauts
on the moon setting gopher traps
wearing swordfish headdresses
moving stars until they reached
twilight's house.
I then floated off the moon
and rode in a canoe till
I reached the planetarium
to swing on the pendulum.
When I went to the exhibit
I couldn't see because
Henry's Beach was in the way!
so I hitched a ride on the
horizon line and returned
to my home made from a basket!
—Ben Browning

Even adults like doing this exercise. It frees them from having to say anything beautiful, wise, profound, or perfect. To get to the heart of us, we sometimes have to go way out to come back in.

4. Free the Poem within Your Name

What inspires children the most is their own inner, secret world where they fantasize about themselves as beings quite different from who they are. A favorite exercise is modeled after a poem by the Native American Pulitzer prize winning novelist and poet, N. Scott Momaday which appears in *Songs From This Earth On Turtle's Back: Contemporary American Indian Poetry* Momaday's poem, "The Delight Song of Tsoai-Talee" begins, "I am a feather on the bright sky/I am the blue horse that runs in the plain.' The children begin their poems with "I am. . . " writing down all the things that they love, admire and respect, extending any image as much as they like.

NICOLE

I listen, I talk, I wish.
I am the eye of a bird
and the body of a sapling. . .
still growing.
Who am I?
Am I pain or defeat?
Am I only a dream?

Am I a person who is alone?
Who will get me when I die?
God? Will I die?
I am a tree, a bird, a song. . .

    —Nicole Talley, gr. 6

Children also love to write poems about their name; what it means, what it is the rhythm of, what it sounds like, what it can do very extraordinary. They do this while I beat the drum. Often they beat their pencils on their desks. As in the cluster exercise, I ask them to find sounds in their names, like the hissing of a snake. The following is a poem by a third grader written during a second poetry session.

My name is the rhythm of a lion running
My name is the sound of a swirl of colors
It swirls round, round faster it goes
it never stops till you let it go
My name goes flowing through the air
it soars and dives
feels like power floating on like a red ribbon
it drips through the sky down it goes
My name means a clock striking twelve
it gives me ideas when I need them

    —William Holbrook

The portrait poem is also popular. It may begin by stating your name, the same as above, or what you'd like your name to be, and then go on to include all of the following or a combination; the animal inside you and what you can do as that animal you could not be before, the object in your heart; sounds, colors and smells you love; a wish you have, your favorite kind of weather, your favorite time of day and why, the word on your forehead, if your hands could speak what they would say, an often expressed saying of a parent or grandparent or anything else that comes to mind. Many times they will pick their favorite part of this idea, like the animal inside of them, and write the whole poem from that.

ALEX

Silent
A summer breeze
    whirling
A panther
    striking
A falcon
    diving
A worn key
    forged from life
An eagle
    screaming

FAR AWAY

When I'm far away
from people
by myself
I'm happy
If I'm really far
I like to scream
or shout
Maybe I'm mad
or confused
so I run fast
as I can and think

126

Eyes
　　piercing
　　gazing onward

　　—Alex Hunt, gr. 6

about everything
that happened.
If I'm by a river
or a waterfall
I feel so good
I can't tell you.

　　—Jessica Stevens Gr. 6

5. Wake Up Imagination with Similes

Poetry is rich with similes, when we compare one thing to another to describe its *similar properties.* Writing similes, comparisons using *like* or *as,* awakens *images* in our mind and activates *imagination,* which is what creative writing is all about.

A first session in creative writing will often begin with children doing comparisons orally. Objects and pictures in the classroom are a good starting point. What does a stapler look like? a pencil? a scissors? The comparisons do not have to make sense.

Have students write as many comparisons as they can think of in five minutes. After that, they can write a whole poem about their favorite one. In a fourth grade class, a child said about a paper star hanging from the ceiling, "Stars are like shoes." From that we did a group oral poem I wrote on the board as they excitedly offered suggestions.

Stars are like shoes
as they walk across the sky
Stars are like shoes when they
are new, so clean and shiny
My eyes are like shoes running across
the sky as I watch the stars
like shoes when they get worn out
with holes in the bottom and
your socks poke through
Stars are like shoes looking up at us
and stars are shoes giving the night
a way to get around

One day we did this exercise while it was raining.

Rain is like feathers
falling from the sky
making my heart beat
faster and faster.
I want to fly
like a bird.
When the rain stops
my heart slows down
and I wait for the next
rain.
　　　　—Luke Clausen, gr. 4

When the children extend their comparisons, I ask them to write what their image feels, tastes, sounds, moves and smells like. A model that works well to incorporate these senses follows. They are to use words that you usually can't touch or necessarily feel. We list some on the board; light, air, love, anger, a mountain, even life or death. First we do a group poem and I stress to reach for the unusual image. The repetitions get them used to the idea of a chantlike quality often found in poetry.

If I could hear the _____ it would sound like _____
If I could feel the _____ it would feel like _____
If I could taste the _____ it would taste like _____
If I could smell the _____ it would smell like _____
If _____ could move it would move like _____
If I could see the _____ it would look like _____

Reading a model poem before they write is vital. I find if I do not provide a structure and some ideas they can include but don't have to, they won't know what to write. When I do give a model, they rarely follow it, because they feel safe to explore and become inspired to write, not having to worry about failing.

THE MOUNTAIN

*If I could see the mountain
it would look like a
Hover craft crossing the sea.
If I could hear the mountain
it would sound like the sea
crashing against the rocks
on the shore.
If I could feel the mountain
it would feel like solid gold,
If I could smell the mountain
it would taste like fresh
smoked salmon right by
the rushing river's edge.*

—Jerry Weslander, gr. 4

SPACE

*As I was walking in space
I felt as I never had before
a madness
        a sadness
                a happiness
I felt thin as ice
yet big as an apple.
I backed up, felt something
coming over, a wave not in space.
I screamed as it was just
my imagination.
The stars are dangerous
as they tell me. As I walk by
they say I cannot hear.
I walk to the moon and
am not seen ever again.*

—Amanda Kull, gr. 4

6. Create "Songs to Heal the Heart"

Earlier I mentioned creative writing can be integrated into any classroom activity. Some third and fourth grade classes were studying the California Chumash Indian culture. An article appeared in the paper about a Chumash elder named "Sky Eagle." I phoned to see if he would consider giving my students a "teaching." He agreed. Seventy children sat spellbound for two hours.

He talked about the power of the four directions, the meaning of ceremony, the significance of the Great Spirit, Wakantanka, and Mother Earth and Father sky. He burned sage to bless the students and their lives, chanting that now their wishes and prayers were a part of the world and would live on top of the mountain. He told them stories of his youth and the importance of never hurting a living thing because when we do, we hurt ourselves, because we are connected to and part of everything that is. One child wrote to him, "You are a man to respect. I will never forget you." Another wrote:

TO SKY EAGLE

I will listen
to the birds that sing
I will I will
I won't hit
the turtle on his shell
I won't I won't
I won't kill anything
I will respect the right
for living
I will I will

      —Casey Sims, gr. 4

Shortly after his visit, Sky Eagle had a heart attack. The children felt like they wanted to do something to help. Because words can be like medicine, particularly in connection with the chant, the idea came to me to write " Songs to Heal the Heart." This poem's joy is in mixing the senses, that is you can feel what you see and hear what you taste. When Sky Eagle grew well, the children felt that they had made a difference.

SONG TO HEAL THE HEART

Oh Sky Eagle
brave as the wind
hear the wind whistling
hear your heart beating
Oh Sky Eagle
taste the middle of your heart
taste Mother Earth
Oh Sky Eagle
smell a rose sweet like your life
smell Mother Earth and her sage

touch Mother Earth with your feet
touch the Great Spirit

—Kajsa Medak, gr. 3

7. Use the Medicine Wheel as Metaphor

One way to begin a poem is to say one thing is something else. This is metaphor, the heart of poetry, where one thing is given the properties of something else, without using like or as, in order to see it in a new way. The "I am. . ." poem is an example.

Besides the drum, I use the Medicine Wheel as a metaphor to inspire children's creative writing.

What I attempt to convey to all my students is that this land is rich in our own mythology. What we are looking for is not over there, in some other country or culture, but right here. We are related to all the great heros, heroines and warriors of American heritage. Children gain respect for themselves by learning to revere their own origins, whatever they are.

The Medicine Wheel is a circle comprised of the four directions. Each direction represents not only one of the basic elements necessary for our survival, but a human element. The East is symbolic of the sun and fire and our own creative spirit. The South represents water and our emotions. The West is the place of Mother Earth and our intuition; the place of magic and dreams. North represents air and our minds filled with wisdom as we learn about the mystery of life.

I explain when we write creatively we get under the labels of words and discover their essence, starting with our emotions, in the South. We connect these with our minds and inner wisdom of the North. Our creative spirit is connected with our bodies which hold all memory. In the center is the mystery which we allow to happen in creativity, blending all of the elements. A second grader wrote, after hearing my explanation, "A circle can't do nothin' cut in half." I use the Medicine Wheel for many writing ideas, one already mentioned, "Songs to Heal the Heart." Another is to have them write metaphors for each of the four elements or other things that are a part of nature.

WHAT WE ARE

Sky is a bird as sapphire flying overhead
Night is a lady with her black cloak outspread
Water is a jewel shimmering and sparkling like gold
Sun is a leaf on the tree of life
and we are specks of sand on the beach of forever

—Shannon Moore, gr. 6

Metaphor can be used in many ways. Feelings can be metaphors. For example, write about loneliness as a series of images. "Loneliness is a tadpole looking for its legs." They can write about numbers as people or animals as people. "One is an arrow straight and true." They can also mix any two properties, such as color and sounds. "Red is the sound of fire flames roaring in me."

A particularly successful technique to incorporate with metaphor is what Kenneth Koch calls the "Swan of Bees" exercise described in *Wishes, Lies and Dreams.* As in "herd of cows," start with combining two unusual images; "tree of talk," or "lake of shadows." After they write a list of these on paper, have them use as many as they want and weave them into a poem. Often I will give them a beginning line, such as: "Hiking in the woods I find. . . ." " Walking home from school I saw. . . ." "From behind a cloud. . . ." "Sitting around the fire. . . ."

I'M LONELY

In a house full of buffalos
I go no where. I just sit
around like the sadness of the moon.
I get lonely with no one to talk to.
It's like no one cares.
But the rainbow of happiness came
and in a sparkle there was
another house built.

This boy of buffalo house
was very nice and I'm telling you
now it was like the sky was full
of flowers but the people tore
the house down and it became
the sorrow of love.

—Nicole Gillespie, gr. 5

8. Write Chants to Release Emotions and Share Feelings

Once children are used to the idea of working with comparisons, free association, repeating sounds, metaphor, and rhythms of the heart, they can begin working on patterns. I have them write chants while I beat the drum. They begin by closing their eyes, and seeing someone or something that they wish to speak to. They can describe it, if it is an animal or something else in nature, comparing it to other things, and then invoking its spirit to give them something. or, they can command it to do something. One child who wrote to a tree, ended her poem, "Tree, release us from all evil/Make us grow tall enough to pick the rainbow from the sky when it comes/Help us wear the colors in our hearts."

FIREBIRD

Come firebird
Come out of the sky
Swoop down low
and light our lives
Firebird Firebird
stay forever and lift the sky
with your shining red body
and glowing hot eyes
Come down low so that
I might have a feather
to light my heart
and put the pale face
soldiers to fright

—Eric Crookston, gr. 6

131

When the Challenger exploded in January of 1986, I was just walking into a class. We talked about what we all felt for about fifteen minutes. Everyone was upset. I jotted single words on the board as they spoke. Anger. Confusion. Perfect morning. Stupid. Waste, Hypocrisy. They I simply said they could give their feelings metaphor, free associate, and write quickly in spurts, combining what they saw outside with what they felt inside. Remember to repeat as in a chant.

There were many tears, but afterwards all expressed a certain "lightness." Crisis is a good subject for creative writing because emotions are high. It is only when we are trying to hide something, or are afraid, that writing is difficult. When we have some tools, writing creatively is as natural as saying our names. In closing, I would like to quote one of those poems.

THE CHALLENGER

One beautiful sunny morning
the eagle was leaving its nest
Everything was fine
The eagle was proud
and flying high and then....
he was shot down
the beautiful proud eagle fell
into the ocean and the hunter
was never found

—Bryan Garrick, gr. 6

REFERENCES FOR FURTHER READING

Bay Leaf and Fool's Gold: The California Heritage Poetry Curriculum. Oakland Unified School District, 1982–83.

Bruchat, Joseph. *Songs from this Earth on Turtle's Back; Contemporary American Indian Poetry.* Greenfield Review Press, 1983.

Downey, Bill. *Right Brain Write On,* Englewood Cliffs, Prentice-Hall, Inc., 1984.

Highwater, Jamake. *The Primal Mind.* New American Library, 1981.

Koch, Kenneth. *Rose Where Did You Get that Red.* Vintage Books, 1973.

Koch, Kenneth. *Wishes, Lies and Dreams: Teaching Poetry to Children.* Perennial Library, 1970.

Longo, Perie. *The Magic of Metaphor.* Available on request from author, 987 Barcelona Dr. Santa Barbara, California.

Pearce, Joseph Chilton. *The Magical Child.* Bantam, 1978.

Rico, Ottone M. *The Intimate Art of Writing Poetry.* Prentice Hall, 1980.

Rothenberg, Jerome, ed. *Shaking the Pumpkin: Traditional Poetry of the Indian North Americas.* Doubleday and Company, 1972.

Storm, Hyemeyohsts. *Seven Arrows.* Ballantine Books, 1972.

Zavatsky, Bill and Ron Padgett, eds. *The Whole Word Catalogue 2.* McGraw Hill Paperbacks published in association with Teachers and Writers Collaborative, 1977.

Chapter 14

Teaching English to the
Native American Student

by Rachel Schaffer

Many Native American students speak dialects of English which are nonstandard, differing from Standard American English in grammar and pronunciation. The differences may stem from native language influences on bilingual speakers for whom English is their second language, and from linguistic isolation of the speakers. native American students may therefore have special problems and needs when they study English grammar, composition, and speech in schools that require special sensitivity and teaching methods. This chapter is meant to offer practical suggestions for becoming aware of your students' special needs and for teaching English to your students as effectively as possible.

GENERAL RECOMMENDATIONS

1. Learn Some Basic Linguistics

Taking an introductory linguistics course is important for all teachers of English, but especially for teachers of minority students, who usually speak differently from what we are used to thinking of as "proper English." A basic linguistics course is valuable because it will tell you about the analysis of language structure, not just of English, but of languages in general, and because it will tell you about the various attitudes toward language varieties, attitudes which have nothing to do with the varieties themselves, but rather with their speakers.

Linguists talk about Standard American English (SAE), the dialect used by people educated in the dominant culture in formal writing and speaking, and about nonstandard (never substandard) dialects (regional, rural, or ethnic varieties of English), which may differ slightly or greatly from SAE. Linguists also talk about the attitudes SAE speakers have toward the nonstandard dialects, which usually are *prescriptive* ones: nonstandard speech or writing is "bad," "wrong," or "incorrect." Too often, these attitudes also extend to the speakers themselves; as Madelon Heatherington describes this feeling.* "A child who uses correct language is presumably neat, polite, well groomed, and a paragon of virtue, whereas a child who uses incorrect language probably falls asleep in church, plays hooky from school, dissects cats, and takes dope."

*Heatherington, Madelon. 1980. *How Language Works*. Cambridge, MA: Winthrop Publishers, Inc., p. 216.

When you know more about how languages are structured, you realize that every variety of language, every dialect, has rules of its own. They may be different from SAE, but it is impossible to claim that they are better or worse (that would be like claiming that "plural" is better than "singular" or that addition is better than subtraction); each system meets the needs of its speakers equally well. Linguists therefore prefer to take an objective, *descriptive* attitude to all language varieties, one where you make no value judgments, but appreciate each variety on its own terms. Once you accept this attitude toward language variation, you can appreciate langauge differences in your students without condemning them, and your classroom will be an open, accepting, and constructive place for language learning. Native Americans have a special history of suffering from negative attitudes toward their languages (after all, for many years they were sent to boarding schools to learn English and forbidden to speak their native languages, even in private). By understanding language structure, you can help reverse such negative attitudes and encourage Native Americans to become more enthusiastic about learning English by being enthusiastic; yourself about their own languages and dialects.

2. Learn Something about Your Students' Native Languages

I also recommend, if at all possible, that you learn something about your students' first language(s). I don't mean that you should become fluent (although that would be a valuable learning experience for its own sake), but if you know what kinds of word endings the language has, or what features in general are very different from English, you will be in a better position to explain areas of English (pronunciation, sentence structure, vocabulary) that students have trouble with. It should be possible to find out about your students' language by reading articles or books written about it or by asking native speakers who are familiar with how to describe their language structure. You could even ask your students, comparing how their langauge does something with how English does it.

3. Learn Something about Your Students' Native Culture

It's also very important to learn as much as possible about your students' home culture, a point made over and over again throughout this book. In a language class it is even more important to encourage students to participate and practice their speaking skills than in other subject areas, since the goal of the class is improvement in all language skills. The cultural differences in the use of silence and leadership roles, or competition vs. cooperation, can affect the entire atmosphere of a langauge class. If you understand those aspects of your students' cultures that can affect their willingness to speak or write in class, then you can help increase their willingness to do so.

Many Native American cultures, for example, make use of a silent learning period during which children observe and listen, but do not speak. For students used to such a learning method, the Natural Approach, with its built-in silent period, may feel like the most comfortable (and indeed, natural) method of learning English (see the chapter on bilingual education in this book for a discussion of Krashen and Terrell's Natural Approach). The Natural Approach also stresses the importance of a low-anxiety classroom atmosphere where language mistakes are easily tolerated. For cultures where learners wait until they are ready before demonstrating skill (rather than go through the learning process and mistakes in public), this atmosphere will be friendlier and less intimidating to beginning speakers and writers.

4. Use a Variety of Teaching Methods

Once you know something about your students' native language, culture, and learning styles (see Chapters and 5 of this book for discussion of learning styles), you will have a better idea of the teaching techniques that will be most effective for your class. But every class and every student is different, so using a variety of methods and approaches will ensure that every student will get involved at some time, and you will quickly develop a feeling for the most enjoyable and effective techniques. You should feel free to experiment and to let the students know that you are trying something new. Teaching techniques that I have found to be effective for Native American students in composition classes (and for most of my students, in fact) involve the use of written and spoken models, culturally relevant examples and topics, group work, and individual tutorials outside of class.

5. Use Culturally Relevant Models

Most people feel more comfortable learning by example, rather than being asked to try something totally new with no model to follow. For many Native cultures, especially, this is one of the primary learning strategies. I therefore give my composition students several written models of each kind of assignment I ask them to write, whether grammar exercises, one-paragraph essays, or full-length essays. We do written examples on the blackboard; for oral exercises, I do some examples first or ask for a group response from the entire class so that students who are not quite sure what is expected can see others do the task. We discuss the models in terms of both strong and weak points, avoiding excessively negative terms like "bad" or "wrong," and I make a special effort to make my expectations for each task very clear before we begin.

Many of my Native American students have been surprised that they can actually write an acceptable essay about topics from their everyday lives and cultural backgrounds. They often think that they should write only about suitably academic (technological? mainstream American?) topics, rather than about topics closer to their own experiences, such as family, hometown life, and cultural events, or about differences they have noticed between Indians and non-Indians, or benefits or problems of being Indian. If students have trouble thinking of essay topics, I help them focus on possible areas by asking them about home, friends, family, hobbies, interests, knowledge of their culture and first language, and other personal topics. Students who write about subjects they know and like will write longer, more interesting compositions.

I also try to use culturally relevant topics in my writing examples and grammar exercises. I use student essays as samples as much as possible, and I have made up a sentence-combining exercise based on a Navajo short story ("Chee's Daughter," by Juanita Platero and Slyowin Miller), a part-of-speech exercise taken from a biography of a Sioux warrior (*Crazy Horse, the Strange Man of the Oglalas,* by Mari Sandoz), and sentences that describe activities familiar to my students (riding horses, going to school) or that use their names as examples of various grammar points or even as test questions. An unlimited source of other adaptable materials for many different grade levels is provided by the publications of the council for Indian Education.

6. Give Group Assignments

For students whose cultures encourage cooperation over individual competition, class activities and assignments that use group work may be especially effective and enjoyable learning experiences. In teaching grammar and writing, I have students work in pairs to help each other edit and proofread work, and in groups of three or four to produce short pieces of writing or to do exercises, sometimes with the same grade assigned to each member of the group. In teaching students to do research writing, I use the group activities to prepare and practice various skills such as paraphrasing or quoting, and follow the class activities with an individual take-home assignment. Most of my students have liked the variety in activities and have appreciated the extra feedback from another person. Students weak in one area receive help from someone other than the teacher, and usually are able to help their partners in a different area, a good way to build confidence and self-esteem. Strong students who don't need help still receive valuable experience in teaching others and in clarifying their own knowledge. Above all, students accustomed to cooperative living can work together in their own way, without needing to make one student "group leader."

Group work is also valuable in encouraging participation from otherwise quiet or passive students. Shy or insecure students usually feel more comfortable speaking in small groups rather than in front of the whole class; lazy students are usually forced to contribute something by other group members or by their own pride, and you can thus rely on peer pressure to save you from playing the role of manager and heavy. If you assign the group one grade for all members, you encourage cooperation even more, since all members then work toward a common reward.

7. Offer Individual Assistance

As part of the course requirements, many college-level ESL programs have weekly *tutorials,* individual meetings between teachers and students ranging from 15 minutes to an hour. These meetings are used to discuss the students' particular problem areas, explain comments on papers in more detail, and find out how students feel about their class progress. In large classes, students can be paired for slightly longer tutorials, each listening to the other's session, but for teachers who have several large classes, scheduling occasional individual conferences may be the best they can do.

For elementary and secondary school classes, where there may be very little free time during the day for outside tutorials, see if you can work some individual time with your students into the English class itself, or into a study hall or free period. I realize that this sounds like a tremendous additional burden, but the potential benefits from improved rapport with students and warmer class atmosphere may be worth taking up the time.

8. Make Your Expectations Clear

For some students (and not just minority students, by any means), each new class or new teacher is a mystery. What a teacher considers to be good or bad writing or speaking, satisfactory progress, appropriate behavior,effective evaluation measures for assignments or progress—in general, everything a teacher expects from the students—will vary from teacher to teacher and class to class. If you treat your students as partners in the learning process rather than adversaries, you can help to diminish the mystery—and the anxiety that can accompany it—by making your expectations very clear at the beginning of the course and by remaining consistent from then on. This includes explaining the usefulness of course requirements, whether content-related or grade-related, and explaining the methods of evaluation to be used—letter grades vs point values vs. check marks—and criteria for evaluation—what is considered to be a serious problem (in writing or participation, for example) and what doesn't matter. As much as possible, students need to know how your mind works so that they know what you will expect from them.

Students also need feedback from you on their performance in the form of honest but diplomatic comments, written or oral. Comments should be both positive and negative, with emphasis on the former. It is easy to see mistakes and correct them, but it seems harder for people to realize that good points also can and should be noticed and praised. When I write comments on students' papers, I use two columns, on marked + and one marked -, and I try to make the + column as long as I can. It may never be as long as the minus column (it usually takes longer to explain how to fix a problem than to explain why something is done well), but it should *always* have several items and words of encouragement.

9. Encourage Exposure to English

When children acquire a first language fluently and naturally, they do so simply by being exposed to native speakers of that language. It is useless to try to teach children to speak by teaching them formal grammar rules: no native speakers stop to think about a particular rule before they speak. The same principle of natural language learning is true for less fluent speakers of English: they need constant contact with native English speakers, interacting in normal conversations where they can both speak and listen. It is therefore extremely important that you arrange extra social contacts with native English speakers if possible, perhaps through field trips, regular social events, or guests for one-on-one conversations in the classroom.

10. Address Problems Created by Different Language Structures

Bilingual students most often have problems with those second language areas that differ most greatly from their first language structure—and such differences can be extreme. Not all areas of greatest difference occur often in English, so spending a lot of time on infrequent problems will not help students' fluency very much. Problem areas should be covered in detail when they interfere with the student's communication of ideas or when they appear often enough in the student's speech or writing to be distracting (which in itself can impair communication).

Two major areas of English that cause problems for second langauge learners are idioms and word endings, especially inflectional (grammatical) endings. Idioms are difficult because they are essentially multi-word vocabulary items: phrases of two or more words that have a completely arbitrary meaning rather than the literal meaning found by combining the meanings of each of the words in them. Thus, the idiom "you're *pulling my leg*" has nothing whatsoever to do with pulling legs, but instead has the special idiomatic meaning "you're *joking.*" Students therefore have to memorize sometimes very long strings of words with only one short, arbitrary meanings, and sometimes when they want to use an idiom from their first language, they will translate it *literally,* word for word, into English. since most languages have completely different idioms for the same idea (where they even *have* idioms for the same idea), the results may be unsatisfactory, frustrating, and frequently humorous (but at the speaker's expense).

Idioms must therefore be taught in the same way as single-word vocabulary items, with your careful explanation that *all* of the words in the expression go to make up one completely different meaning. using vocabulary-building exercises, working idioms into class and informal discussions, and giving examples of the appropriate use of idioms can all help students become familiar with the most common ones in English.

Word endings in English also cause a great many problems for speakers of other languages because morphology (which deals with words, prefixes and suffixes, and how they are arranged) is the most variable level of language structure, differing tremendously from language to language in terms of what grammatical features languages mark with morphemes (affixes of some kind) and which they ignore. English has affixes that mark nouns as plural or possessive (-s, -'s); verbs as singular, past tense, perfect or progressive (-s, -ed, -ed or -en, -ing); and adjectives as comparative or superlative (-er, -est), and other affixes that can change the meaning and/or part of speech of a word (pre-, un-, -ive, -ment, to mention a few). Many Native American languages handle verbs and nouns in an entirely different way, so that the distinctions marked in English are not at all natural or intuitive to second language learners, or the arrangement of morphemes seems strange. Furthermore, English has many words that take irregular endings that must be memorized separately as special cases (for example, *children, spoken,* etc.). You will therefore find it necessary to explain these endings carefully and constantly and give your students frequent practice before their usage becomes clear, and it will probably be years before the errors in your students' speech and writing are reduced to a significant degree.

One area of strong difference between language endings is illustrated by Crow, a Montana Indian language which has one ending for singular verbs (with singular subjects) and another for plural verbs.* English, on the other hand, marks singular verbs only in the present tense and only for third person verbs, as in *she walks, he sleeps, it looks rainy;* there are no separate singular/plural endings for any other tenses or persons (*I walk* vs. *we walk, he walked* vs. *they walked*). If you taught Crow students, you could therefore expect them to frequently omit the -s ending on third person singular present tense verbs in English, or to add -s to other persons of singular verbs in the present tense, in an effort to make the english verb forms more regular (as in *he go* or *they sits*). Crow also does not mark verbs for tense (past, present, future), as English does, and Crow speakers therefore frequently shift tense in writing or omit the -ed, -en, or -ing endings.

Other Indian languages also mark grammatical distinctions different from those in English. Hopi has different forms of the plural marker for concrete concepts such as "10 men" vs. cyclical concepts (repetitions of the same event) such as "10 days" or "10 strokes on a bell".** Navajo has verb stems which differ depending on the physical shape (flat

---

*Kates, Edith C., and Hu Matthews. 1980. *Crow Language Learning Guide.* Crow Agency, MT: Bilingual Materials Development Center, pp. 30–31.

**Whort, Benjamin Lee. 1956. *Language, Tlhought, and Reality,* ed. by John B. Carroll. Cambridge: The M.I.T. Press, p. 139.

sheet, cylinder, wire-shaped, etc.) of the subject or object.* Speakers trying to learn a second language do not usually try to impose their first language's distinctions on the second language, adding markers where there are none, but they do omit markers in the second language for which their first language lacks distinctions. These areas in particular will require you to offer much discussion, much practice, many examples, and where possible, direct comparison to the students' first language.

CONCLUSION

Because the classroom environment and interaction with the teacher have such a strong effect on students' willingness to speak and write, they can play a major role in the success and progress of students' language learning. The more you know about sources of influence on your students' learning process, the better prepared you will be to meet your students' needs. Students will learn under virtually any circumstances *if the motivation is there,* and a true understanding of the students' culture, language, and learning styles will help you to encourage and bring out; your students' natural love of learning.

REFERENCES FOR FURTHER READING

Cazden, Courtney B., Vera P. John, and Dell Hymes (eds.). *Functions of Language in the Classroom.* New York: Teachers College Press, 1972.

Celce-Murcia, Marianne, and Lois McIntosh (eds.). *Teaching English as a Second or Foreign Language.* Rowley, MA: Newbury House Publishers, Inc., 1979.

Fromkin, Victoria, and Robert Rodman. *An Introduction to Language.* 3rd ed. New York: Holt, Rinehart and Winston, 1983.

Krashen, Stephen, and Tracy D. Terrell. *The Natural Approach: Language Acquisition in the Classroom.* Hayward, CA: Alemany Press, 1983.

Ohannessian, Sirarpi. "The Language Problems of American Indian Children." in *The Language Education of Minority Children.* Bernard Spolsky, ed. Rowley, MA: Newbury House Publishers, Inc., 1972, pp. 13–24.

Oxford-Carpenter, Rebecca, "Second Language Learning Strategies: What the Research Has to Say." *ERIC/CLL News Bulletin, 9* (1), 1985, 1, 3, 4.

Schaffer, Rachell. "English as a Second Language for the Native Student." In *Teaching the Indian Child: A Bilingual/Multicultural Approach.* Jon Reyhner, ed. Eastern Montana College, Billings, Montana, 1986, pp. 114–133.

*Hale, Kenneth. 1973. The Role of American Indian Linguistics in Bilingual Education. In *Bilingualism in the Southwest,* Paul R. Turner, ed. Tucson, AZ: The University of Arizona Press, pp. 207–208.

Schooling and Language Minority Students: A Theoretical Framework. Los Angeles: Evaluation, Dissemination and Assessment Center, California State University, Los Angeles, 1981.

Shaughnessy, Mina. *Errors and Expectations*. New York: Oxford University Press, 1977.

Stewner-Manzanares, Gloria, et al. *Learning strategies in English as a Second Language Instruction:* A Teacher's Guide. Rosslyn, VA: National Clearinghouse for Bilingual Education, 1985.

Other Resources for Further Information

Organizations and Journals

Teachers of English to Speakers of Other Languages (TESOL), TESOL Central Office, 201 D.C. Transit Building, Georgetown University, Washington, D.C. 20057. Has an annual meeting and Summer Institute. Publishes the *TESOL Quarterly* and *TESOL Newsletter*.

National Council of Teachers of English (NCTE), 1111 Kenyon Road, Urbana, Illinois 61801. Has regional and national meetings annually. *Publishes College Composition and Communication, College English, English Journal* (secondary level), and *Language Arts* (primary level), and offers special member discounts on books and other publications.

Clearinghouses

Educational Resources Information Center/Clearinghouse on Languages and Linguistics (ERIC/CLL), Center for Applied Linguistics, 3520 Prospect St. NW, Washington, D.C. 20007. Publishes the ERIC/CLL *News Bulletin* and a wide variety of monographs and specialized bibliographies.

Bibliographies of ESL Materials

Aronis, Christine. *Annotated Bibliography of ESL Materials*. TESOL, Washington, D.C., 1983.

LeCertua, Patrick J., Carolyn M. Reeves, and Keith Groff (eds.). *ESL Source Book: A Selective Bibliography for Second Language Teachers*. Department of Education, Idaho, 1986.

Reich, William P., and Jennifer C. Gage (compilers). *Guide to Materials for English as a Second Language*. Rosslyn VA: National Clearinghouse for Bilingual Education, 1981.

Chapter 15

Teaching the Native Language

by Jon Reyhner

WHY BILINGUAL EDUCATION?

Many Indians see the loss of their language as "one of the most critical problems" facing Indian people today. They consider it essential that their children be taught in two languages, their own and that of the dominant society.

The opportunity to become fluent and be educated in both languages is important for four reasons.

1. The Native Language Is Essential to the Maintenance of the Culture

Although facts and information can be stated in any language, the beliefs, feelings, and way of looking at the world of a culture are diluted or lost when put into another language. Language and culture develop together. The words and structure of a language express completely the feelings of a people and their culture. Supposedly parallel words in another language do not accurately portray those feelings. Therefore changing to a different language necessarily results in a loss of part of the culture.

2. The Loss of Language Leads to a Breakdown in Communication Between Children and Their Grandparents and Denies Children Their Heritage

Tribal heritage provides a sense of group membership and belonging that is badly needed in an overly individualistic and materialistic modern society. In the words of John Collier, modern society has lost the "passion and reverence for human personality and for the web of life and the earth which the American Indians have tended as a central sacred fire."

3. Repression of the Native Language Is Destructive to Self-Concept

Forcing Indian children to suddenly give up their language and speak only English reinforces the idea prevalent in many schools that the native language and culture are of little or no value, thus effectively destroying the self-concept of many students.

4. Bilingual Instruction Results in Higher Academic Achievement

Research on bilingual education substantiates the conclusion that subtractive educational programs that seek to replace native language and culture with the English language and culture cause students to fail while additive educational programs which teach English language and culture in addition to the native language and culture create the conditions for students to succeed in their schoolwork.

In a review of the research on bilingual education, Cummins (1981) found a lot of studies reporting "that bilingual children are more cognitively flexible in certain respects and better able to analyze linguistic meaning than monolingual children." Bilingual education has effects beyond increased English and mathematics achievement scores. In Chicago's bilingual-bicultural Little Big Horn High School the dropout rate was reduced from the city-wide public school rate of ninety-five percent for Indians to eleven percent.

Many Indian parents, believing it will help their students in school, encourage their children to speak only English. Bernadine Featherly (1985), after research on Crow Indian students and an extensive review of the research, concluded that native language speaking parents should not try to "teach" their children to speak English. If the parents are not fluent in English, the children cannot become fluent by listening to them so if they do not learn the Native language, they will start school without fluency in any language for the type of thought and expression school requires. Children who are fluent in one language have no difficulty learning a second or a third language, but the children who do not become fluent in a language before entering school are usually handicapped throughout their lives. A well planned maintenance bilingual program as described below can teach native language-speaking children the English language skills they need to live and work in the dominant English speaking society, if they so desire, on an equal basis with native English speakers.

TYPES OF BILINGUAL PROGRAMS

There are four basic types of programs for bilingual students: (1)submersion, 92) immersion, (3) transitional, and (4) maintenance.

Submersion type programs have historically been used with Indian students. They are placed in regular all-English classrooms with little or no special attention and left to "sink or swim." The result of traditional English-only "submersion programs" for Indian students is that their achievement in schools falls further behind whites as they progress through their school years. The whole history of Indian education is proof of the ineffectiveness of this system.

Immersion bilingual programs use the second language extensively to give students an environment where they are "immersed" in the second language. Immersion teachers speak to the children only in the language to be learned but, unlike in the "submersion" classroom, students are exposed to special second language teaching methods.

This type of program has been found to be very effective in teaching French and Spanish to middle-class English speaking students with no long term negative effects on children's skills in using English. However, such programs are not intended to replace the home language. English language instruction is continued in school or is brought back after an initial period of all second language instruction. This could be an effective means of teaching native language fluency to Indian students who are not fluent in their own language, or to non-Indian students in Indian communities. It has been effective in teaching their own languages to Native people in New Zealand and Hawaii. However, such programs used to teach English to Indian students lack the advantage of the students' own languages being the accepted language of society as is true for English speakers, nor do students revert back to their native languages as the main language of instruction. Therefore they tend to lose their first language skills.

For Indians, immersion programs can reinforce feelings of inferiority and worthlessness by ignoring the home language and culture of the child. Dominated minorities such as Indians do better in school if their language and culture are a part of the school's curriculum.

Transitional bilingual programs are designed to teach English to language minority students as quickly as possible. While children are taught extensively in their native language during their first year of school, instruction in English is quickly phased in so that by about fourth grade all instruction is in English. Transitional programs do little to promote native language skills. Even though they are the most common form of bilingual programs in the United States, Cummins, who reviewed a great deal of research on bilingual education, found no educational justification for transitional bilingual programs. He also found that quick exiting of students from transitional bilingual programs to the regular English-only program had negative effects.

Maintenance bilingual programs place the most emphasis on developing children's native as well as English language abilities. They are designed to teach reading, writing, and some other subjects in the native language of the child while adding English language skills and instruction in some subjects. Begun in 1967, the maintenance bilingual program at Rock Point Community School on the Navajo Reservation in Arizona graduates students who can read and write in Navajo and who also test out on English language standardized achievement tests superior to comparable Indian students who have not had a bilingual education. At Rock Point most students enter school speaking mostly or only Navajo, and they are taught to read first in Navajo. Students add English reading instruction starting in the middle of the second grade. In kindergarten seventy percent of the instruction is in Navajo with the rest of the time spent teaching students oral English. By second grade students are receiving half their instruction in English and half in Navajo. In the upper grades fifteen to twenty percent of the instruction is in Navajo with the rest in English. In the early grades, mathematics are taught first in Navajo and then the specialized English vocabulary is taught later. By teaching content area subjects in the early grades in Navajo, Rock Point students are not held back in those subjects until they learn English. The concepts they learn in Navajo are retained and usable by the student later in either language, and almost all basic reading skills learned in the Navajo reading program transfer into the English reading program.

In 1983 Rock Point students by eighth grade outperformed Navajo students in neighboring public schools, other Navajo speaking students throughout the reservation, and other Arizona Indian students in Reading on the California Achievement Test. On the grammar (written English) portion of the test the results were much the same. In mathematics, the Rock Point students did even better, outperforming the comparison groups and approaching or exceeding national averages. It is important to remember these excellent results did not appear right away, but after sixteen years of a maintenance bilingual program.

Bernard Spolsky of the University of New Mexico summed up the results of the Rock Point School's educational program:

In a community that respects its own language but wishes its children to learn another, a good bilingual program that starts with the bulk of instruction in the child's native language and moves systematically toward the standard language will achieve better results in standard language competence than a program that refuses to recognize the existence of the native language. (Rosier & Holm, 1980, p. vi)

THE NATURAL APPROACH TO LANGUAGE ACQUISITION

Linguists and educators warn against a translation approach to teaching any language. Krashen and Terrell (1983) have developed what they call "The Natural Approach to learning languages." This method is equally effective in teaching English to Native language speakers and in teaching an Indian language to students more fluent in English.

The first principle of this approach is that *"comprehension precedes production."*

This implies,

1. The instructor always uses the target language (the language to be learned).
2. The focus of the communication is on a topic of interest to the student.
3. The instructor strives at all times to help the student understand.

The second principle is that *language production* whether oral or written *is allowed to emerge in stages,* first nonverbal communication, second by single words such as yes or no, third by combinations of two or three words, fourth by phrases, fifth by sentences, and finally by more complex discourse. In the beginning students use a lot of incorrect grammar and pronunciation. Krashen and Terrell emphasize in their method that "the students are not forced to speak before they are ready" and that "speech errors which do not interfere with communication are not corrected."

The third principle is that *the goal of language acquisition is communication.* Each classroom activity or lesson is organized around a topic rather than a grammatical structure. Topics can include field trips students are taking, classroom science activities students are doing, or games students are playing. Students need to do more than just talk about a topic, they need to participate in associated activities. Children learn from their own experiences, not other people's.

Krashen and Terrell's fourth principle is that classroom activities must not put any kind of stress on the students to perform beyond their capabilities:

An environment which is conducive to acquisition must be created by the instructor—low anxiety level, good rapport with the teacher, friendly relationship with other students—otherwise acquisition will be impossible. Such an atmosphere is not a luxury but a necessity. (p. 21)

By not focusing on vocabulary, such as memorizing the names of numbers and colors, or grammar, students acquire language skills they can use. Only if students use the language skills they acquire will they remember them. It is important that an environment both inside and outside of school be provided where a student can use newly acquired language skills.

146

The home is an obvious place to use the native language, but some tribes have also started radio and television stations with native language programming.

Students must also have environments where they can use the language they are learning in conversation. One of the important factors in the success of the Rock Point Community School curriculum is that students are encouraged and required to talk and write a lot in both languages. One Cheyenne family whose children never spoke the Cheyenne language set aside two days each week, Friday and Saturday, in which no English would be spoken in the home. If anyone spoke English, they were ignored as if they were not heard. It became an enjoyable activity for the children and parents together, and the children soon became relaxed in the use of their native langauge.

TEACHING MATERIALS FOR BILINGUAL PROGRAMS

A spoken language can be taught without written materials, but the attempt is seldom successful in the school setting. However, it is pointless to teach reading in an Indian language if only a few books are available in that language. The amount that teaching reading and writing are stressed will depend upon the amount of printed material available in the language. Commercial publishers are not interested in the small markets which even the largest tribes represent. However, you may find some material available from missionary organizations and the Wycliffe Bible Translators, both of which have a long history of missionary interest in translating religious works into Indian languages.

Recently Bilingual Materials Development Centers have been funded by Title VII of the Bilingual Education Act to produce materials that are not available through commercial sources. These Centers have printed materials in many Indian languages. However, native langauge materials are hardly adequate for real bilingual teaching even for the Navajos, who are by far the largest tribe and have a history of concern for the preservation of their language. Even less material is available in the native languages of other tribes.

Even when Native langauge material is available, it seldom has the controlled vocabulary needed to make beginning reading easier for students. Stories transcribed from elders may contain words with which Indian children are unfamiliar. An excellent method for avoiding inappropriate vocabulary in beginning reading is the "language experience" approach to teaching reading, discussed in more detail in the chapters on Whole Language and developing reading skills. The methods discussed there are equally applicable to either English or the Native language.

EXAMPLES OF MATERIALS DEVELOPMENT AT THE LOCAL LEVEL

As a director of a bilingual program on the Blackfeet Reservation, I arranged for the taping of some elders telling traditional and historical stories in the Blackfeet language. These stories were then transcribed by a Blackfeet linguist working with the Blackfeet Dictionary Project at the University of Lethbridge. A selection was then made from these stories to make up a booklet, *Stories of Our Blackfeet Grandmothers,* for use with intermediate grade students (published by the Council for Indian Education in 1984).

As another approach to language experience, in addition to having students draw pictures with the kindergarten teacher writing down the students' captions for their pictures, photographs can be taken of the community and made into a book with student supplied text from what they answer when asked, "Tell me about this picture." Two examples of materials that can be produced with the help of younger students are *Heart Butte: A Blackfeet Indian Community* (1984) and *We Live on an Indian Reservation* (1981), both of which are available from the Council for Indian Education. Older students can take pictures, interview elders and other community members, and write their own book. An example that includes work of older students at Rock Point Community School is *Between Sacred Mountains* (published by The University of Arizona Press in 1984).

The poet Mick Fedullo has edited a number of booklets of expressive poetry by Indian students. Some of the students' teachers believed that their students had no ability to write expressive poetry in English until they observed the enthusiasm for writing under Mick Fedullo and saw the results. While this poetry is in English, the same expressive language activities can be done in the native language. A good example is the booklet, *Hman Qaj Gwelnuudja*, done in Havasupai at Havasupai Elementary School in 1985 with the assistance of Akira Yamamoto, a Yuman language linguist.

For primary grade children self made books, hand printed and student illustrated, work fine and are appreciated by parents. For older children, more elaborate books are also useful. Only a few years ago, to publish such language experience books would have required expensive professional typesetting and printing. The special characters required by most Indian language orthographies added to that expense. Today with micro-computers and dot matrix printers, good quality material can be produced in school at a fraction of the former costs, and, using photocopying machines, an unlimited number of copies can be made relatively inexpensively.

A note of caution needs to be given to teachers who want to publish native language material with cultural content. Some tribes require prior approval of such material by a tribal cultural committee before it can be printed. In all cases, local people should be involved in producing and editing traditional stories.

THE ROLE OF LINGUISTS

A full fledged bilingual program requires teaching reading in the native language. There are over two hundred Indian languages still in use in the United States. A writing system (orthography) has to be developed for each of these languages if it is to be written. Robert St. Clair (1982) feels that while professional linguists tend to develop sophisticated orthographies that reflect the grammatical structure of the language, literacy programs for elementary schools need simple, practical writing systems similar to the Initial Teaching Alphabet (i.t.a.). A linguist with an educational background is to be preferred in developing a simplified orthography suitable for use with children. Sources of linguistic help for schools and tribes include universities, the Wycliffe Bible Translators who are found on many reservations, and a number of Indian linguists who have been trained at the Massachusetts Institute of Technology, University of Arizona, and other schools with linguistic departments that have shown an interest in Indian languages.

In addition to simple, practical phonetic orthographies, St. Clair sees the need for simple classroom dictionaries of frequently used words, an "experience based dictionary," which only includes common definitions of words and uses them in sample sentences. Missionaries have researched and published dictionaries such as the Franciscan Fathers' *An Ethnologic Dictionary of the Navajo Language* (St. Michael's Press, St. Michael's AZ, 1910) and the *English-Cheyenne Dictionary* (distributed by the Council for Indian Education, Billings, MT), produced in 1976 with the help of the Wycliffe Bible Translators, which serve as basic sources of information on Indian languages. Competing tribal dialects are not a problem since the same orthography can be used with different dialects.

Robert St. Clair feels that tribal elders have an important role to play in a bilingual program:

> *If there are any tribal members who can really save the program [of language renewal], they are the elders. These are people who may be in the sixty- to eighty-year-old range who have actually spoken the language fluently as children and who fully participated in the ways of the tribe. They still know the ceremonies and are the most valuable elements in any language renewal program. The secret is to get them to work with young children. They can teach them to speak the language and, if circumstances permit, the children can teach them how to read and write in the new system. This program, then, requires parental as well as communal support. (1982, p. 8)*

In New Zealand, Maori grandparents are running a volunteer program of day care centers which feature an immersion program in the Maori language. A similar program with university help is being run in Hawaii.

CONCLUSION

Kenji Hakuta concluded a historical study of bilingual education with the thought that,

> *Perhaps the rosiest future for bilingual education in the United States can be attained by dissolving the paradoxical attitude of admiration and pride for school-attained bilingualism on the one hand and scorn and shame for home-brewed immigrant [and Indian] bilingualism on the other. The goals of the educational system could be seen as the development of all students as functional bilinguals, including monolingual English-speakers. The motive is linguistic, cognitive, and cultural enrichment. . . . (1986, p. 229)*

I am not recommending native language instruction as a substitute for English language instruction or English as a substitute for the Native langauge, but the development of truly bilingual students, at home in two languages. No tribe has recommended that restoration of their language outrank the importance of teaching English (Leap, 1982, p. 151).

Assimilation is not a one way street to progress and Native Americans can learn to participate successfully in white society *and*, at the same time, retain their language and traditional Indian values to become what Malcolm McFee (1968) has described as the 150% man. This 150% person is the goal of bilingual education.

OTHER RESOURCES FOR FURTHER INFORMATION

Evans, G.E., K. Abbey, and D. Reed. *Bibliography of Language Arts Materials for Native North Americans: Bilingual, English as a Second Language and Native Language Materials 1965–1976.* Los Angeles, CA: American Indian Studies Center, UCLA. 1977.

Evans, G.E. and K. Abbey. *Bibliography of Language Arts Materials for Native North Americans: Bilingual, English as a Second Language and Native Language Material, 1975–1976: With Supplemental Entries for 1965–1976.* Los Angeles, CA: American Indian Studies Center, UCLA. 1979.

National Association for Bilingual Education (NABE), 1201 16th St., N.W., Room 407, Washington, D.C. 20036, Phone 202 822 7870. Has annual meetings with workshops for teachers. Publishes *NABE News* and *NABE Journal.* Has state affiliates.

REFERENCES FOR FURTHER READING

Cummins, Jim. *Bilingualism and Special Education: Issues in Assessment and Pedagogy.* San Diego, CA: College-Hill Press, 1984.

Cummins, Jim. "Empowering Minority Students: A Framework for Intervention." *Harvard Educational Review,* 56 1986, pp. 18–36.

Cummins, Jim. "The Role of Primary Language Development in Promoting Educational Success for Minority Students." In California State Department of Education, *Schooling and Language Minority Students.* Los Angeles: California State University at Los Angeles, 1981.

Collier, John. *The Indians of the Americas.* New York: W.W. Norton, 1947.

Featherly, Bernadine. "The Relation between the Oral Language Proficiency and Reading Achievement of First Grade Crow Children." *Dissertation Abstracts International,* 46, 2903A.

Fuchs, Estelle and Robert J. Havighurst. *To Live on This Earth: American Indian Education.* Garden City, NY: Anchor Books, 1973. (Reprinted by the University of New Mexico Press, 1983).

Hakuta, Kenji. *Mirror of Language: The Debate on Bilingualism.* New York: BAsic Books, 1986.

Krashen, Stephen. *Inquiries and Insights.* Hayward, CA: Alemany Press, 1985.

Krashen, Stephen and T.C. Tracy. *The Natural Approach: Language Acquisition in the Classroom.* Hayward, CA: Alemany Press, 1983.

Leap, William. "Roles for the Linguist in Indian Bilingual Education." In *Language Renewal among American Indian Tribes* edited by R. St. Clair and W. Leap, pp. 19–30. Rosslyn, VI: National Clearinghouse for Bilingual Education, 1982.

McFee, Malcolm. "The 150% Man, A Product of Blackfeet Acculturation." *American Anthropologist,* 70–6, 1968, pp. 1096–1107.

Ovando, Carlos J. and Virginia P. Collier. *Bilingual and ESL Classrooms*. New York: McGraw-Hill, 1985.

Rosier, Paul and Wayne Holm. *The Rock Point Experience*. Washington, D.C.: Center for Applied Linguistics, 1980.

St. Clair, Robert. "What Is Language Renewal." In *Language and Prospects* edited by Robert St. Clair and William Leap. Rosslyn, VI: National Clearinghouse for Bilingual Education, 182.

Studies on Immersion Education: A Collection for United States Educators. Sacramento, CA: California State Department of Education, 1984.

Trueba, Henry T. and Carol Barnett-Mizrahi. (Eds.). *Bilingual and Multicultural Education and the Professional: From Theory to Practice*. Rowley, MA: Newbury House, 1979.

Chapter 16

Mathematics for the Native Student

by David M. Davison and Duane E. Schindler

A classroom of Indian students is working on problems based on data collected from an arrow throwing contest. The students are graphing distances arrows are thrown by different individuals. They are involved in discussions about comparing the distances the arrows were thrown. The idea for these problems did not come from a mathematics textbook or typical teachers' guide. This teacher is answering the challenge to make her classroom responsive to the mathematics learning needs of her students.

American Indian students are typically not culturally in tune with the mainstream Anglo system of learning. Traditionally the history of mathematics serves to illustrate how man has interacted with his environment in a quantitative way. For example, early American mathematics history is rich with situations such as the Aztec calendar and Mayan numeration that can be used to motivate classroom learning. However, only Western mathematics history is treated in the classroom.

The respect of native students for their past, and their understanding of how mathematics can influence their present and their future, calls for more serious attention to ways of presenting classroom mathematics in more appropriate ways.

THREE WAYS OF INCREASING MATHEMATICS LEARNING

Native students will learn more mathematics if the concepts presented in the classroom are culturally relevant, are responsive to their preferred learning styles, and emphasize the learning of English language mathematics terms.

1. Use Culturally Relevant Materials

As Hap Gilliland pointed out in the first chapter of this book, a culturally relevant curriculum should value the students' heritage and build on ideas that are meaningful to them. One way a teacher can make mathematics meaningful is by using culturally relevant materials. The use of such material is advantageous for two reasons. First, the students see mathematics applied to *their* real world. All too often Indian students see no relation between school mathematics and reality and therefore have little motivation to apply themselves to the study of mathematics. Through the use of examples like the one described above, the teacher is able to stimulate the interest of the students in mathematics. Second, students have a strong interest in learning about their own culture. The use of culture-based mathematical illustrations provides the students with the opportunity to learn about their culture while studying mathematics. This problem is addressed in the National Science Foundation funded project "Increasing Participation of Native American Students in Higher Mathematics" directed by Doug Aichele of Oklahoma State University and Carl Downing of Central State University.

In the arrow throwing contest, the Crow Indian students were actively involved in the learning because the situation described is a regular part of the tribal culture. Other events that have strong cultural significance can also be used as a basis for teaching mathematics to American Indian students in a more motivating manner. Phenomena such as bead frame loomwork, hand games, and sand paintings can be used to teach many mathematical ideas.

In a unit involving a study of buffalo, for example, many mathematics related activities are possible. Some sample activities include: comparing the size of buffalo herds at different periods; estimating the amount of grazing land needed to support these buffalo; calculating the number of people that can be fed from a large buffalo; discussing ways of estimating size and weight of buffalo; and estimating the distance a herd can travel in a given time period.

A collection of culturally relevant materials, whether Indian or non-Indian, cannot be substituted for a coordinated mathematics curriculum. It behooves the curriculum planner to begin with a well-integrated mathematics program and to explore as many ways as possible to make the curriculum meaningful. Meaningful examples could describe situations in which Indians might be involved, such as one dealing with horses. We have found that Indian students regard school mathematics as meaningless, as having no bearing on their lives. The way mathematics is presented in text books only serves to reinforce this belief. If the students are to learn the mathematics that they need, the concepts will need to be presented in a more appealing manner. The use of culturally relevant stimulus material to illustrate the application of these concepts will help to attain this objective.

2. Adapt to Native Learning Styles

The native students' learning of mathematics is also influenced by differences in their learning styles. The native student is more typically a visual/kinesthetic learner than an auditory learner. Most school instruction is more auditory/abstract in its emphasis and does not respond to the native student's preferred style of learning. Native students process mathematics in a less abstract way because their view of the world is more practical.

Typical mathematics learning materials are prepared on the assumption that all students learn mathematics in the same way. An examination of such materials indicates that the dominant mode of presentation of mathematics is abstract. Available evidence indicates that most native students do not process mathematics in an abstract way, but depend on tactile and visual stimuli to facilitate learning. In a society where most curriculum is abstract in focus, the student whose focus is more visual will have difficulty dealing with the material.

The elementary mathematics curriculum emphasizes competence in work with number and its operations. Geometry assumes a less prominent place. Chapters in geometry are usually near the end of the book and may possibly be treated in a superficial manner. Geometry is the one branch of mathematics that can stress Indian rather than non-Indian approaches to mathematics. Success in geometry is related to a kinesthetic processing of the environment. For example, we found that when given the geometric attribute pieces containing the primary colors, four shapes, and two sizes, non-Indians classify primarily by color first. Indian students, on the other hand, mostly classify by shape first. This observation supports the notion that these Indian students' preferred style of mathematical processing is essentially kinesthetic.

Few curricular efforts have been devoted to addressing different learning styles in mathematics. Perhaps the best known approach to primary mathematics stressing tactile methods is found in Mary Baratte-Lorton's *Mathematics Their Way*. This program is activity-oriented; students learn mathematical ideas by working with familiar objects. While the program is intended to help all primary students learn mathematics, its emphasis is such that minority students now have a chance to learn mathematics in an understandable way.

Another project which deals with the way native students learn mathematics is "Math and the Mind's Eye," a National Science Foundation funded project under the directorship of Gene Maier in Portland, Oregon.* Maier points out that many people, in the Anglo as well as in the American Indian culture, find mathematics devoid of meaning—nothing more than jargon and symbol manipulation. The result is mathematics under achievement, anxiety, and aversion. Many of the people who do succeed in post-school mathematics use sensory perception, models and imagery. This is very different from the views of school mathematics described above. Maier's project stresses the use of manipulatives and activity methods in the middle grades as well as in the primary grades. Certainly, an emphasis on a hands-on approach to mathematics learning would help Indian students make more sense of the way mathematics is presented.

Curriculum designers are being made aware that not all students learn mathematics in the same way. Materials that place emphasis on the use of hands-on activities will help students whose primary learning mode is kinaesthetic, not abstract. The use of an activity-centered approach in working with native students is one way of responding to their different learning style.

3. Emphasize the Learning of Mathematical Language

A third way in which the native student relates differently to the mathematics curriculum is in the use of language. In the mathematics classroom many terms are used in ways that differ from normal English usage. For example, the word 'product' in mathematics refers to the result of multiplying two numbers, whereas in conventional English it connotes something that has been completed. Students who come from homes where the English language is not used extensively are less likely to be aware of the varied meanings of such terms. Further, the student whose first language is not English is not accustomed to hearing the mathematics vocabulary outside of the mathematics classroom.

Bilingual education programs stress the use of the native langauge to help teach English language concepts. This is true in mathematics as well as in other subject areas. We would expect, then, that competence in the mathematics terms in the native language would help the students learn these terms in the English language. However, in our work with Crow Indian children we found that the knowledge of Crow counting number names was limited. The students knew Crow names only for the fractions one-half and one-fourth, they did not differentiate between the cardinal and ordinal uses of number even though the terms exist in the crow language and, apart from the words for circle, square,

*For further information about this project, contact Gene Maier, Project Director, Math and the Mind's Eye P.O. Box 1491, Portland, Oregon 97207.

155

and triangle, names for geometrical figures were not known. This led us to conclude that some of the expected benefits of bilingual education are not occurring insofar as the mathematics vocabulary is not being mastered.

In his work with the Navajo Indians, Douglas Garbe found that the students were not getting enough appropriate instruction in mathematics vocabulary. He recommended that vocabulary to be mastered be clearly identified, and that information on each student's performance in vocabulary be passed on to the teacher of the next grade. This teacher should try to use the student's past experience with each term to help give the term meaning in a mathematical context. The introduction of new terms should be carefully orchestrated. A term should be used in context over and over—students should show that they can pronounce the word, spell it, and use it in a correct context. Attention needs to be paid to the interference caused by 'sound alike' words, those that differ in spelling, pronunciation, and meaning, for example, sum, some, sun. Important vocabulary should be reviewed regularly. Mastery of this mathematical vocabulary should be taught, not as an end in itself, but as a means of mastering more mathematics.

Even students who are no longer bilingual, or who have only residual vestiges of their native language, still have trouble processing English language mathematics. Bill Leap (1982) speaks of 'residual cultural processing'. the students use the English language but they do not understand the nuances of English language thinking with facility. Accordingly, they need procedures such as those recommended by Garbe to improve their grasp of English language mathematics vocabulary.

SUMMARY

We have seen that three factors influence the native student's ability to learn mathematics. While these factors to some extent affect the mathematics learning of all students, the consequences can be quite serious where minority students are concerned. American Indian students view mathematics differently, and their mastery of the English language is less sophisticated. If we are to succeed in teaching more mathematics to native students, we should consider three ways of adapting the way mathematics is typically taught.

First, culturally relevant stimulus material should be used wherever appropriate to stimulate the interest of the students. This is particularly critical as most native students see little relevance for their lives in the mathematics they study. Second, different students have varying preferred styles of learning. The conventional curriculum stresses mathematics as an abstract discipline and, therefore, excludes from the attainment of success those who process mathematics in a more visual/kinesthetic manner. Third, the native student, whether bilingual or not, experiences difficulty with the subtleties of the English mathematics terminology. Deliberate instruction in English language mathematics vocabulary is needed to overcome this difficulty.

It is assumed by many that the native student cannot handle mathematical ideas. We suggest that this assertion is unfounded. We believe that native students will experience success in mathematics if appropriate strategies are used to present the concepts to them.

REFERENCES FOR FURTHER READING

Baretta-Lorton, Mary. *Mathematics Their Way.* Menlo Park, CA: Addison-Wesley, 1976.

Bradley, Claudette. "Issues in Mathematics Education for Native Americans and Directions for Research." *Journal for Research in Mathematics Education,* 15, 1984, pp. 96–106.

Cantieni, Graham and Roger Tremblay. "The Use of Concrete Mathematical Situations in Learning a Second Language." In Henry T. Trueba and Carol Barnett-Mizrahi (Eds.). *Bilingual Multicultural Education and the Professional.* Rowley, MA: Newbury House, 1979.

Closs, Michael P. *A Survey of Mathematics Development in the New World* (Report 410–77–0222). Ottawa, Canada: University of Ottawa, 1977.

Davison,David M. and Duane E. Schindler. "Mathematics and the Indian Student." In *Teaching the Indian Child* edited by Jon Reyhner, pp. 178–186. Billings, MT: Eastern Montana College, 1986.

Drew, Nancy and Else Hamayan. "Math and the Bilingual Student." *Bilingual Education Service Center Newsletter,* 7–1, 1979, pp. 9–10.

Garbe, Douglas G. "Mathematics vocabulary and the culturally different student." *Arithmetic Teacher,* 33–2, 1985, pp. 39–42.

Green, Rayna and Janet Welsh Brown. *Recommendations for the Improvement of Science and Mathematics Education for American Indians.* Washington, DC: American Association for the Advancement of Science. ED 149 896, 1976.

Johnson, Willis N. *Teaching Mathematics in a Multicultural Setting: Some Considerations When Teachers and Students Are of Differing Cultural BAckgrounds.* ED 183 414, 1975.

Leap, William L., Charles McNett Jr., Joel Cantor, Robert Baker, Laura Laylin, and Ann Renker. *Dimensions of Math Avoidance Among American Indian Elementary School Students,* (Final Report). Washington D.C.: The American University, 1982.

Leap, William. "Semilingualism as a Form of Linguistic Proficiency." In Robert ST. Clair and William Leap (Eds.), *Language Renewal among American Indian Tribes: Issues, Problems and Prospects,* pp. 149–159. Rosslyn, VI: National Clearinghouse for Bilingual Education, 1982.

Schindler, Duane E. and David M. DAvison. "Language, culture, and the mathematical concepts of American Indian learners." *Journal of American Indian Education,* 24–3, 1985, pp. 27–34.

Chapter 17

Science for Native Americans

by Sandra M. Rubendall, Jon Reyhner, and Hap Gilliland

Teachers of Indian students need to demonstrate the importance of science to their students. Many Native American students see little or no relationship between their lives and what goes on in the classroom. The importance of science to their personal health and future, to their tribal future, and to the future of the world must be made explicit through meaningful classroom activities. A problem solving, hands-on approach to science which emphasizes the skills of science and de-emphasizes simple memorization of facts is most likely to provide the intrinsic motivation Indian students need to learn science. If science lessons become memorization sessions, students tend to develop an antagonism towards science by the time they reach high school. The resulting poor attitudes toward science may cause discipline problems which may also lead to safety problems if a better teacher later tries to introduce them to laboratory experiments.

SCIENCE AS GROUP PROBLEM SOLVING

A good way to show students the utility of science is to teach it as a problem solving activity (Guthridge, 1986). Starting with environmental or other problems or just student questions, students can learn the scientific method of making hypothesis (educated guesses), controlling variables, collecting and recording evidence in a systemic way to test the hypothesis, and drawing conclusions from the evidence. Group experiments focused around group problem solving can be emphasized with students.

Computer simulation games like *O'Dell Lake* and *O'Dell Woods* can allow students to make decisions in a controlled environment. Students need to be taught how to observe, classify, and categorize information in a meaningful way (Smith, 1982). Bilingual teachers and teacher aides can help explain difficult concepts in both English and the native language.

For example primary grade students can make guesses about the growth of plants in milk cartons with varying degrees of sunlight, water, different types of soil, or different amounts of fertilizer. They can then observe and record their observations about the actual growth of the plants. Intermediate students can hook up simple electrical circuits using batteries, flashlight bulbs, and wire. They can discuss and predict whether various wiring patterns will work and the intensity of light that might result in advance. Circuits can be

159

drawn, labeled, and then actually tried. Then students can explain in their own words why each wiring pattern did or did not work.

The Science Teacher as an ESL Teacher

Along with teaching the methods and content of the sciences, the science teacher needs to be concerned with developing the listening, reading, speaking and writing skills of Native students. Science is an ideal subject for teaching English as a Second Language (ESL) as it can be taught as "experiential learning, capitalizing on hands-on activities." Through field trips, demonstrations, and student experiments students can work individually and in groups. In their science activities they can see concrete examples of what they are talking about which is a necessity for Limited English Proficient students (Chamot & O'Malley, 1986).

Do not assume that students are aware of English syntax and science vocabulary. Indian languages differ greatly from English in these and other ways. Even if the children are not fluent in their native language, they will probably not speak standard English. For example, in the Northern Cheyenne language the present tense of verbs is emphasized and this carries over into the students use of English. Some examples of words students may not be familiar with, but which are much used in current science textbooks are: accomplish, constantly, exactly, differs, requires, process, identical, and original. Teachers cannot rely solely on lists of new vocabulary to be taught that textbooks provide. They need to read the selection, looking for words that are not in their students working oral vocabulary, especially for words that express abstract ideas. The meaning of these words need to be discussed with the students in pre-reading activities before reading in the textbook is assigned. The use of local examples and teacher demonstrations of the meaning of new vocabulary are helpful. Students need to be given a lot of opportunity to use the new vocabulary in discussing their science lesson along with periodic followup activities if they are to make the new vocabulary a part of their working vocabulary.

DO NOT NEGLECT SCIENCE

Often science lessons are left to the last twenty or so minutes of the school day because reading and other subjects have a higher priority. This neglect can be avoided by integrating as many subjects as possible in order to make education more lifelike and less compartmentalized. Teaching in a self-contained elementary classroom provides many opportunities to integrate not only science and Native American culture, but also math, social studies, reading/language arts and so forth. Because life is an integration of these subject areas, they are more relevant if they mimic life as a whole rather than as isolated activities. For example, students studying nutrition in a Health lesson usually engage in reading and writing although this is a scientific subject. Similarly, measurement in terms of daily nutritional requirements can be taught along with concepts of what nutrients the body requires for health and related problems can be developed as part of their math lesson. Students can bring to class empty cereal boxes and compare the nutritional information on them. Since social relations are influenced by how we feel physically and emotionally and since advertisers through the mass media try to influence patterns of consumer consumption, nutrition is obviously related to social studies topics. Furthermore, many wars and political situations have arisen because of the human need for food.

While students may learn a concept in math or another subject, they may not transfer the meaning of the concept to science. For example while a student may know what "environment" means in social studies, they may not understand how this same concept applies to science.

INTEGRATE SCIENCE WITH NATIVE AMERICAN CULTURE

The task in predominately Native American classrooms is to integrate Science and technology with Native American culture in order that they may cope with modern living as consumers, producers, and citizens. Teachers need to understand traditional Native views, and they need to foster curiosity, problem solving skills, information gathering skills, and recording techniques. Preparation of teachers at the college level to teach science all too often emphasizes the theory of science rather than its practical applications. This leaves it up to the teacher to demonstrate science's practical applications in the lives of students, and to demonstrate to students how theory can be developed from studying and generalizing from a number of observations or experiments.

Whether we like it or not, science and its outcome, technology, touch all of our lives. Because of our daily encounters with science and technology, on and off reservations, science and technology need to be understood and used wisely. All Native people are exposed to lighting, heating, modern medicine, telephones, television, video games, electrical appliances, automobiles, and so forth either in their every day life or through attending school and visiting nearby towns. Students need to understand how these technologies work rather than viewing them as mysteries to be turned on and off.

Use examples that are familiar to students to illustrate scientific concepts. Use readily available materials such as chicken eggs, local plants and animals, local rocks and fossils. Locate and use resource people within the school, tribe, and scientific community to aid in your science program. Many tribes have forestry, energy, or soil conservation departments which could provide speakers.

Most of the concepts of biology taught in the elementary level, and many of those taught in the elementary level, and many of those taught at the secondary level, can be taught through or applied to the plant and animal life of the local community. Concepts of physics, such as friction, inertia, centrifugal force, and center of gravity can be related to things the students have first hand experience with. *Village Science* by Dick (1980) is an excellent source for information on science applied to Alaskan village life. A good source for studying birds and animals and their tracks is *A Guide to Nature in Winter* by Stokes (1976).

Secondary students can study the ethnobotany of their region. Several schools have developed guides to the plants and animals of their region which include descriptions of both the traditional and modern uses. A good example is Watahomigie, Powskey and Bender's *Ethnobotany of the Hualapai* (1982). This book can be used both as a resource for the teacher and as an identification guide for the student. Another way to localize science is to study how various tribes measured time and the seasons. this could include the study of the Aztec calendar and Mayan and Incan astronomy.

161

PRACTICAL PROBLEMS

Practices such as dissection of laboratory or other animals may be against tribal traditions. If so, plastic models and movies could be used to teach anatomy and physiology. although Native peoples often use plants and minerals for medicine, many of these medicines could only be administered by a medicine man or woman who was trained in these matters. The rituals which accompany the use of the medicines and even some of the medicines themselves are considered sacred. These beliefs need to be respected.

A study of the effects of the use of drugs, alcohol, and tobacco is especially important, and should be included in the science program at every level in a non-preaching, objective manner.

SUMMARY

To become scientists, Native American students need to recognize the importance of science in their lives and develop a lasting interest in science. The goal for teachers is to give their students the feeling they can do science and to provide them the opportunity to learn the necessary skills and knowledge base. Requiring the memorization of scientific "facts", whether related or unrelated, to be used in answering questions on objective tests has little relation to developing scientific aptitude in students. Students will tend to remember classroom material when it is presented in a well-thought out unified curriculum where they get to practice science and they feel it is interesting or important to their lives.

Teachers are encouraged to contact groups that are dedicated to the improvement of science instruction for Native American students. Two of these are the Native American Science Education ASsociation [1228 M. Street, NW, Washington, D.C. 20005. Phone (202) 638–7066] which publishes *Kui Tatk,* a quarterly newsletter and the American Indian Science and Engineering Society (1085 14th St., Suite 1220, Boulder, CO 80302) which publishes *Winds of Change* quarterly. And, of course, teachers should not forget that many Native people have a broad knowledge of nature including the plant and animal life of their homeland. The knowledge of these people should be utilized as a classroom resource whenever possible.

REFERENCES FOR FURTHER READING

Brown, Roger. "Science Teaching in the Bilingual Classroom." In *Bilingual Multicultural Education and the Professional* edited by H. Trueba, pp. 228–245. Rowley, MA: Newbury House.

Butterfield, Robin. "The Development and Use of Culturally Appropriate Curriculum for American Indian Students." *Peabody Journal of Education,* 61–1, Fall 1983, pp. 49–66.

Chamot, Anna U. and J. Michael O'Malley. *A Cognitive Academic Language Learning Approach: An ESL Content-Based Curriculum.* Rosslyn, VA: InterAmerica Research Associates, 1986.

Cole, K. C. "Things Your Teachers Never Told You About Science (Nine Shocking Revelations)." *Kui Tatk,* 2–2, Fall 1986, pp. 4–5.

Dick, A. *Village Science,* Iditarod, AK: Iditarod Area School District, 1980.

Gilliland, Hap. *The Flood.* Billings, MT: Council for Indian Education, 1978.

Guthridge, G. "Eskimos Solve the Future." *Analog,* April 1986, pp. 67–172.

Hart, Jeff, and Jacqueline Moore. *Montana: Native Plants and Early Peoples.* Helena, MT: Montana Historical Society Press, 1976.

Mala, Theodore. "Indians and Science—A Natural Mix." *Kui Tatk,* 2–1. Winter 1986.

Ovando, Carlos. "Teaching Science to the Native American Student." In *Teaching the Indian Child: A Bilingual/Multicultural Approach* edited by Jon Reyhner, pp. 159–177. Billings, MT: Eastern Montana College, 1986.

Smith, Murray. "Archaeology as an Aid in Cross-Cultural Science Education," *Journal of American Indian Education,* 19–2, January 1980, pp. 1–7.

Smith, Murray. "Astronomy in the Native Oriented Classroom." *Journal of American Indian Education,* 23–2, January 1984, pp. 16–23.

Smith, Murray. "Science in the Native Oriented Classroom." *Journal of American Indian Education,* 21–3, May 1982, pp. 13–17.

Stokes, D. W. *A Guide to Nature in Winter.* Boston: Little, Brown, 1976.

Taylor, Gene. "Making Science Exciting," (Dear teacher section). *Winds of Change,* December 1986, pp. 26–31.

Vecsey, Christopher and Robert Venables (Eds.). *American Indian Environments: Ecological Issues in Native American History.* Syracuse, NY: Syracuse University Press, 1980.

Watahomigie, L. M. Powskey, and J. Bender. *Ethnobotany of the Hualapai.* Peach Springs, AZ: Hualapai Bilingual Program, 1982.

Wayne, Mitchell and Kenneth Patch, "Indian Alcoholism and Education." *Journal of American Indian Education,* 21–1, November 1981, pp. 31–33.

Chapter 18

Teaching and Learning with Computers
by Ruth Bennett

Computer instruction is a widely accepted strategy for focusing on teaching and learning. It has gained widespread acceptance among educators, since computer skills are necessary in virtually every profession. A survey of businesses in California found that 80% of the computer usage is in the area of word processing, with graphics, data bases and spreadsheets following in popularity. (Hopkins, 1987)

Computer competencies are being written into Educational Codes and required for teaching credentials in California, New York, and many other states (DuBois, 1986 p. 41). From the perspective of the American Indian child, computer instruction means an increase in the desire and ability to learn language-based skills. These skills are increased because of the computer's power to move the child from the concrete world of images to the abstract world of conceptual thought.

The computer offers an interactive approach to learning as the child works with a program, follows instructions, offers input, and receives feedback. In general, this sequence of guided choices holds regardless of the type of program, although there are differences in the degree of guidance. The most highly guided type of program is represented in the tutorial type of software, where a student is asked for a certain response, and the computer reacts to both right and wrong answers. A right answer results in praise: "Excellent," or "You win," or a similar expression flashes on the screen, whereas a wrong answer requires the student to try again.

In word-processing or graphics software, fewer guided choices are provided, and the student makes decisions about correctness. Here, the advantage of the computer is that the student can change something with considerably more ease than with a typewriter. In a word-processing program, if the student wants to change the wording of a sentence, for example, the computer provides a way to cut out chunks of words in a text that exists only on the screen, thus eliminating the tedious process of retyping on paper. Some word-processing programs also offer extras, such as Spelling Checkers that note incorrectly spelled words and Text Editors for noting repetition of terms, length of sentences, and types of sentence constructions. Students who are involved with these programs in public school are learning reading and writing skills that will transfer directly to higher education and careers.

In addition to guided choices and ease of modifying information, the computer offers a visual language and a range of types of instruction that have been proven effective with Indian children, such as private, self-testing or cooperative learning. Emphasis on the visual facets of learning, private self-testing, and cooperative learning are more effective in general for Indian children than public testing in front of a teacher where each child is forced to compete with others. A study of the Warm Springs Indian children in Oregon showed that these two types of instruction produced more interest in learning, resulting in increased participation in classroom activities (Philips, 1972, p. 379).

In California, the Hupa, Yurok, Karuk, and Tolowa have found a cooperative learning methodology effective in teaching reading and writing, and have developed a computer curriculum for cooperative learning. Sponsored by Humboldt State University, these tribes have installed their own phonetic alphabet on the Macintosh computer, and produce their own bilingual instructional materials. Research conducted with the children have shown that those classroom teaching methods that follow the traditional education practiced in the Indian home are successful with the Indian child. Strategies that are founded on an Indian curriculum have been found to build self-esteem for the Indian child and are therefore crucial to language learning (Gilliland, 1986, p. 90).

Cooperative learning that utilizes teamwork and peer teaching more closely parallels the Indian home teaching style. Computer instruction appeals to the Indian child because it brings her/him into contemporary American society. Cooperative learning on a computer has an appeal to the Indian because it combines the old and the new, being a sign of the Indian's evolution and successful adaptation to change. Besides the benefits of computer instruction for the child, there are benefits for the public school teacher. Teachers are interested in knowing how computer instruction can help them teach. Teachers ask, "How can it assist me in teaching reading, social studies, math, and other subjects?" "Can it teach a lesson on natural history?" The next section provides an example of how teachers have used computer instruction to get children to write bilingual books, a technique that can be used with any subject.

CREATING A BILINGUAL NATURAL HISTORY DICTIONARY

The computer provided a way for two American Indian classrooms to develop a communicative approach to learning about natural history. It enabled us to focus on language as it is used, to avoid drill, and to let the successful completion of an interactive goal be the reward.

This resulted in completion of children's natural history dictionaries by students in grades 3 through 8 in public schools in two Indian communities on the Hoopa Indian Reservation in Northwest California.

The goal of the project was to develop dictionaries in Hupa/English and Yurok/English. Instructional objectives were to develop sentence-building skills, to increase knowledge about the natural world, and to incorporate cooperative learning methodology into computer instruction. There were several steps in the process.

We chose the Macintosh computer because it has the unique capacity for creating and installing fonts. A font is a set of characters that comprises all of the symbols that represent all of the sounds in any one language. This capacity enabled us to create and install a Unifon phonetic front as well as the English alphabet. The Unifon font was created for use with the Hupa, Yurok, Karuk, and Tolowa languages, and is used for teaching bilingual literacy in classrooms conducted in these languages. Since each of the four Indian languages has a different phonemic system, and a unique combination of letters in its alphabet, a font was created for each of the four languages (Cogan, 1986). Installation of the fonts into a wordprocessing and a graphics program (MacWrite and MacPaint) was the next step.

Then, groups of elementary school children, grades three through eight, were divided into teams of 2–3, and each team was told that their task for the day was to create one page in a dictionary. The dictionary was to contain names for plants or animals familiar to them. Each of the children chose one dictionary entry, and the children were told to "tell what they knew about that animal or plant." The children then composed sentences that were transcribed in Hupa or Yurok, using the Unifon fonts, and translated into English with the help of the bilingual resource teacher.

The project offered a learning experience based upon cooperation, as the children learned what choices were available in the design of the entries, and worked together designing the layouts of the pages.

On the following two pages there are three sets of dictionary entries: Those created by teams of students in grades 3–5 those created by teams of students in grades 6–8 and those created by teams of students combining the two age groups.

These dictionary entries demonstrate how strongly language learning for Indian students occurs through imitating models. These students managed to express individual creativity within a framework of imitation through an assortment of choices: In addition to the composition of the sentence, there were formatting choices: choice of fontsize, fontstyle, and font type. Choices to be made fell into the following three areas:

1. Writing: Sentence building
2. Computer literacy: Doing word processing tasks, operating the graphics program, MacPaint
3. Cooperative learning: working together on a common task, an entire class sharing one computer.

The perception of so many choices may have been a strong influence in the children's decision to imitate models. Modeling has been found to be a major learning role for Indian students. One study showed that teacher as role model is the most important teacher function. (Andreoli, 1987) Cooperative learning offers a variation on the teacher as role model, since the older peer becomes the role model, and the teacher is a resource. The following figure illustrates:

ROLE MODELS IN COOPERATIVE LEARNING

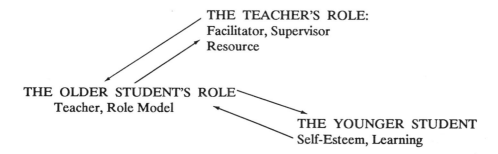

THE TEACHER'S ROLE:
Facilitator, Supervisor
Resource

THE OLDER STUDENT'S ROLE
Teacher, Role Model

THE YOUNGER STUDENT
Self-Esteem, Learning

Dictionary Entries from Students in Grades 3-5

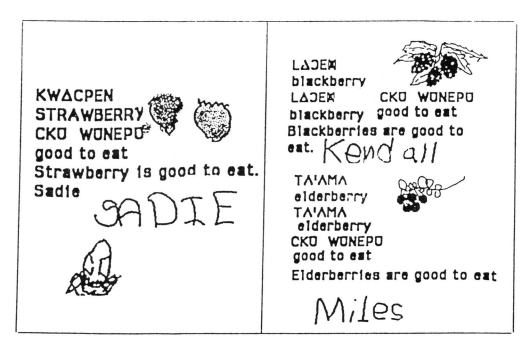

KWᐃCPEN
STRAWBERRY
CKꙨ WꙨNEPꙨ
good to eat
Strawberry is good to eat.
Sadie

SADIE

LᗋꙨEᕏ
blackberry
LᗋꙨEᕏ   CKꙨ WꙨNEPꙨ
blackberry good to eat
Blackberries are good to
eat. Kendall

Tᐱ'ᐱMᐱ
elderberry
Tᐱ'ᐱMᐱ
elderberry
CKꙨ WꙨNEPꙨ
good to eat

Elderberries are good to eat

Miles

Dictionary Entries by Students in Grades 6-8

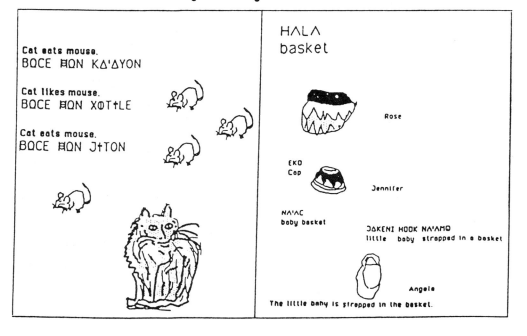

Cat eats mouse.
BꙨCE ᴴꙨN Kᐃ'ᐃYON

Cat likes mouse.
BꙨCE ᴴꙨN XꙨTᵻLE

Cat eats mouse.
BꙨCE ᴴꙨN JᵻTON

HᐱLᐱ
basket

Rose

EKꙨ
Cap

Jennifer

Nᐱ'ᐱC
baby basket

JᗋKENI HꙨꙨK Nᐱ'ᐱMꙨ
little baby strapped in a basket

Angela

The little baby is strapped in the basket.

168

First entry by a 7th grader   model for 3rd graders' entries

RIGAꟼ NI HONEM' HΛGOPΛ
shore it grows cottonwood

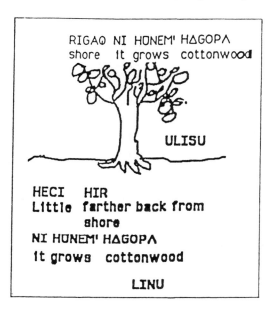

ULISU

HECI   HIR
Little farther back from
            shore
NI HONEM' HΛGOPΛ
it grows cottonwood

              LINU

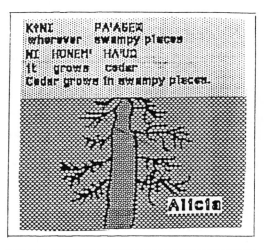

KᵻNI   PA'AGEꟼ
wherever   swampy places
NI HONEM' HΛ'Uꟼ
it grows   cedar
Cedar grows in swampy places.

Alicia

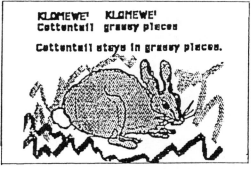

KLOMEWE'   KLOMEWE'
Cottentail grassy places

Cottentail stays in grassy places.

PA'AGEꟼ   NI HONEM'
swampy place it grows
TΛWΛL NI TΛPΛ
      spruce

Spruce grows in swampy
places.

Angela

ꟼIKAL'   NᵻNI HONEM'
everyplace it   grows
Ʊ TΛPΛ
     fir   RᵻꟼERD

ULᵻSU

As the model on page 167 shows, the advantage of cooperative learning is that it involves teacher, older student, and younger student in a triad of participation that utilizes the teacher's knowledge, but it emphasizes the older students' expertise as teacher. It offers a bridge to the teacher for the younger student, and the chance for the older student to engage in the satisfactions of teaching while still a learner.

Older students involved in the dictionary activity were able to provide a model for younger children, who could feel more comfortable about their contributions, knowing that they were making guided choices. This is not to infer that in all cases the younger children followed the examples of their older peers. In fact, we were able to distinguish between the types of definitions created by students at three age levels. Younger children were prone to create definitions that referred to eating. Students in the upper elementary grades were more likely to refer to the environment. Adults, in contrast, reflected a concern with environmental issues. Students took advantage of the cooperative nature of the project to communicate with each other and with the instructor. Further, when a code for communicative competence was used to analyze the older students were more likely to offer than to ask for help (42% offering help, as compared with 4% asking for help). In addition, older students were more likely than younger students to be concerned with information about the task (37% of the older children, as compared with 32% of the younger children.) further, there were two areas where older children expressed themselves, and there was no talk from the younger students: (11% of the older students' talk was evaluation and 6% was to tell others about the project.) Finally, for both groups, 2/3 of the talk was information-centered talk.

INTEGRATING COMPUTER INSTRUCTION INTO THE BILINGUAL CLASSROOM

When Indian children in rural areas are taught how to use a Macintosh, they have knowledge that will assist them in pursuing a higher education, and in developing professional skills. Thus, the Macintosh is providing career education for these children at an early age, and can supply them with a growth in skills related to any career where computers are used.

There are three basic categories of computer software: a tutorial, a simulation, and a tool (Miller, p. 198). The task of the teacher is to find a way to use the tools within the framework of public school education. The bilingual teacher can view this task as (1) finding ways to teach standard subjects (writing, reading, math, science), and (2) pre-college training. What the teacher needs first are programs appropriate for a given subject area.

There are thousands of commercially available computer programs, covering virtually any subject area. Before examining these, however, I offer this suggestion: Since most teachers who are searching for software are budget-minded, shareware is an important resource to be investigated. There are shareware brochures available through electronic bulletin boards, and in book form through commercial outlets, and computer User Groups. (One round of checking the local bulletin board came up with programs teaching vocabulary-building (Hangman8), world geography (Earthplot), concentration and visual memory (Concentration), and biology (animals).

Finding programs that are relevant to American Indian culture is a more difficult task, but commercially available programs can be used as tools to explore such topics. For example, if a teacher of Northwest California Indian children wants a science lesson relevant to the local culture, the teacher might want to start with the life cycle of the salmon, using a word processing program to tell the myth of how the salmon were released.

Then she can use a data-base program to show how many salmon are released in a particular creek to swim up to spawn each day for a period of two months.Or she can use a spread sheet program to display the relationship between the survival of young salmon and weight at birth. In sum, the computer can help in the visual presentation of information, it can handle simulations of the voyage of many salmon to a creek to spawn, it can display through spreadsheets what the chances of survival of any one salmon egg are, it can display the importance of the salmon by a graphics display that labels the parts of the salmon in the Indian langauge and discusses their use, and finally, it can provide a way to integrate cross-cultural perspectives.

Using any software program that has a Font menu, and that has a capacity for installing an additional font, a student can write a bilingual text. For example, Macintosh has software for word-processing (MacWrite, Microsoft Word), for graphics (MacPaint, FullPaint), for data-bases (Microsoft File and Filevision are both data-bases with capacities for graphics displays built-in), for spread sheets (Jazz), and for desk-top publishing (Ready, SEt, Go, and pagemaker).

Tutorials that allow for the installation of bilingual fonts are particularly useful because they provide a greater degree of guidance to the student, and can be used by the student to create bilingual text. Some of these programs combine tutorials with word processing or graphics: both Kids Time and Kids Talk, for example, have bilingual capabilities, and have storywriting word-processing programs on them.

Reading, writing, and math practice are offered directly in available software, and there is available software aimed at specific disciplines, such as history, geography, and other areas in the social, biological, and physical sciences. For the teacher, however, getting started using programs, it may be more useful to think of available programs in terms of developing thinking skills.

Teachers who find that there are limits to the number of programs with bilingual capacities, and virtually no bicultural software for American Indians, may want to develop new software or modify existing software to meet the needs of the American Indian population (Strickland, 1986, p. 188).

CONCLUSION

In discussing teaching and learning on the computer, I have given an account of the process that lead to the development of a computer curriculum in one bilingual teacher training program. By offering some information about the Humboldt State University bilingual computer curriculum, I hope to have provided a starting place for those teachers of Native Americans who are interested in implementing computer curriculum into their classrooms. For those teachers who are already implementing bilingual computer curriculum, there is information on how to proceed in further development. Because this method is general, it can be tried by any teacher interested in developing writing and other language skills using a computer, with any group of children in need of a new method of instruction. It is especially applicable to children from oral cultures such as the American Indian.

REFERENCES FOR FURTHER READING

Androli, A. *Multicultural Education and American Indian History.* Humboldt State University, CA, April 1987.

Bell, F. "Classroom Computing: Beyond the 3 R's." *Creative Computing,* 5, 1981, pp. 68–70.

DuBois, P. and J. Schubert. "Do Your School Policies Provide Equal Access to Computers? Are You Sure?" *Educational Leadership.* March 1986, pp. 41–44.

Cogan, M. "Font Designing." *Wheels for the Mind.* Winter 1986.

Gilliland, Hap. "Self Concept and the Indian Student." in J. Reyhner, ed. *Teaching the Indian Child: A Bilingual/Multicultural Approach.* Eastern Montana College, 1986, pp. 57–69.

Guilford, J. "Creativity." *American Psychologist,* 5, 1950, pp. 444–454.

Hopkins, J. "Computers in Business." Humboldt County Office of Education, May 1987.

Levy, S. "What Every Parent Needs to Know about Computers." *Computers: An Apple Application Special,* 5–5, 1987, pp. 26–30.

Miller, I. "How Schools Become Computer Literate." in S. J. Taffee, ed. *Computers in education,* Dushkin Group, 1986, pp. 197–200.

Morgan, C. *Hidden Powers of the Macintosh.* New American Library, 1985.

Philips, S. "Participant Structures and Communicative Competence." in C. Cazden, V. John, and D. Hymes, eds. *Functions of Language in the Classroom.* Teachers College Press, 1972, pp. 370–394.

Rietz, Sandra. "Preserving Indian Culture through Oral Literature." in J. Reyhner, ed. *Teaching the Indian Child: A Bilingual/Multicultural Approach.* Eastern Montana College, 1986.

Underwood, J. *Linguistics, Computers, and the Language Teacher: A Communicative Approach.* Newbury House, 1984.

Chapter 19

Teaching the Indian Child Art

Lori Sargent and Jo Reid Smith

Art has always been a natural part of life with the Native American people. An innate sense of design interwoven with a delicate natural balance prevails in Native American artifacts. The tools of daily life not only were prepared for the task at hand, but incorporated a spiritual presence, a medicine prayer which was often reflected in a pleasing design.

Recognizing the art with which we live is important. Items that should be considered traditional are as diverse as the shape and surface decoration of clothing, tools, furniture, and dwellings. The way in which we organize and design our environment involves much the same types of aesthetic processes that were used by our ancestors.

By studying these forms of art we are given the opportunity to understand and appreciate remarkable cultures. Art is a form of communication at its best because it may appeal to all the senses—touch, sight, and often sound, smell, and hearing. It involves the objects of everyday life—tools, clothing, and living environment—along with items used in ceremonies and for special occasions. For example, clothing was and is shaped and decorated to communicate additional meaning to those who use or see it. The movement of a person wearing particular items may create sound. The art of today has become much more decorative. It should be our goal to help reestablish art as an integral part of everyday life.

1. Become Well Informed in Historical Native American Art

It is imperative that teachers be familiar with the history of Native American art and all its ramifications, and most importantly the fact that historically, art was not a separate entity from the rest of Indian life, but a closely interwoven part.

Native American art has great variety. Many tribes had their own unique artistic expressions and concepts, and the artifacts which remain reflect these differences. However, there are also a great many similarities, an example of which is the circle, a prevailing motif which was constant, symbolic of the fact that all of life depended upon all of life, that all was a part of the beginning and the end. This symbol reminds us that the history of Native American art includes all aspects of life.

2. Relate Art to Tribal Legends and History

There are many legends about the beginning of arts and crafts, such as the story of Spider Woman, who came to the Anasazi with the art of weaving. Whenever possible, share these legends. Ask students to share the legends they know and ask elders for others. By trying the work at hand with the legends of the past, the student will feel a sense of continuity and pride.

Legends can lead into the history of all art. Begin with simple assignments, perhaps asking children to bring in clippings or items that they find beautiful. Show the students how art has been part of life for all cultures for a very long time and can be a part of everyday life now.

History is rich with examples and influences still relevant in today's societies: Pottery of the Mimbres, a southwestern prehistoric tribe long since vanished, remains as an outstanding example of early pottery. The weavings of the Hopi remain unexcelled although their neighbors, the Navajo, adapted the method of weaving and are today more famous for weaving than their predecessors. Basket weaving, carving, mask making, painting, dancing, flute making, belt weaving, dyeing of fibers, beadwork, rawhide, and other uses of natural materials are as important in art today as they were in the daily life of the earlier people.

3. Use Slides and Field Trips

Use any method available to exhibit the quality of creative concepts of early Native American and contemporary artists of all cultures. If possible, obtain the use of a projector and slides to illustrate the collections of Indian artifacts, contemporary art (Indian and non-Indian) as well as historic non-Indian art. It would be worth your while to accumulate a small collection of slides whenever the opportunity arises. Handout sheets of examples from books, or posters and photos can suffice if no slides are available. Encourage discussion of the items shown so students will observe carefully to encourage their own creative expression.

Artifacts are available through museums and galleries and, when possible, tours to these places offer good experience. There are also art objects which can be seen or borrowed within every Native American community. Functional and non functional ceramic examples abound in homes, books, galleries, and museums. Traditional ware often combines utility with sculptured forms and surface enrichment.

4. Explore Materials and Encourage Personal Expression

Basic skills development should lead toward better expression of artistic perceptions. A variety of mediums such as paint, clay, and fiber should be offered for exploration. Instruction in their use can be done through demonstration, showing examples of historical and contemporary interpretation of historical themes and techniques, but most importantly by challenging the student to relate to these in a personal way.

Students taken out-of-doors may choose the most interesting stone, leaf, or twig they can find and then return to the classroom to draw it. Talk with the students about why they chose the object—color, texture, or personal meaning. Why do they draw it large or small, in multiples, abstracted, photographically or expressively, by itself or in an environment? The drawing tool—pencil, pen, charcoal, or brush-ink—makes a dramatic difference.

Watercolor or other color can bring added vitality into drawings. Introduce it by washing color over sheets of paper before drawing, adding bits of magazine pages for color or texture, gluing on part of the object for collage. Paint part of the drawn object with bright color for added emphasis. The entire page is important. Does the object fill the page, run off the page, or use a small area? Does the page include a border? Repeating design elements in several places helps unify the presentation.

Weaving may be introduced by cutting paper that has been water-colored or drawn on into strips and weaving them together. Variations are limited only by the imagination of the student. Cut strips may vary. They may curve, be cut with geometric designs and different widths, be folded, overlapped, and twisted. Other materials—yarn, string, horsehair, grasses, and leaves—can be added. Man-made materials—plastic strips, wire, newspaper—may add to a student's expression. These may progress from flat to three dimensional objects by binding edges or corners, or weaving them over non-flat surfaces. The weaving should not be restricted to "over one, under one," and the explorations using a variety of materials will encourage creativity. After initial explorations, examples of traditional or contemporary basketry and clothing may spark further interest.

Clay is found over all the earth and has been used to create pottery since 2000 B.C. Clay has a natural response to the hands which rarely fails to captivate students. It is easily dug where vegetation fails to grow and the earth is cracked into "chunks." This clay may be mixed with water to a workable consistency. In this way students are given an understanding of traditional culture which is not possible by using only prepared clay. Pinching and coiling forms from clay is another means of introducing students to three dimensional art.

Students' hands are of different sizes, shapes and strengths, and their thoughts are also unique. This will be reflected in their work so that each piece of work is an expression of its creator's personality and skill.

Moist clay may be decorated with natural clay colors or commercial products. Firing may be completed in a traditional outdoors fire but will be more durable and with less loss if pieces are pre-fired in an electric kiln at 1800 to 2000 degrees Fahrenheit.

Allowing the student to feel at ease with the media is important and with experience and encouragement in a positive environment the student's ideas will grow and mature.

5. Stimulate Curiosity and Creativity

Native American arts came from a society that accepted intuition and feelings as important elements of reality. Intuition and feelings are an integral part of creativity and should be encouraged in art classes.

Demonstrations by local artists are a good resource. Craftspersons within the community may be given the opportunity to pass their knowledge on to the children. Most artists are willing to share time with children and encourage the children to participate with materials similar to those the artist is using. Learning by watching and doing is natural and familiar to Native American children.

Advanced students could be encouraged to further research materials through their school library. Searching for the origins sometimes helps students define themselves in the present. They are led by the attempt to solve the mysteries of life through art and learn that every concept began with what we have available to us today, the human mind and soul.

6. Allow Freedom of Vision and Artistic Expression

Once the students have achieved some skill with different media, they should be encouraged to explore their interests in more depth. Creative thinking and expression is easily incorporated into all activities and subject matter. It also takes courage for a teacher to offer tools without demanding a specific product; to allow freedom and use of creative energy. Too often instruction equates quality with control, but in art that can be destructive. It takes courage to support the student in areas where the teacher may not be knowledgeable.

Art can offer a profound involvement and understanding of our culture. The degree of accomplishment is secondary to the thrill of exploration. It is through searching that cultures are spanned and continue as viable shared experiences. Perhaps the greatest accomplishment of the art instructor is to teach skills which will help students realize that art enhances their lives.

Art is not an isolated activity. Successful teaching comes from sharing experience, understanding, and vision. The open exchange of ideas is foremost in the development of creative expression.

REFERENCES FOR FURTHER READING

Brown, Joseph Epes. *The Spiritual Legacy of the American Indian.* Crossroad, 1984.

Highwater, Jamake. *Ritual of the Wind.* The Viking Press, 1977.

Holm, Bill, and Bill Reid. *Indian Art of the Northwest Coast.* Univ. of Washington Press, 1976.

James, George Wharton. *Indian Blankets and Their Makers.* Rio Grande Press, 1967.

Laubin, Reginald, and Gladys Laubin. *The Indian Tipi.* Univ. of Oklahoma Press, 1975.

Mails, Thomas E. *The Mystic Warriors of the Plains.* Doubleday and Co. 1972.

Mason, Otis Tufton. *Aboriginal American Indian Basketry.* Pergrine Smith, 1976.

Miles, Charles. *Indian and Eskimo Artifacts of North America.* Henry Regnery Co., Chicago, 1968.

Morrow, Mable. *Indian Rawhide.* University of Oklahoma Press, 1975.

Wright, Barton. *Hopi Kachinas, The Complete Guide.* Northland Press, 1977.

Chapter 20

Incorporating Native American Activities into the Physical Education Program

by Robert N. Grueninger

Adding traditional games and activities to your physical education program offers opportunities to promote greater enthusiasm on the part of your Native American students. It also will enhance their self esteem and help to preserve a valuable part of their culture.

TEACH NATIVE AMERICAN GAMES

An account of the games played by Indians would fill several books, and several have been written that list games and tell how they were played (Culin, 1907; MacFarlan, 1958). Such activities that have roots in Indian culture would include, for the elementary grades, games such as Blind Man's Bluff, prisoner's Base, Crack the Whip, Hide and Seek, and Follow the Leader. For the upper grades, lacrosse, field hockey, ice hockey, soccer and football each have their place in Native American history.

EMPHASIZE THE HISTORY OF NATIVE AMERICAN GAMES AND SPORTS

It also supports the needs of Native Americans if you teach the history of the games and sports being introduced. Help the child to recognize that, in the past, the values and skills which a Native American needed for survival were perpetuated through games and sports. Thus, activities often simulated hunting, food gathering, tipi building, relaying vital messages, or fighting. Skills emphasized were those of throwing spears, shooting arrows, riding horses, and running. Games both developed and tested the strength, stamina, speed, pain tolerance, and courage required for life.

TRY THESE INDIAN GAMES FOR ELEMENTARY SCHOOL CHILDREN

Blind Man's Bluff (Kindergarten—Primary Grades)

A blindfolded player stands in the center while all of the others skip around the perimeter of the circle. The "blind man" points at a player with the stick and asks the child to make an animal noise. "Quack like a duck", or "Whinny like a horse," etc. Then the blindfolded player tries to guess who the player is. If he guesses right, the two exchange places. If not, everyone starts skipping again. To allow more players the chance to take part and to avoid embarrassing the "blind man", limit the number of unsuccessful attempts.

Fish Trap Game (Primary Grades)

Among Northwest Coast Indians, a tag game was played in which somewhere between 4 and 12 children would hold hands and form a fisherman's net, and three or four others would be the fish. The object was to trap the fish by touching them with any part of the net. Once caught, a fish became part of the net. The game continued until all of the fish were caught.

To begin the game, separate the players into two teams and have them line up facing each other, about 25 ft. apart. Designate one side as fish, the other as the net, and pretend to throw the net in.

Hoop Race (Primary Grades)

The Beaver Clan of the Seneca Nation enjoyed a circle relay involving passing a 24 inch diameter hoop over the head, body, and legs of each player around the circle and back again in reverse sequence (step in to the hoop, over the trunk, and off over the head). The first team to complete the hoop passing without missing a person or step was the winner.

Corncob Darts (Primary Grades)

Darts made of shelled corncobs and feathers were tossed underhand at a circular target drawn on the ground at various distances. Twenty feet was common, although the target could be nearer or farther depending upon the skill level of the participants. A suitable dart may be improvised by tying a knot in a bandanna; tie a stone inside the knot to increase the weight, if necessary.

Dodge Ball (Upper Elementary)

Mandan, Pawnee, and other prairie tribes played a form of dodge ball in which a batter would toss up and bat a rawhide ball with a 4 ft. hardwood stick. If any of the 8 or so fielders encircling the batter caught the ball, that fielder would throw it from that spot at the batter. The batter had to dodge the ball while staying inside a 4 ft. diameter circle. If hit, the batter became the fielder, and the thrower, the batter. Design your variation, using a rubber playground ball.

Pin Guard (Upper Elementary)

In Louisiana and Arkansas, the Caddo Indians played an interesting team game, not unlike what is now known as "Pin Guard". A field about 30 ft. by 70 ft. was marked out, and 6 clay "Indian clubs" were placed side by side along each end line. Two teams of 7 players each competed, each being confined to its own half of the field. The object was to bowl or throw a basketball-sized ball so that it would knock down the pins. When a team possessed the ball, the other defended its pins. Play continued until one team had knocked over all the pins on the other team's end line.

Hoop and Pole Games (Upper Elementary)

Sports implements often were derived from weapons used in hunting or in war. Thus, the shield became a hoop in the hoop and pole game, and the spear became the pole. Sometimes arrows or darts were thrown at the rolling hoop.

For physical education classes today, the "Buffalo Hunt" game of the Oklahoma area seems most adaptable. The objective is to throw a blunt spear through a 10 in. (i.d.) ring made of green branches wrapped with rawhide. Children are divided into groups according to available equipment, so as to allow maximum participation consistent with good safety practices. The groups may be further subdivided into two lines, throwers and retrievers. The last person in the throwers' line rolls the hoop, and the first throws the pole at it. Each child is given five trials. Throwers become retrievers, and retrievers join the throwing line as rollers, etc. Close supervision is advised, to prevent someone from being hit by a pole. Vary the throwing distance according to the players' skill.

Prisoner's Base (Upper Elementary)

Any number of players are divided into two teams, each team defending one half of the play field. Each team has an area designated as its prison, somewhere near its own end line. Within the prison are placed three blocks or balls. The object of the game is to steal the opponents' blocks without being caught in enemy territory and thrown into prison. Once caught, prisoners may be freed only by being tagged by a member of his own team.

INCLUDE THESE ACTIVITIES FOR INTERMEDIATE AND HIGH SCHOOL

Archery

The following progressions in learning archery have their historical precedents among Native Americans: (a) standing and shooting at a stationary target, (b) standing and shooting at a moving target, such as a ball of yucca (Navajo), (c) standing and shooting at a buffalo hide being dragged by rawhide, (d) trying to have more arrows in the air at one time than could your opponent, in a rapid fire technique, and (e) launching a piece of straw into the air and trying to hit it with an arrow, similar to trap shooting (Crow). The Blackfeet had their own version of archery golf, consisting of shooting an arrow into the ground, shooting a second arrow at the first, and so on. The Pawnee variation consisted of shooting an arrow about 50 yards ahead to land flat; other archers then attempted to shoot so that their arrows would come to rest across the first.

Shinny and Ice Shinny

Shinny was the forerunner of both ice and field hockey, and was popular from Canada to Mexico, from the Atlantic to the Pacific. Teams competed by defending goals located at opposite ends of the field or by taking turns and counting the number of strokes that it took to score a goal by hitting the ball along the ground with the stick. The crooked sticks were similar to the ice hockey sticks of today, although skates were not used. Introduce shinny as a lead-up game to field hockey.

Lacrosse

While ancestral forms of bowling, hockey, baseball, wrestling, and football may be found in many parts of the world, lacrosse is uniquely American Indian. The Iroquois called the game Tokonhon, the "little brother of war." But, French settlers thought that the curved sticks used by the Senecas resembled their bishop's staff, which was called "lacrossier." Therefore, they named the game lacrosse.

Lacrosse was a violent sport, with much running, quick starts, and often involved injury. The rules have been refined through the years, first to teams of 30 or so per side, and eventually to the current 10-a-side for men, 12-a-side for women, and a field the size of a soccer pitch. Rules of safety and protective equipment have been added. Modern Lacrosse is played widely in North America, by both men and women. A variation, Box Lacrosse, is played in iceless hockey rinks, adopting rules from ice hockey, lacrosse, and "murder ball".

Football

Games played with the feet included foot catch, soccer, and both kick ball and kick stick races.

Footbag Games

Foot catch was played by tribeswomen, who balanced a small deerskin ball on top of the foot, kicked it into the air, and then caught it again on the foot. Among the Eskimo, the ball was 1 1/2 to 2 in. in diameter, made of buckskin, somewhat skin to the popular hackeysack now possessed by hordes of American teenagers.

The World Footbag Association gives several tips on skills and drills using a small footbag. (Hackeysack is a trademark name.) First, the primary volleying skill consists of lifting the ball up and towards the body gently with the top of the foot, and not kicking it away as in soccer. The basic kicks consist of contacting the footbag (1) with the top of the foot near the toes, and (2) with the knee. After setting up the ball with these kicks, try the (3) inside kick, with the instep, (4) the outside kick, with the lateral border of the foot, and the (5) back kick, with the outside of the foot over your back or shoulder. Begin play by a courtesy hand toss to another player.

Kick Ball Races

Tekmu Puku means, in Moquelumnan tribal language, "to kick little dog", and was one of many kick ball and kickstick races. Two parallel lines were marked 6 inches apart, extending 50 to 100 yards or more; a post was placed at each end of the lines. The object was to keep the small, buckskin ball between the lines while foot racing; if the ball went out of bounds, it was restarted from that point.

Running

For many tribes, running was and still is an important part of life. Pueblo children were told to "Look to the mountain tops and the running (will) be easy." Hopi children and adults would get up before dawn and run to the fields to cultivate, as far as 35 miles, and then back again by nightfall. Each season had its running races, such as for corn planting in the spring and harvesting in the fall. Then there were the ceremonial runners who ran messages from village to village.

The physical educator should feel confident in emphasizing running as a fitness activity which is part of the Native American heritage. Instruction in common track and field events, too, would be most appropriate. A similar overhand throwing pattern is used whether the implement is a spear, throwing arrow, or javelin, for example.

DEMONSTRATE TRADITIONAL EQUIPMENT

Of the many books on Native American sports and games, several describe the equipment used by different tribes, sometimes with detailed instructions on how to make it. Canoes, sleds, snowshoes, moccasins, hammocks, kayaks, ponchos, toboggans, parkas, stilts, swings, tops, and in fact, rubber balls are all equipment invented by Indians. Of course, equipment may be improvised with the use of newer materials. Since Indians continually made the best use of what they could find in their environment, such as by using metal for arrow tips and spear heads when iron became available, it would not seem impure to use synthetics, plastics, or even manufactured equipment in teaching and practicing traditional activities. For example, hoops made of plastic or of rubber hose joined with a wooden dowel and tape could substitute for the traditional wooden hoops in the hoop and spear game. Equipment for field hockey and lacrosse is available from many sporting goods companies that advertise regularly in *Scholastic Coach* or in the *Journal of physical Education, Recreation and Dance*. For retaining that important sense of history, however, show your students some authentic or homemade replicas of the equipment actually used.

TEN SUGGESTIONS FOR PHYSICAL EDUCATION

1. Incorporate activities with a cultural background of Native American participation in a way that promotes physical fitness, through participation of every student. For example, I have observed field hockey with a few players actively involved and the rest standing around watching. Ease into team sports, teach the skills required, drill the students on the skills and their application, and then coach them so that they all are part of the action. (This does not mean everyone should horde around the ball.)

2. When introducing a game or sport, give background information that links current participation with that of the childrens' ancestors. In addition to giving interesting historical anecdotes, show some of the equipment used in the past.

3. Involve Native American students in planning, helping to teach, demonstrating, and officiating activities.

4. Assign players to teams or use a method of choosing team members that will avoid possible embarrassment to students. Blackfeet women had an impartial way to choose teams for shinny. Each player would place her individually carved stick on a pile. A blindfolded person would pick up the sticks from the pile, two at a time, dividing them into two smaller piles which henceforth formed the teams (Whitney, 1977). This way no one's feelings were hurt by being chosen last.

5. In evaluating student performance, use norms specific to the population being tested. It may mean establishing new norms from the test data at a particular school or area, which a student may find more meaningful than standards based on a larger population with little or no representation from Native Americans.

6. Recognize that successful performance in school depends upon a supportive home environment, good health, and proper nutrition. A child who has low self esteem or who has chronic fatigue and depression will not perform well in school either academically or physically.

7. Help students build self-esteem these three ways:
   a. Learn their names; recognize them as individuals. a name gives identity, pride, and is therefore a valuable, personal possession.
   b. Seek opportunities to commend children. Be positive. Research has shown that a 4:1 ratio of positive to negative feedback is most beneficial to student achievement in the elementary grades.
   c. Lead through personal example and through teaching about successful Indian athletes who can serve as additional role models—Jim Thorpe, Billy Mills, Frank Hudson, Bart Starr, Johnny Bench. Further information on outstanding Indian athletes may be obtained by writing the American Indian Hall of Fame, Haskell Indian Junior College, Lawrence, Kansas 6044.

8. Choose activities that are inclusive rather than exclusive. Games such as dodgeball that have the objective of eliminating players from the inside of the circle may be modified so that players once hit become throwers rather than spectators.

9. Plan open houses, sports festivals or other such activities as part of your public relations efforts. These may help to increase parental participation and support for your school programs.

10. Teach for concomitant learnings of fair play, cooperation, skill in observation, courage, patience, humor and self-reliance. Traditionally, Indian games stressed endurance, perseverance, skill, brute force, and the ability to withstand pain. Games and sports, properly planned for and conducted, afford opportunities to teach fair competition, the desire to excel, sportsmanship and respect for self and others.

One final note. These suggestions are not intended to form the basis for an entire curriculum, but only to supplement a good physical education program to make it better. Do not be surprised if your Indian students would rather play softball, basketball, and football than play field hockey and lacrosse. At Eastern Montana College, the most popular fall activity classes for Native American Students re physical fitness and weight training, basketball, tennis, bowling and archery. But a curriculum that offers only what is popular would not be best meeting the educational needs of students or our respective cultures. Not only is there joy in diversity, but a well-rounded curriculum will best serve both individual and societal needs.

REFERENCES FOR FURTHER READING

Blood, Charles. Indian Games and Crafts. New York: Franklin Watts Press, 1981. Tells the young reader how to make signs and symbols, a necklace, an apron, a dancing bustle, a breastplate, plus how to play the Indian games of arrow toss, a stick game, and shinny, 32 pp.

Culin, Stewart. Games of the North American Indians. New York, Dover Publications, Inc. 1975. (Originally published as "Games of the North American Indians", Twenty-Fourth Annual Report of the Bureau of American Ethnology to the Smithsonian Institution, 1902–03, by W.H. Holmes, Chief, and published by the U.S. Government Printing Office, 1907). An excellent historical reference compiled around the turn of the century includes a tabular index of games played by various tribes, and describes numerous games played with implements.

Grueninger, Robert (1986). Physical Education for the Indian Students, in J. Reyhner ed., Teaching the Indian child. Eastern Montana College. pp. 201–213. Discusses additional Indian Games to use in PE.

Laubin, Reginald and Gladys. American Indian Archery. Normal: University of Oklahoma Press, 1980. The physical education instructor with more than a casual interest in archery will find this book helpful in expanding enthusiasm to Indian youth. The authors discuss equipment used by different tribes—arrows, bows, quivers—variations of technique, competition and hunting.

McFarlan, Allan A. Book of American Indian Games. New York: Association Press, 1958. Describes how to play 150 different Indian games, grouped according to age suitability, with suggestions for adapting running, relay, kicking, hunting, tossing and catching, and challenge games and contests.

Meeker, Louis L. "Ogalala Games," reprinted from the Bulletin of the Free Museum of Science and Art, University of Pennsylvania, 3–1, 1901.

Nabokov, Peter. Indian Running. Santa Barbara: Capra Press, 1981.

NCAS. Official Rules of Lacrosse.

NAGWS. Official Rules of Field Hockey. The Indians of Alkali Lake. Film. 1 hr. 30 min. Available from the Inter-Tribal Policy Board. The incidence of alcoholism on a British Columbia reservation was one hundred percent, affecting every man, woman and child. Now that same reservation, once called Alcohol Lake, is completely dry. A fascinating film showing how the destructive force of alcoholism can be overcome, allowing people to live happier, more fulfilling lives.

Wolfe, Karleen. "Things to Do". In Classroom Activities for the Middle Grades. Olympia, Washington: Office of the State Superintendent of Public Instruction, 1982.

World Footbag Association. Official Players' Manual. Pamphlet may be obtained by writing to the World Footbag Association, 1317 Washington AVe., Suite 7, Golden, OC 80401.

THE AUTHORS

Dr. Hap Gilliland. Professor of Education at Eastern Montana College, and president of the Council for Indian Education, has devoted more than twenty years to the Education of Native American people. He has taught Indian, Eskimo, and Aleut students at every level from second grade through university graduate school, in Montana, Alaska, California, and Washington. He is known for his training sessions for teachers of Native American students in most of the western states, Alaska, and Canada, as well as his work with teachers of the Native children of New Zealand, Australia, Venezuela, Hawaii, and the Philippines. His interests in teaching, exploration, backpacking, photography, and Native cultures have led to the publication of five college texts, eleven children's books, and one novel. He has also edited over one hundred children's books on Native American life.

Dr. Jon Reyhner. Assistant Professor of Bilingual Education at Eastern Montana College and his Navajo wife have lived on reservations throughout the west during his years as teacher and administrator in Indian schools.

Dr. Sandra Fox. Oglala Sioux, has twenty years of experience in Indian education. Her emphasis has been the teaching of reading and langauge arts in BIA schools and in IEA Title IV programs.

Dr. Ruth Bennett, although a member of the Shawnee tribe, works with the reservation schools for Hupa and Yurok children in Northern California. She teaches Bilingual Education at Humboldt State University.

Dr. Rachel Schaffer, a specialist in sociolinguistics, is Assistant Professor of English and Linguistics at Eastern Montana College. She devotes a great deal of time to helping bilingual Indian students with their writing problems.

Dr. Adrian Heidenreich. Professor of Native American Studies at EMC, has devoted his life to the teaching of Indian students.

Dr. Perie Longo, poet and teacher, conducts demonstrations of creative writing techniques in schools near her home in Santa Barbara California and elsewhere.

Dr. Robert Grueninger motivates Native students academically through their interest in sports and physical activities. He is chairman of the Division of Health, Physical Education, and Recreation at Eastern Montana College.

Sandra Rubendall teaches science in the Busby Indian school of the Northern Cheyenne reservation.

Dr. David Davison, originally from Australia, is Professor of Education at Eastern Montana College and has had broad experience teaching Mathematics in varied cultural settings, including experimental work with Crow Indian children.

Lori Sargent, professional artist, exhibits in galleries throughout the country. She has taught headstart and art at the elementary school through university graduate levels. She presently teaches ceramics at the University of Missouri.

Dr. Daniel Pearce, Associate Professor of Education at Eastern Montana College, is former editor of *The Reading Professor.* He has worked with teachers in the classrooms on four different Indian reservations on a long time consultant basis.

Dr. Kay Streeter, Assistant Professor of Education at EMC has worked with Indian schools in both Oklahoma and Montana.

Jo Reid Smith, artist/craftsman, works in clay and has taught and exhibited in many states. She was for five years editor of *The Indian Trader,* a publication devoted to promoting American Indian art.

Index

spelling words, use of, 108
  see also Writing instruction
Whole word methods, 53
Wholistic learning, 53–54
WISC, 47
Word parts, 140
Word recognition, 116–118
  see also Reading
Work, objective of, 34
World view, 50
Writing books for children, 98–101
  see also Reading materials
Writing instruction, 107–110, 123–133
  chants, 131
  controlled, 107–108
  cooperative effort, 42
  correcting, 110
  criticism, 123
  daily writing, 107
  dictation, 108
  emotional release, 131
  expectations, 138–139

  group assignments, 138
  inspiring, 123
  independent writing, 108–109
  journals, 110
  language experience, 115
  medicine wheel as inspiration, 130
  metaphor, 130
  models, 137–138
  names as basis for, 125–126
  poetry, 123–133
  shared feelings, 131
  similes, 127
  spelling words, use of, 108
  spirituality, 129
  topics, 137
  vocabulary for, 124
  whole language approach, 107–110
Wynne, Ed, quote, 12

Yanowamo, 32
Youth vs. age in Native culture, 34
Yurok Indians, 166